Communications in Computer and Information Science   1470

More information about this series at http://www.springer.com/series/7899

Selma Boumerdassi · Mounir Ghogho ·
Éric Renault (Eds.)

Smart and Sustainable Agriculture

First International Conference, SSA 2021
Virtual Event, June 21–22, 2021
Proceedings

Editors
Selma Boumerdassi
CNAM/CEDRIC
Paris, France

Mounir Ghogho
Université Internationale de Rabat
Rabat, Morocco

Éric Renault
Laboratoire LIGM UMR 8049 CNRS
ESIEE Paris
Noisy-le-Grand, France

ISSN 1865-0929   ISSN 1865-0937 (electronic)
Communications in Computer and Information Science
ISBN 978-3-030-88258-7   ISBN 978-3-030-88259-4 (eBook)
https://doi.org/10.1007/978-3-030-88259-4

This Springer imprint is published by the registered company Springer Nature Switzerland AG
The registered company address is: Gewerbestrasse 11, 6330 Cham, Switzerland

Preface

The development of new technologies like the Internet of Things and energy efficient devices have led to the concept of smart agriculture or Agriculture 2.0 in which low-cost systems allow plants and animals to grow under the supervision of autonomous robots and intelligent systems. The International Conference on Smart and Sustainable Agriculture (SSA) aimed at providing a top forum for researchers and practitioners to present and discuss new trends in communication and networking, the Internet of Things (IoT), data processing for smart agriculture, long range IoT (LoRa, Sigfox, NB-IoT), satellite communication, time synchronization, self-configuration, service discovery, sensor networks, quality-of-service, protocol optimization, prototype systems and real-world deployment experiences, secure services and protocols, energy efficiency, standards and norms, security and privacy, machine learning and big data, application for smart agriculture, autonomous systems, image processing, testbeds and platforms, robotics and energy efficient devices, renewable-energy based devices, low-cost solutions for wide-area exploitations and developing countries, smart agriculture and urban farming, smart irrigation, application for small-size and large-size exploitations, application of ancestral farming to smart agriculture, waste management for Agriculture 2.0, and the census of regional ancestral farming. Due to COVID-19 and the special health situation all around the world, all presentations at ssa 2021 took place remotely.

The call for papers resulted in a total of 25 submissions from authors all around the world: Algeria, China, France, Germany, Kenya, India, Indonesia, Morocco, New Zealand, Portugal, and the USA. All submissions were assigned to at least three members of the Program Committee for review. The Program Committee decided to accept 11 papers. The technical program was completed with two keynotes, the first one from Christopher Bryant, University of Guelph, Canada, and the second one from Anand Nayyar, Duy Tan University, Vietnam, and two tutorials, the first one from Mustafa Kishk and Mohamed-Slim Alouini, King Abdullah University of Science and Technology, Saudi Arabia, and the second one from Christophe Maudoux, CNAM, France.

We would like to thank all who contributed to the success of this conference, in particular the members of the Program Committee and the reviewers for carefully reviewing the contributions and selecting a high-quality program. Our special thanks go to the members of the Organizing Committee for their great help. We hope that all participants enjoyed this successful conference.

June 2021

Selma Boumerdassi
Mounir Ghogho
Éric Renault

Organization

SSA 2021 was jointly organized by CNAM Paris, the International University of Rabat, the Laboratoire d'Informatique Gaspard-Monge (LIGM) and ESIEE Paris of Université Gustave Eiffel, and the EVA Project at Inria Paris.

General Chairs

Selma Boumerdassi   CNAM, France
Mounir Ghogho   UIR, Morocco

Steering Committee

Selma Boumerdassi   CNAM, France
Paul Mühlethaler   Inria, France
Éric Renault   ESIEE Paris, France

Technical Program Committee Chair

Éric Renault   ESIEE Paris, France

Technical Program Committee

Aissa Belmeguenai	University of Skikda, Algeria
Mohammed Boulmalf	Université Internationale de Rabat, Morocco
Selma Boumerdassi	CNAM, France
Christopher Bryant	University of Guelph, Canada
Ikram Chairi	Mohamed VI Polytechnic University, Morocco
Mohamed Amine Ferrag	Guelma University, Algeria
Mounir Ghogho	Université Internationale de Rabat, Morocco
Aravinthan Gopalasingham	NOKIA Bell Labs, France
Alfredo Grieco	Politecnico di Bari, Italy
Viet Hai Ha	University of Education, Hue University, Vietnam
Sofiane Hamrioui	ESAIP Engineering School, France
Majdoulayne Hanifi	Université Internationale de Rabat, Morocco
Imran Ali Lakhiar	Jiangsu University, China
Cherkaoui Leghris	Hassan II University of Casablanca, Morocco
Ruben Milocco	Universidad Nacional del Comahue, Argentina
Paul Mühlethaler	Inria Paris, France
Anand Nayyar	Duy Tan University, Vietnam
Edmond Nurellari	Lincoln University, UK
Tran Thi Phuong	Hue University of Agriculture and Forestry, Vietnam

Éric Renault	ESIEE Paris, France
Essaid Sabir	Hassan II University of Casablanca, Morocco
Christian Salim	Inria, France
Lei Shu	Nanjing Agricultural University, China
Mounir Tahar Abbes	University of Chlef, Algeria
Shahab Tayeb	California State University, Fresno, USA
Van Long Tran	Hue Industrial College and Phu Xuan University, Vietnam
Yu-Chia Tseng	NOKIA Bell Labs, France
Pham Huu Ty	Hue University of Agriculture and Forestry, Vietnam
Bogdan Uscumlic	NOKIA Bell Labs, France

Organization Committee

| Lamia Essalhi | ADDA, France |
| Nour El Houda Yellas | CNAM, France |

Sponsoring Institutions

CNAM, Paris, France
ESIEE, Paris, France
Inria, Paris, France
Université Gustave Eiffel, France

Contents

Fuzzy Logic Based Pasture Assessment Using Weed and Bare Patch Detection

Hossein Chegini$^{(\boxtimes)}$ ⓘ, Fernando Beltran ⓘ, and Aniket Mahanti

University of Auckland, Auckland CBD, Auckland 1010, New Zealand
h.chegini@auckland.ac.nz

Abstract. Precision agriculture has provided supporting applications for farmers with the use of Artificial Intelligence (AI) for processing farming data. Pastures are one of the main sources for dairy farming that have a great share in economy of agriculture. Weeds are the main issue of pastures, which impose a huge cost to dairy farmers annually. This paper proposes designing a software framework based on a fuzzy logic system for pasture assessment and pasture clean-up. Once weeds and empty spots of any pasture reduce its productivity, we considered them as two uncertainties that affect the weed management process. Applying our system to any pasture can measure the weed density and bareness through images and score the state of pasture's productivity. With the aid of our software framework we can produce 2D weed density maps, 2D bareness maps, and scoring maps, which provide a better insight into the pastures. The types of 2D maps and the yield score can help and support dairy farmers to schedule, organize, and manage pastoral weeds.

Keywords: MaskRCNN · Weed detection · Fuzzy system · Agriprecision · IoT · Smart decision-making

1 Introduction

Pastures are a great source of food for livestock. Producing grass and ryegrass for cattle, they greatly impact dairy farming, the meat industry, and the milk industry. According to Destremau and Siddharth [19] the dairy products has an export value of 17 billion dollars in 2017, with an 8.2 billion dollars contribution to the New Zealand economy. Increasing pasture production is the primary goal of dairy farmers. Once dairy farmers do labor tasks to maintain pastures for grass production, there exist problems that limit any pasture productivity.

Weeds are one of the major problems in pastures. Dairy farmers spend 1.2 billion dollars to monitor and clean up weeds according to Bourdot et al. [17], and Saunders et al. [18]. Weeds limit the space, nutrients, and resources of ryegrass, significantly leading to loss of revenue. This will have a tremendous negative impact on dairy production.

The works on weed management are mainly about a discussion on weed detection models. Zhang et al. [20] shows an in-pasture image processing by

This paper received the certificate, title, and the award of the best paper in smart and sustainable agriculture conference in 21-22 June 2021, Paris, France

S. Boumerdassi et al. (Eds.): SSA 2021, CCIS 1470, pp. 1–18, 2021.
https://doi.org/10.1007/978-3-030-88259-4_1

examining several Machine Learning (ML) models. Kulkarni and Angadi [21] uses a Convolutional Neural Network to classify weed in a crop environment. There is no study to process pastoral images for recommending in-field actions for weed management to the best of our knowledge. Some studies are focused on developing a high-level decision-making system for weed management with no technical aspect. The papers on weed detection models are also limited in showing the results with no practical study on decision-making for farmers. Our proposed solution for weed management is an integration of a technical model and a fuzzy system. Fuzzy systems do not process crisp data and are based on linguistic variables, which score them as the best explainable systems for decision making. In addition, they are flexible and allow modifications in rules. Therefore, we proposed a fuzzy system for weed management based on the 14 results of an object detection model.

We designed and developed a model for monitoring pastures based on two image objects that significantly affect pasture productivity: weeds and bareness. Then we developed a fuzzy system based on models for weed detection and bareness detection. We used the idea of bareness or empty soil detection for the first time to increase the awareness of our system to the pastures. There are many works on detecting weed objects, but according to our review, we did not see any detection study on bareness spots, which causes negative impacts to the pastures as well.

With detecting weeds and bareness, we added a quantification module to measure them as crisp values. Using this idea, we could measure weed density and bareness on each image and use them as two random variables for analysis and scoring. The flow of data image to quantification and yield scoring is the main contribution of our system. Besides yield scores, our system can produce 2D maps of weed density, which is a great desire of dairy farmers.

The rest of the paper is organized as follows. Section three shows the methodology of our work. Section four shows the results and 2D maps of our system framework. Section five shows our ideas on adding more components to increase the accuracy of our system. Section six is the conclusion. Section seven explains a limitation of our study, and section eight is the future work.

2   Related Work

Studies on weed management are mostly on models for weed detection and classification. To the best of our knowledge, there is no focus on using the results of weed detection models for decision-making on weed management. Thanh V. Le et al. [1] is an example of using a FasterRCNN model trained with realistic weed images for latency improvement in testing mode. X. Jin et al. [2] train a Mobile net, VGG, and a CNN model with 15000 training images for feature extractions of weeds and detecting 10 weed types in crops. M. Abdulsalam et al. [4] uses You Only Look Once (YOlO) and a ResNet model for classifying four types of weeds. Once the mentioned models are focused on weed detection in in-crop environments, they have not propose how to use the models inside a system as a Decision Support System (DSS).

P. G. Cox et al. [9] count some attributes for a DSS model for farmers, such as being predictable and evaluated. There exist examples of DSSs in agriculture for different tasks. C.L. Susilawati [5] demonstrates a DSS model which senses the size of irrigation levels in lands and figures the locations of bores to predict the cultivated lands and optimize water supply usage. Another example, A. Bonfante et al. [6] shows a DSS for predicting and optimizing maze production based on three methodologies: analyzing soil data, crop remote sensing, and water flow modeling. Rinaldi and He [7] propose a DSS for managing water supply and field irrigation. S. Fountas et al. [8] propose a Data Flow Diagram (DFD) based on three main types of decision-making: strategic, tactical, and operational. The motivation of the studied papers is to implement a DSS for automating a part of a farming task based on collecting a selected sensor data such as soil or water supply.

For weed management, the proposed DSSs are designed based on farmers' behavior for weed control. A simple behavioral framework for weed control would have three stages: observing the pasture, doing actions (e.q. spraying, mowing), and evaluating the pasture. The proposed DSSs aims to capture the mentioned tasks (or sub-tasks) and their related data into models. For observing the pasture we used our weed detection model and we thought of a fuzzy system inference for evaluating the pasture.

Once fuzzy systems are among powerful systems in decision-making and handling uncertainties in a process, we have applied them in our DSS model. Some studies have used fuzzy sets and systems in various applications to overcome other complexities and uncertainties. S. Sivamani et al. [13] propose a fuzzy system for controlling and managing animals. They use two factors - age and weight - as membership functions and have four output decisions - change diet, change diet schedule, need health check-up, and ready for a sale. Nguyen-Anh and Le-Trung [14] study the problem of adaptive programming in an IoT environment. They show how to use a fuzzy inference system for controlling complex contexts in IoT for decision-making.

There exist a few fuzzy applications in the domain of agriculture. Khanum et al. [15] uses a fuzzy system for gaining knowledge on the context of leaves

Table 1. Key findings of reviewed papers

No	Paper	Findings
1	[3]	In-crop study with realistic images
2	[4]	In-crop study with No DSS study
3	[8]	Weed management DSS with data flow diagram with no detection
4	[12]	Utilizing fuzzy system in causation
5	[15]	Leave fungi detection with a fuzzy system
6	Our paper	Designing a DSS weed management with a fuzzy logic

and their disease to detect fungi. They used five factors of crisp input into their fuzzy system and evaluated the accuracy of each. Pandey et al. [16] is another example of using fuzzy systems for agricultural data processing. They use crop data for disease detection to improve decision-making on exact timings of sprays and reduce the error and bias of human decision-making in agriculture. They used fuzzy membership functions for two input data: wind and temperature. Their fuzzy system then triggers the fuzzy rules for detecting crop disease. These examples show how fuzzy systems can be used for different agricultural problems to help the farmers to improve their accuracy and timing of routine crop, stock and pasture management tasks.

Table 1 shows the key findings of the papers, which studied weed management. Papers [3] and [4] have used a model for weed detection in an in-crop environment with a lack of weed decision-making system. [8] showed a DSS model for weed management, but they did not use any weed detection model in their proposed system, which is an indication of a technical gap in their study. [15] shows a fuzzy system for detecting fungi in leaves, and [12] shows how to use fuzzy logic for implementing causation. Our study shows an integration of a weed detection model and a fuzzy system to estimate accurate actions against weeds. We have used a weed detection model and a fuzzy system for recommending actions, which represent a complement DSS for weed management.

We adapted the fuzzy rules for our weed system framework based on analyzing the conditions of a pasture based on weed density and bareness. The fuzzy rules are a flexible part of a fuzzy system once we can increase or decrease the rules or change the input data based on dairy farmers' suggestions or notions. For this work, we surveyed dairy farmers and asked various questions about their pastoral maintenance to learn their weed management.

This paper proposes a weed system framework based on a weed detection model designed for pasture environments. Our system uses the outputs of a MaskR-CNN weed detection model for scoring the productivity of the pasture. Analysis of the survey data revealed much uncertainty around weed management on New Zealand dairy farms, including how weeds affect pasture productivity. Therefore, we decided to add a decision-making component to a weed detection model for scoring pastures and convert the model to a Decision Support System (DSS).

3   A Proposed DSS Weed Management

In this section, we explain the design and implementation of our DSS weed management system. We used a state-of-the-art object detection model to process weed images. Once a weed detection model is used for detecting an individual weeds in the pastures, a fuzzy inference system process the weed outputs and recommend actions for pasture cleanup.

From the DSS point of view, we thought of the role of weed information acquired from images in decision-making. We realized seeding could help to constrain weed invasion. We knew from our survey data that identifying empty spaces and seeding them with ryegrass can compete with weeds' growth. Therefore, we included bareness objects to complement our dataset. We integrated our

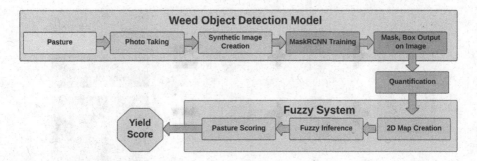

Fig. 1. Flowchart of our weed system framework: weed detection, quantification, and fuzzy inference

weed/bareness detection model with a fuzzy system for assessing a pasture. We chose fuzzy systems because they are highly explainable to a problem.

We have used a fuzzy inference system for processing the image output of the MaskRCNN model. Figure 1 shows the flowchart of our DSS system components. We created two synthetic datasets for weed and bare patch. We developed a weed detection model for the first component and trained it with datasets.

We improved the model's accuracy by hyperparameter tuning. We then recorded the masks and image outputs in an array. The quantification component converts weed output masks into crisp ratios and connect the weed detecting software to fuzzy inference system. The fuzzy inference system receives the weed and bareness crisp values and assesses the pasture.

3.1   MaskRCNN

This section describes our object detection model, which we have used for processing pastoral images for detecting weeds and bareness. We used two synthetic datasets of weed and bareness for training our MaskRCNN model. In our synthetic methodology, we created foreground objects and attached them to background images.

Figure 2 shows a schematic process of creating our synthetic dataset. The left part of the figure shows empty backgrounds that we took from pastures. Then we added extracted weed objects and attached them to the background. This

Table 2. Precision, Recall, and F1 score values for weed and empty models

Model	Training images	Epochs	mAP	Precision	Recall	F1Score
Thistle	500	200 * 100	0.856	0.72	0.52	0.61
Empty	500	200 * 100	0.75	0.7	0.6	0.64
Thistle	2500	200 * 100	0.93	0.78	0.61	0.7
Empty	2500	200 * 100	0.84	0.74	0.62	0.7

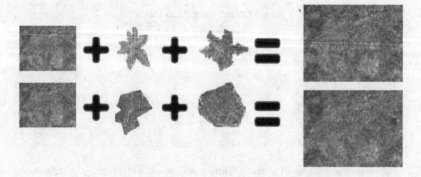

Fig. 2. The schematic diagram of synthetic creation

Fig. 3. A weed image with its output results on weed and empty spot. The upper picture is a photo of a real pasture. The small image in the left shows the weed detections and the right image shows the empty spots detected by the bareness model

way, we created our synthetic dataset. Figure 3 shows the output of our weed and empty models on an image. The top image shows two weeds in the middle and several distributed empty spots. The bottom images represent the mask outputs of the weed and bareness model that we used to process the pastoral images in our software system.

For improving the accuracy of our MaskRCNN model, we conducted multiple training and hyperparameter tunings. We adjusted MaskRCNN config parameters and hyperparameters to their optimized values. We experimented with hyperparameters such as learning rate, RoI, maximum instance, and resenet backbone. We also experimented with epochs and image resolutions. We discovered the scale of 640 × 480 as the best resolution for accuracy. We also recorded the accuracy metrics for weed density and bareness models. Table 2 shows our experiments on the number of images and epochs in the training set. The table shows the precision, recall, and f1score for each experiment.

3.2   Weed and Bareness Quantification

This section describes the module we have designed and coded to measure the ratio of weeds and bareness in an image. After producing the mask results of weed images, we applied a quantification module for calculating the pixel counts of masks and then the ratio of weed/grass. If, for example, we have an image with seven weeds, a mask array with the shape (480, 640, 7) represents the image. We use the image resolution of 640 * 480 pixels with seven 2D arrays corresponding to a detected weed in our output image. Each of the mask arrays in the 480 * 640 scale has a value of 1.

$$T_{weeds} = if \sum_{i=1}^{weeds} r[640, 480, i] > 0 \tag{1}$$

$$T_{bareness} = if \sum_{i=1}^{empty} r[640, 480, i] > 0 \tag{2}$$

$$The\,coverage\,ratio\,of\,Weed = \frac{Total\,weed\,pixels}{Total\,image\,pixels} = \frac{\sum T_{weeds}}{640 * 480} \tag{3}$$

$$The\,coverage\,ratio\,of\,Bare\,patch = \frac{Total\,bare\,pixels}{Total\,image\,pixels} = \frac{\sum T_{bare\,patch}}{640 * 480} \tag{4}$$

Each of the masks is contained within a bounding box, and the model's output includes the coordination of the top left and bottom right of the bounding boxes. These coordinations allow us to compute the area of each box, hence giving us an estimate of the total area covered by a weed or bareness. However, we need to calculate the intersectional region for two overlapping weeds and subtract it from the total area of boxes. We ignored the calculation to reduce the complexity of our quantification module.

Another plausible approach for quantification is to consider the mask arrays. We devise a method that allows us to stack the mask arrays and count non-zero pixels in the flattened 2D array. Dividing the count of non-zero pixels by the total pixels in an image will give us a weed coverage ratio.

Equations 1–4 show the quantification stages for calculating the weed/grass ratio. The sigma in Eq. 1 counts the pixels of a detected weed. Equation 2 shows the condition we used to count the pixels of bareness, which should be greater than 0. Equation 3 shows the formula for calculating the weed/grass ratio according to Eqs. 1 and 2. Equation 4 shows the same approach for calculating the bareness/grass ratio. This way, we achieve two scalars, which we use as the crisp input of our fuzzy system.

3.3 Fuzzy Inference System

This section describes the implementation of our fuzzy inference system in our DSS weed management. Before introducing fuzzy systems, traditional tools for formal modeling, reasoning, and computing were inherently crisp, deterministic, and precise. The outcomes were known to be dichotomous, which is yes/no or 0/1 rather than more/less. However, real situations are very often not deterministic and cannot be described precisely. As the complexity of a system increases by non-deterministic values, We need to define systems for managing uncertainties as stated by [10] and [11].

We construct our fuzzy logic model with two inputs for weed and bareness as two uncertainties of our system. We then defined our fuzzy rules according to changes of inputs and pasture productivity. The reasons for choosing a fuzzy system are the following:

1. Fuzzy systems are one of the best models for handling uncertainties in a process.
2. They are very clear and explainable because they use fuzzy membership functions for presenting input data which are very close to human reasoning and linguistic.
3. The rules of fuzzy systems are very flexible and can be adjusted according to process changes. Farmers can define new rules if they see other factors that might affect their pastures and weed management
4. Fuzzy systems are one of the best models for decision making.

Fuzzy Sets. A fuzzy set is a pair *(U, m)* where U is a set and $m{:}U \rightarrow [0,1]$ is a membership function. For each x *in* U the value $m(x)$ is called the degree of membership of x *in (U, m)* with membership functions we can describe different degree of a member. For instance, we can assign a degree close to 1 for "large" and a degree close to 0 for "small". Equation 5 shows a simple example of mathematical formula of a fuzzy membership function.

$$\mu_{Sf} = \begin{cases} 0, & \text{if } s \leq 1 \\ 1 - e^{-s}, & \text{otherwise} \end{cases} \tag{5}$$

There are different types of fuzzy membership functions, which can be defined and constructed in a fuzzy system according to the nature of a problem. Figure 4 shows six examples of fuzzy membership functions: triangular, trapezoidal, gaussian, pending, linear, and bell.

We have used the set of [0, 1] for weed density and bareness as two inputs of our fuzzy system. The sets of two inputs are *LO, MO, and HI* for weeds, which

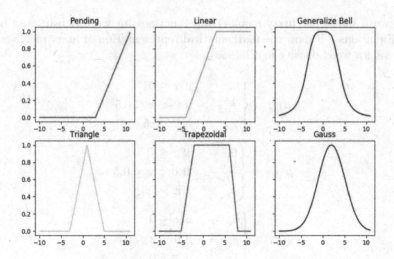

Fig. 4. Six types of fuzzy membership functions

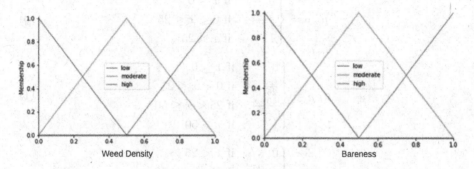

Fig. 5. Two triangular fuzzy membership functions for weed density and bareness

represent *low weed coverage, moderate weed coverage,* and *high weed coverage* respectively. We have used the same notations of *LO, MO, and HI* for bareness, which represent *low barrenness, moderate barrenness,* and *high barrenness* respectively.

The set of linguistic values for the system's output of pasture yield is *EX, GD, AV, PR, and VP*, which represents *excellent yield, good yield, average yield, poor yield* and *very poor yield* respectively. We chose the triangular membership function for our fuzzy membership function in input and output due to its simplicity. Equation 6 shows the triangular formula for our fuzzy membership functions.

$$\mu = \begin{cases} 0, & \text{if } x \leq A_1 \\ \frac{x-A_1}{A_2-A_1}, & \text{if } A_1 < x \leq A_2 \\ \frac{A_3-x}{A_3-A_2}, & \text{if } A_2 < x \leq A_3 \\ 1, & \text{if } x > A_3 \end{cases} \tag{6}$$

Figure 5 shows the fuzzy membership functions for weed density and bareness. Equations 7–9 show the mathematical representation of fuzzy membership functions for weed density and bareness.

$$
\mu_{LO} = \begin{cases} 0, & \text{if } x \leq 0 \\ \frac{0.5-x}{0.5}, & \text{if } 0 < x \leq 0.5 \\ 1, & \text{if } x > 0.5 \end{cases} \tag{7}
$$

$$
\mu_{MO} = \begin{cases} 0, & \text{if } x \leq 0 \\ \frac{0.5-x}{0.5}, & \text{if } 0 < x \leq 0.5 \\ 1, & \text{if } x > 0.5 \end{cases} \tag{8}
$$

$$
\mu_{HI} = \begin{cases} 0, & \text{if } x \leq 0 \\ \frac{0.5-x}{0.5}, & \text{if } 0 < x \leq 0.5 \\ 1, & \text{if } x > 0.5 \end{cases} \tag{9}
$$

$$
\mu_{VP} = \begin{cases} 0, & \text{if } x \leq 0 \\ \frac{25-x}{25}, & \text{if } 0 < x \leq 25 \\ 1, & \text{if } x > 25 \end{cases} \tag{10}
$$

$$
\mu_{PR} = \begin{cases} 0, & \text{if } x \leq 0 \\ \frac{x}{25}, & \text{if } 0 < x \leq 25 \\ \frac{50-x}{25}, & \text{if } 25 < x \leq 50 \\ 1, & \text{if } x > 50 \end{cases} \tag{11}
$$

$$
\mu_{AV} = \begin{cases} 0, & \text{if } x < 25 \\ \frac{x-25}{25}, & \text{if } 25 < x \leq 50 \\ \frac{75-x}{25}, & \text{if } 50 < x \leq 75 \\ 1, & \text{if } x > 75 \end{cases} \tag{12}
$$

$$
\mu_{GD} = \begin{cases} 0, & \text{if } x \leq 50 \\ \frac{x-50}{25}, & \text{if } 50 < x \leq 75 \\ \frac{100-x}{25}, & \text{if } 75 < x \leq 100 \\ 1, & \text{if } x > 100 \end{cases} \tag{13}
$$

$$
\mu_{EX} = \begin{cases} 0, & \text{if } x \leq 0 \\ \frac{x}{25}, & \text{if } 0 < x \leq 25 \\ \frac{50-x}{25}, & \text{if } 25 < x \leq 50 \\ 0, & \text{if } x > 50 \end{cases} \tag{14}
$$

Figure 6 shows the triangular fuzzy membership functions for pasture yield. We defined five attributes for the output: very poor, poor, average, good, and excellent. Equations 10–14 show the mathematical representation of fuzzy membership functions for pasture productivity or yield a score.

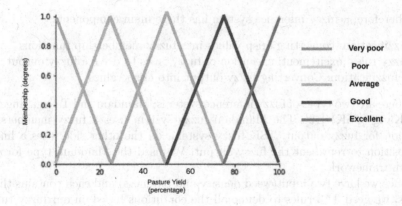

Fig. 6. Five fuzzy membership functions for pasture productivity

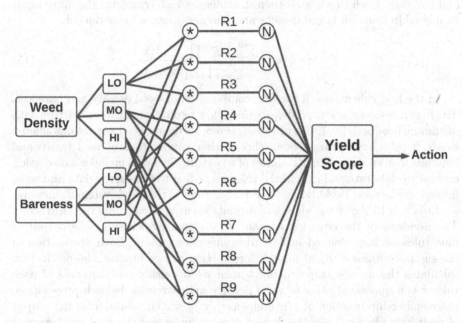

Fig. 7. Our fuzzy network for yield scoring based on weed density and pastoral bareness

Fuzzy Rules. Fuzzy rules represent fuzzy logic, and they are the internal part of a fuzzy system to conduct reasoning and inference. Fuzzy logic resembles approximate human reasoning for checking uncertain conditions, hence allowing the representation of vagueness. Another to say, the fuzzy rules are the logical bridge between fuzzy inputs and fuzzy output. Each fuzzy rule has the structure of *if-then*. With each rule, we can check the input conditions and conclude a fuzzy output. Once we have two inputs in our fuzzy system, we have defined the structure of *if-and-if-then* in our system for each of our rules.

Therefore, a fuzzy inference system has three main components:

1. Fuzzification: converting crisp values into fuzzy membership functions
2. Fuzzy rules' excitement: execution of fuzzy rules to drive a fuzzy output
3. Defuzzification: Converting fuzzy output into crisp values

There are two types of fuzzy inference systems: Mamdani and Takagi, Sugeno, and Kang (TSK) [12]. The Mamdani fuzzy system uses a fuzzy membership function for fuzzy output. TSK fuzzy system, on the other side, uses a linear proposition to represent the fuzzy output. We used the Mamdani type for our system framework.

Once we have two input(weed density and bareness) and each contains three states, we need 3 * 3 rules to define all the conditions based on our fuzzy rules. Figure 7 shows our fuzzy network for scoring yield score based on weed density and bareness. Each rule is an if-then statement, which translates the fuzzy input membership function (weed density and bareness) into a fuzzy output.

$$Yield\,score = \frac{\sum_{l=1}^{9} y^{-1} \prod_{i=1}^{2} \mu_i^l(x_i)}{\sum_{l=1}^{9} \prod_{i=1}^{2} \mu_i^l(x_i)} \tag{15}$$

In the first rule we check the first combination of weed density and bareness. The first rule says a low weed density and a low bareness indicates a pasture with maximum productivity. If this rule is triggered, we do not need any actions against weeds. In rules 2–8 the fuzzy system checks other combinations of weed density and bareness to overcome all uncertainties of a pasture. Section 5 includes a discussion on how to elaborate and extend the rules according to the survey data and weed influencing factors. Table 3 shows our defined rules in the weed system framework.

Equation 15 shows the Mamdani formula we used to calculate the yield score. The dividend of the equation has an outer sigma, which sums the output of nine rules we have defined in our fuzzy inference system. Each proposition in the sigma contains a y and internal production of two inputs. The production calculates the membership functions μ, of weed density and bareness of each rule. x is a quantized value of weed density and bareness. In each proposition, the membership function of x is multiplied by y, which results from the output of each individual rule. In the divisor, there is no y and the final yield score is achieved after the dividing operation.

4   Weed Knowledge: Pasture Assessment

This section shows the results, scores, and 2D maps we produced with our weed software system. For implementing our fuzzy inference, we used python skfuzzy and skfuzzy control packages. Figure 8 shows the scores of our weed framework system on five pastoral images. The first column shows the pastoral images, and the second and third columns reflect its weed density and bareness. The fourth column shows the fuzzy output, and the fifth column represents the yield score.

For recording a pasture with images, we need to define its coordinates. We can programme a robot or a drone to cover a field and take pictures of each

Table 3. Fuzzy rules of our weed system framework

Rule no.	Rule
1	IF (weed density (WD) is low) and (barrenness (BR) is low) THEN Yield is excellent
2	IF (WD is moderate) and (BR is low) THEN Yield is excellent
3	IF (WD is high) and (BR is low) THEN Yield is good
4	IF (WD is low) and (BR is moderate) THEN Yield is good
5	IF (WD is moderate) and (BR is moderate) THEN Yield is average
6	IF (WD is high) and (BR is moderate) THEN Yield is poor
7	IF (WD is low) and (BR is high) THEN Yield is poor
8	IF (WD is moderate) and (BR is high) THEN Yield is very poor
9	IF (WD is high) and (BR is high) THEN Yield is very poor

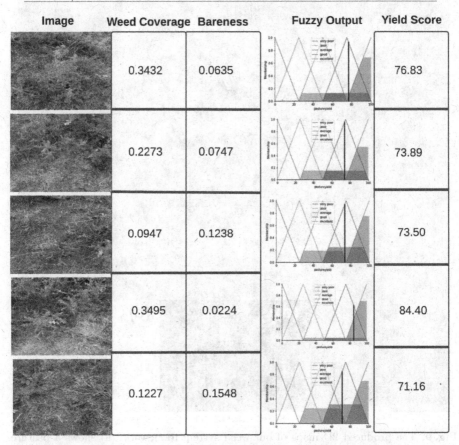

Image	Weed Coverage	Bareness	Fuzzy Output	Yield Score
	0.3432	0.0635		76.83
	0.2273	0.0747		73.89
	0.0947	0.1238		73.50
	0.3495	0.0224		84.40
	0.1227	0.1548		71.16

Fig. 8. The scores of our weed framework system on five pastoral images

tile. The drone can fly over a building, land, or a farm and record the landscape with captured images. The application records each tile with an image, and our system can use the individual images for score processing.

We have simulated a land with images representing each tile with different states of weeds. Figure 9 shows one example of land with three 2D maps we created of weed density, bareness, and yield productivity. Top image is a top view of a pasture represented in tiles of images taken with a drone, which has flown in one meter of height to the ground. The left red 2Dmap shows the state of its weed density. The blue map shows the bareness, and the green one shows the productivity of each tile. Darker squares represent lower profitability, while the lighter squares indicate more productive parts. The produced score for the studied land is **84.27**.

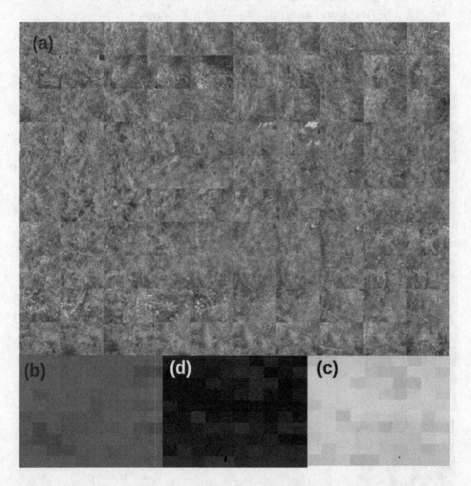

Fig. 9. The produced 2D maps of our weed system framework. (a) shows a pasture divided into 100 individual images. (b) shows the 2D map of weed density. (c) shows the bareness 2D map and (d) shows the 2D map of yield score. For this studied pasture the yield score is 84.27 (Color figure online)

Algorithm 1: The algorithm of calculating a yield score for a pasture

---

Input: N: Extract number of images for a pasture
Image processing section
for *1 to N* **do**
| Calculate the weed density of image(i)
| Calculate the bareness of image(i)
end
Fuzzify the weed density and bareness values
Incite the rules
Calculate the fuzzy score for each image
Defuzzify
Average the scores of all images of pasture
Result: Scoring section

---

5   Weed Management System Extension

In this section, we provide our thoughts on extending our software system with more practical components required by dairy farmers. With the coordinates and area of a piece of land, we can calculate an exact scaling to estimate the areas of weed coverage and bareness from the images collected by the drone. We can assess much information from the 2D map with an exact scaling number. We need to adjust the scaling number after fixing the image resolution. The scaling number is the proportion of land's area to the 2D map.

Once we have the score, we can record it for a specific time. By adding more scores, we can create a dataset of our scores. We need to save the pasture's coordinates in a config file and map a pasture into a 2D array of individual images. The farmers can then use the time-series data to see the weed growth or the pasture's yield score over time. We can also predict the weed growth with a time series and apply a proactive spray schedule accordingly.

With our proposed maps, farmers can have much greater granular insight into their pastures and identify the unproductive areas. They could then take actions only on those parts instead of taking overall and uniform action. In other words, our maps will enable farmers to be proactive and "spot-wise".

In the rule section of our fuzzy system, we can include more factors for decision- making. Through analyzing our survey data, we realized that external factors play a role in weed density. Hence, we can include factors such as wind, humidity, temperature, and seasonal change in our rules. Many of the farmers in our survey stated that monitoring tiny weeds and killing them in a real-time fashion is very important. Our system can detect tiny weeds by a pixel threshold, using the scaling factor explained above. Knowing the number of tiny weeds, we can then assign a threshold in a rule. The following expression shows an example of an extended rule that incorporates some of these factors.

if(weed growth is high) and if(temperature is low) and
if(wind is becoming high) and if(bareness is low) and
if(weed density is high) and if(tiny weeds are above 35%)
then (very low score) and (need a high amount of spray)

6 Limitations

Throughout this research we did not have frequent access to a pasture to fly a drone over it, capture tiled images, and process them with DeployDrone. We, therefore simulated a pasture with images in row and columns.

7 Conclusion and Future Work

This study shows a successful integration of two artificial intelligence models - an object detection model and a fuzzy system - to score a dairy field. Scoring a pasture or dairy farm has not been studied before. Many dairy farmers in New Zealand lack sufficient knowledge for efficient pasture management. They do most of their weed control in person without any tool to support them in monitoring and to score their fields. We have designed and developed a software system that assesses and scores a pasture by processing two random variables that affect the pasture's productivity: weeds and bareness spots. We produced a 2D map that is a representation of pasture quality. Our system can provide farmers with information about their land at a granular scale, thus supporting them to control weeds in their pastures more efficiently.

We can use a python captioning package for 2D maps or the pasture images to create automatic captions, which describe the pasture state. We can also use a nuero fuzzy system or An Adaptive Neuro Fuzzy system (ANFIS) that can be trained by paired data (input weed/bareness and yield score) to increase its accuracy. Once satellite imaging is increasing the image resolutions nowadays, we plan to research their resolution in image processing and automating image capturing from pastures. With satellite images, we do not need to rely on cameras or drones for covering a pasture, and it can increase image processing automation to a great extent.

References

1. Le, V.N.T., Truong, G., Alameh, K.: Detecting weeds from crops under complex field environments based on Faster RCNN. In: Journal ICCE 2020–2020 IEEE 8th International Conference on Communications and Electronics, pp. 350–355 (2021). https://doi.org/10.1109/ICCE48956.2021.9352073
2. Jin, X., Che, J., Chen, Y.: Weed identification using deep learning and image processing in vegetable plantation. IEEE Access **9**, 10940–10950 (2021). https://doi.org/10.1109/ACCESS.2021.3050296
3. Bir, P., Kumar, R., Singh, G.: Transfer learning based tomato leaf disease detection for mobile applications. In: 2020 IEEE International Conference on Computing, Power and Communication Technologies, GUCON 2020, pp. 34–39 (2020). https://doi.org/10.1109/GUCON48875.2020.9231174

4. Abdulsalam, M., Aouf, N.: Deep weed detector/classifier network for precision agriculture. In: 2020 28th Mediterranean Conference on Control and Automation, MED 2020, pp. 1087–1092 (2020). https://doi.org/10.1109/MED48518.2020. 9183325

5. Susilawati, C.L.: Rainwater management model development for agriculture in the Savu Island semi-arid region. J. Civil Eng. Dimension **2012**, 36–41 (2012). https:// doi.org/10.9744/ced.14.1.36-41

6. Bonfante, A., et al.: LCIS DSS—an irrigation supporting system for water use efficiency improvement in precision agriculture. J. Agric. Syst. **2012**, 102646 (2019). https://doi.org/10.1016/j.agsy.2019.102646

7. Rinaldi, M., He, Z.: Decision support systems to manage irrigation in agriculture. J. Adv. Agron. 229–279 (2014). https://doi.org/10.1016/B978-0-12-420225-2.00006-6

8. Fountas, S., Wulfsohn, D., Blackmore, B.S., Jacobsen, H.L., Pedersen, S.M.: A model of decision-making and information flows for information-intensive agriculture. J. Agric. Syst. **87**(2), 192–210 (2006). https://doi.org/10.1016/j.agsy.2004. 12.003

9. Cox, P.G.: Some issues in the design of agricultural decision support systems. J. Agric. Syst. **52**(2–3), 355–381 (1996). https://doi.org/10.1016/0308-521X(96)00063-7

10. Zadeh, L.A.: Toward a theory of fuzzy information granulation and its centrality in human reasoning and fuzzy logic. J. Fuzzy Sets Syst. **90**(2), 111–127 (1997). https://doi.org/10.1016/S0165-0114(97)00077-8

11. Zimmermann, H.-J.: Book Fuzzy Set Theory–and Its Applications. Springer, Dordrecht (2001). https://doi.org/10.1007/978-94-010-0646-0

12. Chen, G., Pham, T.: Book fuzzy sets, fuzzy logic, and fuzzy control systems. J. Fuzzy Sets Syst. (2005)

13. Sivamani, S., Kim, H.G., Park, J., Cho, Y.: A study on decision support system based on the fuzzy logic approach for the livestock service management. J. Int. J. Serv. Technol. Manag. **23**(1–2), 83–100 (2017). https://doi.org/10.1504/IJSTM. 2017.081878

14. Nguyen-ANH, T., Le-Trung, Q.: An IoT reconfiguration framework applied fuzzy logic for context management. In: Journal RIVF 2019 - Proceedings: 2019 IEEE-RIVF International Conference on Computing and Communication Technologies, pp. 1–6 (2019). https://doi.org/10.1109/RIVF.2019.8713619

15. Khanum, A., Alvi, A., Mehmood, R.: Towards a semantically enriched computational intelligence (SECI) framework for smart farming. In: Mehmood, R., Bhaduri, B., Katib, I., Chlamtac, I. (eds.) SCITA 2017. LNICST, vol. 224, pp. 247–257. Springer, Cham (2018). https://doi.org/10.1007/978-3-319-94180-6_24

16. Pandey, P., Litoriya, R., Tiwari, A.: A framework for fuzzy modelling in agricultural diagnostics. Journal Europeen des Systemes Automatises **51**, 203–223 (2018). https://doi.org/10.3166/JESA.51.203-223

17. Bourdôt, G.W., Fowler, S.V., Edwards, G.R.: Pastoral weeds in New Zealand: status and potential solutions (invited paper). New Zealand J. Agric. Res. **50**, 139–161 (2007)

18. Saunders, J.T., et al.: The economic costs of weeds on productive land in New Zealand. Int. J. Agric. Sustain. **15**(4), 380–392 (2017). https://doi.org/10.1080/ 14735903.2017.1334179

19. Destremau, K., Siddharth, P.: How does the dairy sector share its growth?, NZIER final report to Dairy Companies Association of New Zealand, Issue: October (2017)

20. Zhang, W., et al.: Broad-leaf weed detection in pasture. In: 2018 3rd IEEE International Conference on Image, Vision and Computing, pp. 101–105, Issue: October (2018). https://doi.org/10.1109/ICIVC.2018.8492831
21. Kulkarni, S., Angadi, S.A.: IoT based weed detection using image processing and CNN. Int. J. Eng. Appl. Sci. Technol. 4(3), 606–609 (2019). https://doi.org/10.33564/ijeast.2019.v04i03.089

Ensuring Smart Agriculture System Communication Confidentiality Using a New Network Steganography Method

Youssef Nour-El Aine[1,2(✉)] and Cherkaoui Leghris[1,2]

[1] Sciences and Technologies Faculty, HASSAN II University, Mohammedia, Morocco
[2] Laboratoire Informatique de Mohammedia (LIM), Mohammedia, Morocco

Abstract. Nowadays, the demand for natural resources is increasing, which leads to the search for new solutions to prevent its resources from becoming scarce. Indeed, this resources scarcity, such as water one, poses a threat to all of humanity. Thanks to current technologies, we are able to avoid the worst if there are going to be implemented quickly. So, several research projects are being carried out in the field of smart agriculture with the use of advanced technologies such as IoT to optimize production and reduce costs. In parallel to their works, others are focused on solving other problems according to the development of smart agriculture, in particular energy consumption and the security of exchanges between IoT objects to avoid any alteration that may impact the correct exploitation of the Smart agriculture solutions. In this paper, we propose an adaptation of a widespread techniques used in the exchange confidentiality, which is steganography, in the smart agriculture field IoT based. Our approach aims to secure exchanges with a minimum of energy consumption for common objects with a limited energy resource. The results of our experiments show low impact resources consumption when using steganography as a secure exchange solution.

Keywords: Smart agriculture · IoT · Steganography · Confidentiality · Network security

1 Introduction

The purpose of smart agriculture is the use of technologies to strengthen the capacity of agricultural systems by reducing wastage of natural resources and increasing food production. It aims to ensure sustainable development of the agricultural sector. This new direction comes to respond to the population explosion and to feed a growing world population in a sustainable, profitable and environmentally way, there is no other solution than to plant the seeds of an agricultural revolution. Indeed, many studies forecast the imminence of a global food shortage if we do not increase food production. In view of the difficulties encountered with increasing the area of arable land, it would be necessary to improve the yield per unit area (or reduce waste) to achieve this goal. To this end, the use of

S. Boumerdassi et al. (Eds.): SSA 2021, CCIS 1470, pp. 19–29, 2021.
https://doi.org/10.1007/978-3-030-88259-4_2

technologies is proving to be a necessity such as the Internet of Things, which gives rise to what is now called smart agriculture. However, smart agriculture is faced with major challenges such as the exploitation reliability of Smart Agriculture solutions or the data security exchange. For its part, modern security today relies on algorithms and cryptographic methods that provide robust security for communications and exchanges in a network where the communication channel is considered insecure. IoT objects are landing on a large scale in the field of smart agriculture and other fields using IoT technology such as smart cities, health care, etc. These objects have constraints related to performance, energy, memory and the use of cryptographic algorithms which may prove to be unsuitable for these constraints. constraints. To this end, the use of modern security techniques in the field of Smart Agriculture aims to:

- Protect exchanges between connected nodes;
- Authenticate nodes;
- Ensure the integrity of the data collected on which any decisions will be made;
- ... etc.;

The security techniques used in the Smart agriculture field must consider the constraints related to connected objects and the openness of the environment for their implementation. Therefore, there techniques must be performed on objects limited in physical and energy resources. So, we propose, in this article, an approach which is based on the use of the shorthand technique for the security of the exchanges in the field of Smart Agriculture. This is a new method which uses steganography instead of cryptography to ensure the confidentiality of the information exchanged between the sensor nodes. This method optimizes the performance consumption and does not occupy large amounts of memory. The rest of this paper will be organized as follow: The related works are discussed in Sect. 2; Sect. 3 is dedicated to the background; Sect. 4 details the proposed steganographic method. In Sect. 5, we present the simulation environment, the obtained results and their interpretation. The last section is dedicated to the conclusion and perspectives of this work.

2   Related Work

The agriculture sector is a most favorable field for the implementation of IoT solutions. Thus, this IoT mutation should allow Smart Agriculture to cope with the lowering in production. To this end, several connected initiatives - ranging from soil monitoring to irrigation sensors - have emerged and are currently being implemented. This orientation of smart agriculture continues to develop nowadays despite new challenges such as the reliability and security of trade.

The smart agriculture sector is undergoing many developments in terms of monitoring and reliability. Thus, in [1], the authors tried to design a smart IoT based agriculture monitoring system which makes use of wireless sensor network that collects data from different sensors deployed at various nodes and sends it through the wireless protocol. This system acts a protection of the fields from various problems.

The technology, object of article [2], is developed to helps monitoring the environmental surroundings using wireless technology based on MQTT protocol. By utilizing these sensors, the farmers could be able to monitor, in real time, by using web server. With the help of this server, they can be able to monitor the level of water, temperature, humidity and soil moisture.

In articles [3], the authors propose a holistic smart agriculture application that consists of various agricultural sensors, drones, and IoT hardware and software utilities. Several sensors are able to gather specific cornfield data and send it to the coordinator node which is capable of communicating with a drone. The drone flies over the large-scale cornfields at certain times of the day and collects the data from coordinator nodes. It delivers the cornfield data to the gateway as a relay node. The farmers monitor the data on graphical monitoring interfaces with the help of IoT software.

The use of IoT in smart agriculture seems relatively simple and low risk, but it turns out to be very vulnerable. Indeed, one of the objectives of smart agriculture is to automate manual processes and promote practices with reduced interactions that lead to good decisions. This can multiply the easy targets for hackers. Often, these systems fun on unsupervised networks making unreported the action hacking. More seriously, in a field that is still little aware of cybersecurity, unlike the banking sector, security is not included in the specifications. Hackers can easily gain access to irrigation control systems to hijack them or demand a ransom in exchange for restitution of control rights. The administration of highly regulated pesticides can be changed without the knowledge of the farmer. Finally, these Internet-connected systems can be used to access other third-party systems connected and integrated into a network of botnets. Without complying with security standards, manufacturers of smart objects and devices must adhere to the principles of self-regulation and good security practices. When it comes to security, the principles that protect the Internet today will also protect the Internet of Things tomorrow.

With possible IoT security risks in the field of smart agriculture, several research works have recently conducted in the literature aiming to ensure the confidentiality and integrity of exchanges and thus limit unauthorized access that can alter good farmer decisions.

In articles [4], the authors dress some research challenges on security and privacy issues in the field of green IoT-based agriculture. They, particular, provide a classification of threat models against green IoT-based agriculture into five categories, including, attacks against privacy, authentication, confidentiality, availability, and integrity properties. They also tried to present some adapted sécurity solutions for green IoT-based agriculture.

In articles [5], the author presents a holistic study on security and privacy in a smart farming ecosystem. Their paper outlines a multi layered architecture relevant to the precision agriculture domain and discusses the security and privacy issues in this dynamic and distributed cyber physical environment. Furthermore, the paper elaborates on potential cyber-attack scenarios and highlights open research challenges and future directions.

The aim of the paper articles [6] is to propose a system which is useful in monitoring the field data as well as controlling the field operations which provides the flexibility. The authors aim at making agriculture smart using automation and IOT technologies by including Node MCU and Arduino.

In articles [7] the authors discuss three adaptations of cryptographic methods that rely on the development of lightweight cryptography adapted to IoT security: lightweight block ciphers, lightweight stream ciphers, lightweight hash functions, elliptic curve cryptography. Steganography has become a promising field of research for the development of new security approaches adapted to objects with energy and memory performance constraints such as the IoT. The authors articles [8] propose a method of steganography based on storing data in fields, using the fields of the IPv4 packet as a cover medium to hide the message. Their system uses the overflow field of the timestamp option to hide a message by sender A, receiver B of the message can extract the bits hidden in the overflow field to build the message sent by A. This method allows to hide and carry a maximum of 20 bits per packet, if the value of the hidden bits exceeds this threshold, it can raise suspicion on this packet. In addition, if the packet is destined for a remote network, the router that the packet must pass through will not find enough space in the overflow field to write its timestamp value, it will be forced to increment the value of the overflow field, and consequently the message sent by A will not be the same as the one received by B. Finally, the robustness of this method is based on the fact that no one can suspect the presence of a hidden message and that the algorithm used is secret. However, modern security considers that the communication channel is not secure and that the security algorithm used is public known (Kerkhof's principle) [10].

The steganographic method we developed is based on storing data in the IP packet of the IP protocol, using the data field of the payload as a cover medium, which can contain up to 65,515 bytes if the ip header is 20 bytes, and up to 65,472 bytes if the ip header is 60 bytes [11].

3   Background

3.1   Green IoT Based Agriculture Architectures

Among the most popular green IoT based agriculture architectures are: the three-tier architecture, the four-tier architecture and the SDN architecture. [4] explains that the four-tier green based agriculture is the most used and is based on 4 layers: agriculture sensors layer; Fog node layer; core network layer; and cloud computing layer. The sensors node layer includes the IoT objects used as smart meters and sensors nodes... etc., these IoT objects ensure the collection of data concerning the plants, the soil condition, the environment... etc., in order to transmit them to the fog nodes layer. The fog nodes layer receives the data collected by the IoT objects in the sensor nodes layer, and reacts with the environment according to the received values, for example receives the values of the soil moisture and according to these values decides to water or not the plants. The core network layer is responsible for transporting data from the fog layer to the cloud computing layer, it uses interconnection devices such as switches and routers to ensure data transfer. The cloud computing layer is responsible for hosting the data from the lower layers in high-performance servers for use in analysis and synchronization operations.

The communication between the sensors nodes layer and the fog nodes layer is the first step of data exchange in the whole system, it is vital information on which relies the great part of the decisions taken by the system, so it is a communication generally without wires between fragile elements having constraints of performance, energy and memory as the IoT objects, that is why it is the first target of attacks and threats.

3.2   Network Steganography

Steganography is the art of hiding data in a cover media, the purpose behind steganography is to communicate securely and prevent interception of the exchanged data. Many different cover media are used to hide a message such as video, image, audio, text and network. The use of the latter is called network steganography, it uses network protocols and IP packets to hide the data. According to articles [9] this technique can be classified into two bases: The storage of data either in fields or by synchronization and the delay generated between the sending and receiving of packets. Depending on the number of protocols used.

4   Proposed Method

In this work, we proposed a new steganographic method which is based on the technique of storing data in fields. We chose to use the Data (payload) field of the IP packet as a cover media to store and hide the data taken by the IoT object in order to send it to the FOG node. Our method ensures the confidentiality of the exchanged data without touching the IP packet structure.

4.1   Operating Principle

To explain the working principle, we considered the following scenario: An IoT object (client) collects and sends the ambient temperature of an agricultural greenhouse to a fog node (server). The client and the server have a pre-shared list of positions. The operating process at the client level is illustrated in (Fig. 1).

Thus, the IoT object (client) performs the following operations:

- Captures the ambient temperature and stores it in a variable called "Temperature";
- Converts the temperature into binary with a length of 8 bits and stores it in "BinaryTemp";
- Generates a random binary value with a length of 16 bits and stores it in "CoverMedia";

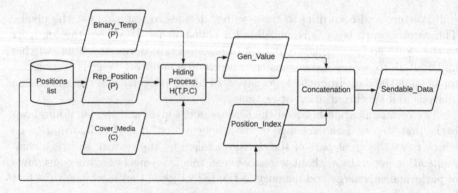

Fig. 1. Hiding Process in the client side.

- Randomly selects a position in the list and stores it in "RepPosition";
- Replaces the bits of the "CoverMedia" variable with the bits of the "BinaryTemp" variable according to the values of the digits and their indexes in the "RepPosition" variable, the new value generated is stored in "GenValue". (Fig. 2) shows the replacement operation;
- Converts to binary (with a length of 8 bits) the index of the chosen position and concatenates it to the left of the "GenValue". To form a new value "SendableData";
- Puts "SendableData" in the data field of the Ip packet and sends it to the server.

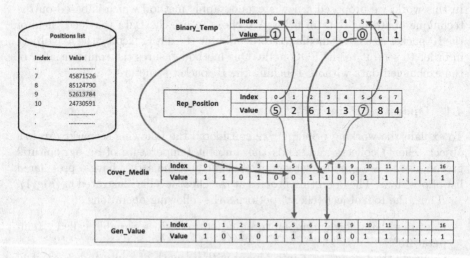

Fig. 2. Replacement operation.

The Server process is illustrated in (Fig. 3).

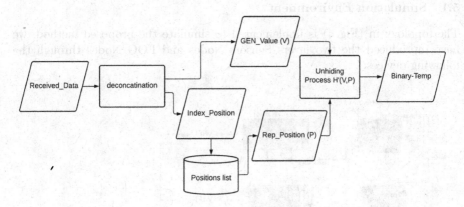

Fig. 3. Replacement operation.

The fog Node (server) receives the Ip packet sent by the client and proceeds as follows:

- Extracts the value of SendableData from the payload;
- Isolates the first 8 bits of the value and converts them to decimal to get the index of the position used by the client and stores the rest of the bits in the GenValue variable;
- Selects the position in the pre-shared list according to the index calculated previously;
- Uses the position to deduce the binary value of the temperature hidden in GenValue;
- Convert the deduced temperature to decimal to get the ambient temperature value of the greenhouse.

4.2 Choice of Parameters

The choice of the payload as cover media comes from the fact that the payload field remains unchangeable even when the packet is destined to a remote network, in addition to its large size which allows to host data of a significant length.

The temperature taken by the IoT object is written in decimal, we decided to present it in 8-bit binary to strengthen the hiding process and make the value prediction difficult. The cover media is randomly generated and presented in 16-bit binary at each exchange to deal with potential traffic analysis by malicious parties.

The list of alternative positions is pre-shared, it reduces the load on the IoT object compared to an alternative solution of position exchange. The choice of the position to be used is random, discrete and does not follow any order.

5   Simulation and Results

5.1   Simulation Environment

The topology in (Fig. 4) is implemented to simulate the proposed method, we have reproduced the two layers Sensors Nodes and FOG Nodes through the following devices:

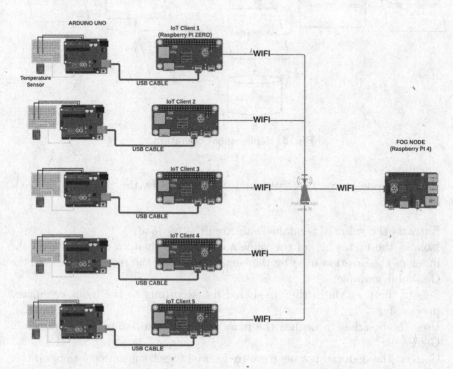

Fig. 4. Used topology for simulation

The IoT (TCP Client) object executes a program written in python allows creating an IP packet and add SendableData by using Scapy Library and send the packet using TCP sockets. The second program also written in python at the level of FOG NODE (TCP Server), allows to receive the IP packet sent by the IoT object, extract the payload from the packet using Scapy library and deducts the Temperature value.

5.2   Results and Interpretation

In a first step we analyzed 100 values generated and sent by each of the five IoT Clients, each value corresponds to the ambient temperature of the greenhouse at a time T, the results in (Fig. 5) show that the generated values are sufficiently random and are resistant to prediction attacks. The results also show that no relationship can be established between the temperature value collected and the value generated and sent using our method, to confirm this we have performed another experiment which consists in generating 100 values for the same temperature (35 °C) by the same IoT Client, the (Fig. 6) shows that indeed and even if it is the same temperature value the output of the method is random, so the method allows to cancel any relationship between the input (temperature value) and the output (value generated and sent).

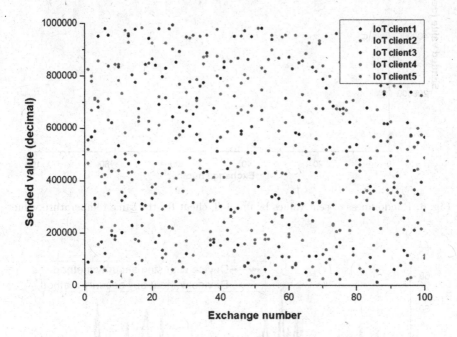

Fig. 5. Randomness of sent values by five IoT clients

Then, we monitored the CPU load of two IoT objects, the first one exchanges data with the FOG NODE using the steganographic model and the second one exchanges the same data with the FOG NODE in plain without using any security layer, (Fig. 7) shows that securing the exchange using our method does not have a considerable impact in the CPU load.

Finally, with comparing our method with the method in [8], it is clear that our method allows to exchange large amounts of data using all the payload field compared to the method that uses only the timestamp field, the method is valid for exchanges in local networks and for exchanges in remote networks and this whatever the version of the IP protocol used (IPv4 or IPv6) and Kerkhof's principle [10] is respected.

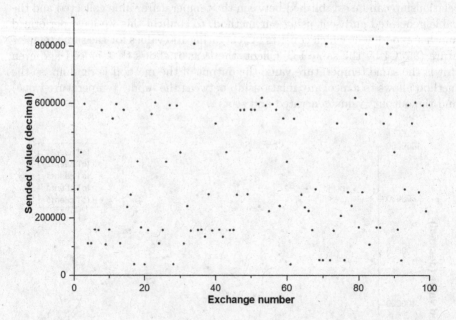

Fig. 6. Randomness of sent values by one IoT client for the same temperature value

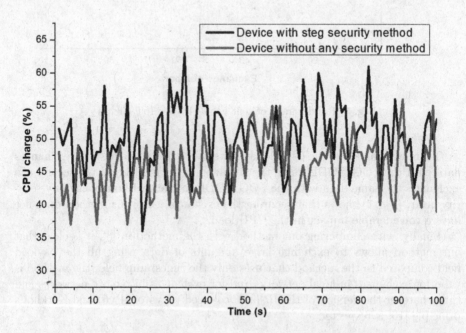

Fig. 7. Randomness of sent values by one IoT client for the same temperature value

6   Conclusion and Future Scope

In this paper, we proposed a new security method, which ensures the confidentiality of exchanges between sensor's node layer and FOG node layer in a smart agriculture system, this new method based on network steganography allows to add confidentiality to the exchanges, while respecting the constraints of performance, energy and memory that characterize IoT objects and sensors used in smart agriculture. The results obtained show that network steganography can offer security at a lower cost, and even become an alternative to cryptographic algorithms and techniques. Its field of application can be extended to cover integrity, privacy and authentication, which can be the subject of an extension of this work with an optimization of energy consumption.

References

1. Rajesh, T., Thrinayana, Y., Srinivasulu, D.: IOT based smart agriculture monitoring system. Int. J. Innov. Technol. Explor. Eng. **9**(9), 325–328 (2020). https://doi.org/10.35940/ijitee.i7142.079920
2. Rameshkumar, S.G.: Efficient method using multi-sensors for smart agriculture using IoT. **8**(06), 350–352 (2019)
3. Cicioğlu, M., Çalhan, A.: Smart agriculture with internet of things in cornfields. Comput. Electr. Eng. **90**(August 2020), 106982 (2021). https://doi.org/10.1016/j.compeleceng.2021.106982
4. Ferrag, M.A., Shu, L., Yang, X., Derhab, A., Maglaras, L.: Security and privacy for green IoT-based agriculture: review, blockchain solutions, and challenges. IEEE Access **8**, 32031–32053 (2020). https://doi.org/10.1109/ACCESS.2020.2973178
5. Gupta, M., Abdelsalam, M., Khorsandroo, S., Mittal, S.: Security and privacy in smart farming: challenges and opportunities. IEEE Access **8**(February), 34564–34584 (2020). https://doi.org/10.1109/ACCESS.2020.2975142
6. Keerthana, B., Nivetha, P., Boomika, M., Mathivathani, M., Niranjan, A.: IoT based smart security and monitoring devices for agriculture. Int. J. Inf. Res. Rev. **05**(04), 5415–5419 (2018)
7. Dhanda, S.S., Singh, B., Jindal, P.: Lightweight cryptography: a solution to secure IoT. Wirel. Pers. Commun. **112**(3), 1947–1980 (2020)
8. Bedi, P., Dua, A.: Network steganography using the overflow field of timestamp option in an IPv4 packet. Procedia Comput. Sci. **171**(2019), 1810–1818 (2020). https://doi.org/10.1016/j.procs.2020.04.194
9. Bedi, P., Dua, A.: Network steganography using extension headers in IPv6. Commun. Comput. Inf. Sci. **1170**, 98–110 (2020). https://doi.org/10.1007/978-981-15-9671-1-8
10. Shannon, C.: Communication theory of secrecy systems. Bell Syst. Tech. J. **28**(4), 656–715 (1949)
11. RFC 791. https://datatracker.ietf.org/doc/html/rfc791

Deploying Deep Neural Networks
on Edge Devices for Grape Segmentation

Mathias Roesler[1], Lucas Mohimont[1,2], François Alin[1],
Nathalie Gaveau[2], and Luiz Angelo Steffenel[1(✉)]

[1] Université de Reims Champagne-Ardenne, LICIIS - LRC CEA DIGIT,
51687 Reims Cedex 2, France
[2] Université de Reims Champagne-Ardenne, RIBP - EA4707 - USC - INRAE1488,
51687 Reims Cedex 2, France
{mathias.roesler,lucas.mohimont,francois.alin}@univ-reims.fr,
{nathalie.gaveau,angelo.steffenel}@univ-reims.fr

Abstract. Deep learning (DL) is a hot trend for object detection and segmentation, thanks to the use of Deep Neural Networks (DNNs). Image recognition is a powerful tool for precision viticulture, having a strong potential in cases such as yield estimation and automatic quality estimation of the grapes. Developing the models is one part of the problem, deploying them in the field, at the edge of the network, is another problem that comes with its own constraints. This paper studies the use of embedded devices to run Deep Neural Network algorithms for real-time grape segmentation at the wine press.

Keywords: Grape detection · Precision viticulture · Deep learning · Edge computing

1 Introduction

Computer vision has helped automate tasks that once required intensive manual labor. In agriculture, it has been used to automatically count fruits and vegetables such as peppers [23] or oranges [17]. Applying this to viticulture is a more challenging problem because each individual fruit, i.e., the grape, is made of several berries with colors that can vary depending on the variety (white or red) or even resemble the color of the foliage before the grapes ripen. Nonetheless, being able to detect grapes automatically is a necessary step for solving other, more complex problems such as yield estimation. Dunn et al. [9] were the first to propose a method for detecting grapes in an image. Since then, a wide range of methods have been developed to achieve better detection rates and to be used on large scales. The latest methods, that show the most promise, are based on deep neural networks and more specifically on Convolutional Neural Networks (CNNs).

Developing the algorithms for the detection of grapes is one major part of the problem. However, once these algorithms have been developed, trained, and

© Springer Nature Switzerland AG 2021
S. Boumerdassi et al. (Eds.): SSA 2021, CCIS 1470, pp. 30–43, 2021.
https://doi.org/10.1007/978-3-030-88259-4_3

tested, they must be deployed in the field. This task comes with its own set of challenges and setbacks. One way to deploy the algorithms is to use specific hardware such as embedded devices, essentially small computers that can operate in remote places like vineyards or wine presses. These small devices have limitations, most notably in computing power and available memory. These limitations, in turn, condition the algorithm, for example which DL architecture should be used, the programming language to write in, etc. Therefore, not only must the developed algorithm be light enough to fit on the device, but it must be able to run with the limited resources available. Other factors can come into play as well, notably the execution speed. Because these systems use less powerful hardware than a standard computer, the time needed to run the algorithm can sometimes be very long, which is problematic when the predictions must be performed in real-time. Luckily, a wide range of readily available boards with various capabilities can be used for deploying grape detection algorithms. The option of creating a board for a specific application is always possible.

This paper focuses on the detection of unwanted elements (green or ripen grapes, leaves, stones, tools) prior to the delivery of the grapes to the press. This paper will be looking at the deployment of a deep neural network for semantic segmentation on two different readily available embedded devices, enabling AI inference at the edge of the network. Different versions of the model will be tested, and the performances of each device will be compared based on these three criteria: inference time, performance loss when compared to the original model, and model size. In addition to this, results must be obtained in less than 15 s in this study case, in order to not impact the winery production chain.

The rest of this paper is divided into four parts. The first one will review the related work about grape detection. The second will detail the method and the tools used (model, dataset, and hardware). The third will present the results that were obtained, and finally, the last section will conclude this paper and present leads for future work.

2   Related Work

This first section will first look at the different approaches to detect grapes in images before explaining which method was selected for this case study.

There are several approaches for detecting the location of grapes on a given image. The most intuitive way is by looking at the color of each pixel. This basic method was first proposed by Dunn et al. in [9] where they use a threshold to detect the grapes in the image. Even though methods using thresholds are simple to implement and have low execution times (which is interesting for embedded applications), they present several drawbacks. Firstly, they are sensitive to the lighting conditions: with variations in the lighting, the pixel values change, and the thresholds will no longer be able to detect the grapes. Secondly, the same threshold cannot be used for different grape varieties—red or white. One solution to address the issue of inconsistent lighting is to shine an artificial light at night at the grapes such as in [19] as well as use an artificial background. However, this will not change the fact that the thresholds will have to differ depending on the variety of grapes that is analyzed. These extra elements are cumbersome and make it difficult to use an algorithm based on pixel thresholds in the field. Because of these drawbacks, this method is well suited for research purposes but not for large-scale applications.

Another approach to detecting grapes consists in trying to detect the individual berries as first proposed by Grossetete et al. in [11]. For this, they use the reflection properties of light on each berry. It will produce a specular reflection pattern that follows a Gaussian distribution that can be used to isolate the individual berries that compose the grape. Methods for detecting the specular reflection pattern vary: in [11] a filter is used to detect it, in [13, 18] a circle detector is used, either a Hough or a fast radial symmetry transform, and in [4] a local maximum detector is used. Filters and classifiers are then used to remove the false positive detections. These methods require specific lighting conditions to be able to produce the reflection pattern on the berries rendering this approach difficultly usable in natural conditions. Although it has been implemented in the field and evaluated on a large scale, this approach requires additional equipment (flash or lamp) and works best at night. Therefore, it is not a practical method for use in the field.

Moreover, methods for counting berries have been implemented on handheld devices [3, 5, 11, 15], but they often have limitations that make them impractical for large scale applications. For instance, the method proposed in [11] can only be used at night with a flash; other methods from Aquino et al. (vitisBerry [3] and vitisFlower [5]) as well as the one from Liu et al. [15] require an artificial background: a black cardboard for the methods in [3] or [5], and a black or white one for the one in [15] depending on the grape variety. In addition, all four of these applications are only able to count the berries of a single grape at a time rendering them inapplicable for large scale detections in the field. Nonetheless, they can be used in real-time requiring only a piece of cardboard and a smartphone, providing important insights for the viticulturists, such as phenotyping information. Aquino et al. have also proposed an application for larger scale grape detection by modifying an all-terrain vehicle [4]. This method has the advantage of being automated and usable on an entire field. Despite this, it requires extra material and can only be used during the night to ensure controlled lighting conditions making it somewhat impractical to use.

Finally, machine learning methods have been developed to produce a binary estimation on each pixel or pixel block of an image. In this case, the selected pixel or block is classified to either be a grape or not a grape. Some methods require a feature extraction process before the classification [8, 16] and others, based on deep learning, combine the feature extraction and the classification within the same model [6, 7]. In this first case, many different features can be used, for example Zernike moments [8], the average of the RGB channels in the pixel block [16] or the color histogram [14]. Several classifiers are possible as well, such as the Multi-Layer Perceptron (MLP) [6], Support Vector Machines [8], Adaboost [16] or even Convolutional Neural Networks (CNNs). Each method will be a combination of these two different algorithms—feature extractor and classifier. One of the main problems with this approach is that the quality of the classification results depends on the choice of the feature extractor, which in turn depends on the choice of the researcher. Convolutional Neural Networks can overcome this problem by combining the feature extraction process and the classification of the extracted features in the same algorithm. CNNs are versatile and can be trained to detect various objects. The major drawback of DL models such as these is that they require large amounts of data to be able to operate correctly; in the case of image recognition, labeled images of the object to be detected in diverse situations. To partially overcome this issue, transfer learning is used on models that have already been trained on other databases such as the ImageNet database. Different architectures have been examined with the objective of detecting grapes using transfer learning which yield good results [7]. Some other models have also been explored, such as the Mask R-CNN by Santos et al. [22], Faster R-CNN, R-FCN, and SSD [12]. These methods detect the location of grapes in the image with bounding boxes. Other approaches use deep learning for semantic segmentation to detect individual berries [10,25] or grapevine flowers [21].

Among these approaches, deep learning methods and, more specifically, CNN architectures for semantic segmentation have been studied. The selected model has a pre-trained UNet architecture that was perfected using transfer learning on specific datasets for it to be able to detect grapes. The output of this model is a binary image the same size as the input, where each pixel has been given the value of 1 or 0. The latter value indicates that the pixel does not belong to a grape, while the first value indicates that the pixel belongs to a grape.

3   Scenario Description and Methodology

This section will detail the resources that were mobilized and provide information on the deep neural network and its variants that were used in the various tests that were undertaken.

In total, three different devices were used. The first one was an NVIDIA DGX-1 server that is part of the ROMEO Computing Center of the University of Reims Champagne-Ardenne, composed of 8 Tesla P100 GPUs. This server was used to train the original model. The results that were obtained using one of its GPUs are the ones selected to serve as the baseline for comparing the performances of the different boards and models. Alongside the DGX, two embedded devices were used: the Jetson Nano 2 GB (Fig. 1a) and the STM32MP157C-DK2 (Fig. 1b).

The first board is the Jetson Nano 2GB, produced by NVIDIA, which comes with a Quad-core ARM A57 CPU and a 128-core NVIDIA Maxwell GPU. The board that was used had the latest SDK installed, JetPack 4.5.1, as well as the version 2.4.0 of TensorFlow and the version 2.4.1 of TensorFlow Lite. Therefore, the Jetson Nano accepts TensorFlow models, TensorFlow Lite (*tflite*) models as well as models based on the TensorRT runtime promoted by NVIDIA [1]. Because it has enough resources, it was also able to run the TensorFlow model.

The second board is produced by STMicroelectronics and has two processors, a dual-core Cortex-A7 32 bits and a Cortex-M4 32 bits. The latest version of the X-Linux-AI package, specifically created by STMicroelectronics to be able to run AI models on their devices, was installed on the board that was used for testing. This package comes with TensorFlow Lite 2.4.1 as well as the necessary support libraries for using Coral Edge TPU accelerators. Since it is unable to have any version of TensorFlow installed on it, the STM32MP157C-DK2 is only able to run *tflite* models. Because this board has no dedicated GPU for artificial intelligence, inferences can only be performed using its CPU unless an external processing unit is connected to the device. To boost its performances, the STM32MP157C-DK2 board was equipped with a Google Coral USB accelerator (Fig. 1c). This tensor processing unit (TPU) is an ASIC processor specifically designed to accelerate the inference of artificial intelligence models, which are provided in the form of TensorFlow Lite models.

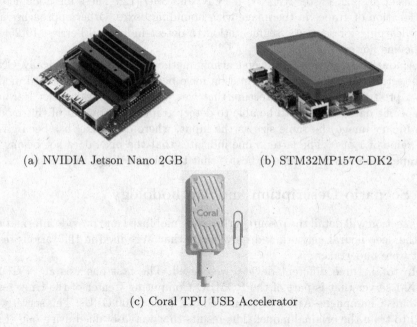

(a) NVIDIA Jetson Nano 2GB   (b) STM32MP157C-DK2

(c) Coral TPU USB Accelerator

Fig. 1. Edge boards and accelerator used in this work

The model that was selected for these experiments had a UNet architecture [20] containing over 8 million trainable parameters. This encoder-decoder architecture used a MobileNet-V2 backbone as an encoder and was downloaded using the *segmentation-models* Python package [24]. The UNet architecture was not designed with the objective of using it for real-time applications. However, because the real-time constraints in this case are relatively relaxed, it is possible to use a larger model that will be slower but slightly more precise than some lighter models that were designed with real-time applications in mind. As explained in the previous section, it is common practice to use a pre-trained model on a large, varied database and use transfer learning to adapt it to other needs. This model was already trained using the ImageNet dataset; transfer learning was then used to specialize it in grape segmenting using 318 images divided into two sets: the training set containing 254 images and the validation set containing 64 images.

The images that were used for training and testing the model were all acquired by our team, for this specific task, at the wine press. Each one was a high resolution (4000 by 3000 pixels) image representing four crates at the wine press containing grapes as well as some of the surrounding environment, an example can be seen in Fig. 2. The model can only accept image blocks of 224 by 224 pixels as input. The images in the training and validation set were therefore split into smaller blocks which corresponds to 12713 image blocks for the training set and 3250 image blocks for the validation set. The training process was performed on one GPU of the DGX server for a total of 30 epochs, with a batch size of 32. The Jaccard index was used as a loss function and Adam as an optimizer. The model was implemented in Python using TensorFlow's Keras API and saved in the *hdf5* format. For this model, all the weights and biases are stored as 32-bit floating-point numbers (float32 datatype).

A specific testing set was created for this case study using images in the validation set. They were cropped to be 900 pixels high by 700 pixels wide and represent only one crate of grapes at the wine press, an example of an image of the testing set is shown in Fig. 3a. The testing set was composed of 28 images, 16 of those were crates containing red grapes and 12 containing white grapes.

Fig. 2. Example of an image in the training set.

The segmentation of an image is done by dividing the provided input into blocks of the required size, in this case 224 by 224 pixels. The final segmentation mask is then reconstructed from the output mask of each block to produce an image with the same dimension as the input. With the full mask and the image, it is possible to extract the grapes from the rest of the image by simply multiplying the input image with the segmentation mask. Since in the latter a pixel considered to belong to a grape is represented with a value of 1 and anything else is represented with a value of 0, the multiplication will turn the value of any pixel that is not a grape on the input image to 0, which will appear black on the final image, and the values of the pixels that belong to grapes will be unchanged, appearing on the final image as they do on the input image. An example of this can be seen in Fig. 3 which shows the different steps of the workflow. Figure 3a shows the input of the model, an image from the testing set, Fig. 3b shows the corresponding segmentation mask that was obtained with the original model using the DGX server, and finally Fig. 3c shows the segmented image after the multiplication process.

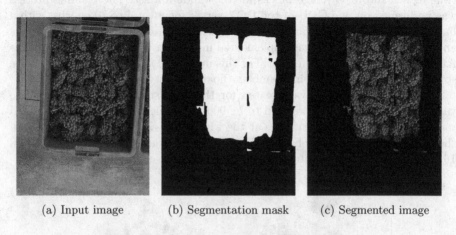

(a) Input image   (b) Segmentation mask   (c) Segmented image

Fig. 3. Example of the model's workflow.

The embedded devices are not necessarily powerful enough to run an AI model written in Python. For efficiency reasons, the applications that are run on these kinds of devices are usually programmed in a compiled language such as C or C++ as opposed to an interpreted language like Python. However, to avoid having to rewrite entire models in one of these languages and yet still be able to deploy them on smaller, embedded devices, Tensorflow has created a conversion process to optimize a *hdf5* model developed using their API. The process converts the model into an optimized FlatBuffer by, for example, fusing layers together when possible. This conversion aims at reducing the overall size of the model while trying to maintain the performances of the original model. Different options are available when converting a model from the *hdf5* format to the *tflite* format. A commonly used one is the quantization of the weights and biases to optimize the model even further. Using this converter, on the UNet model that was developed (hereby referred to as the original model), two variants were generated. Both variants were obtained by using the TOCO converter provided by TensorFlow and saved in the *tflite* format. The first model was converted in the simplest manner using the API provided by TensorFlow's version 2.2. No datatype conversion was performed on the weights, biases or activations for this model therefore maintaining their original datatype of float32.

The second variant, while also being converted using TensorFlow's version 2.2, took advantage of the post-training integer quantization process to convert the datatype of the constant tensors (i.e., weights and biases) and the variable tensors (i.e., activations) from float32 to int8. This quantization process reduces the size of the model and the memory usage while also increasing the inference speed allowing it run on smaller devices. However, it will inevitably affect the global performances of the model in a negative way due to rounding errors that will occur during the conversion. To convert the variable tensors (the output of the intermediate layers), a representative dataset must be provided to estimate the range of the floating-point tensors by running a few inference cycles. A specific dataset does not need to be created for this process therefore, for the original model, the representative dataset was generated using the images in the validation set. Several of the images were cut into blocks of the same size as the model's input. There was a total of 179 images, each of 224 by 224 pixels in the representative dataset. Before being used for the quantization of the model, the images were normalized. This conversion operation is necessary for being able to use the model on a TPU. The accelerator can only run layers that have been converted beforehand. If the entire model is not quantized, then the operations that have not been affected by the process will be run on the CPU.

In this case, all the operations, i.e., the different layers, were successfully converted except for the first and the final one. Because the images are normalized before being fed to the model, the value of each pixel is a floating-point number between 0 and 1. If the input layer only accepted integers, then the pixel values would be rounded off and the input image would only contain values of 0, creating a black image and rendering the inference pointless. For the final layer, even though the model's output is a binary mask with integer values for pixels—1 represents a pixel belonging to a grape and 0 a pixel that does not – the performances were significantly deteriorated if the output of the final layer was of type int8. An example of the impact of the quantization of the final layer is shown in Fig. 4. Therefore, the first and final layers were not converted using post-training quantization.

To evaluate the performances, three criteria were used: the inference time, the overall size of the model, and the intersection over union (IOU) score (see Eq. 1). The inference time is measured to compare the hardware as well as validate or invalidate that a given model on a certain device respects the real-time constraint that has been set – 15 s in this case. The size of the model is given to show how efficient the compression is during the conversion process. The IOU score was calculated relative to the results obtained with the DGX server. The idea behind this approach is to assess how the performances of the different versions of the model vary with respect to the original one. Therefore, an IOU score of 1 means that the performances of the variant model are the same as those of the original

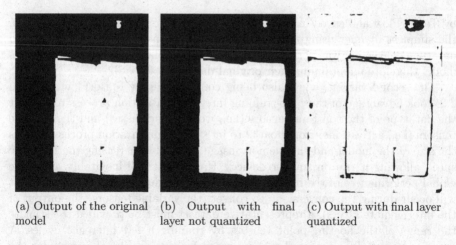

(a) Output of the original model (b) Output with final layer not quantized (c) Output with final layer quantized

Fig. 4. Example of the impact of the quantization of the final layer.

one. The original model obtained a score of 0.97 in training and a score of 0.94 with the validation set.

$$IOU(A, B) = \frac{A \cap B}{A \cup B} \qquad (1)$$

4   Results and Discussions

The obtained results are presented in Table 1. Figures 5 and 6 show an example of the output for each model variant on the Jetson Nano board and the STM32MP157C-DK2 board, respectively. The inference time and the IOU score that are presented here were obtained by averaging the individual inference time and IOU score of all the images in the test set. For each board, three tests were run with different models. On the STM32MP157C-DK2 board, only the *tflite* versions of the model (quantized and not quantized) were tested because the board does not support TensorFlow but only the TensorFlow Lite runtime environment. The quantized model was run twice, once without using the accelerator and the second time with the accelerator. The Jetson Nano board was able to run the original model with TensorFlow and both compressed ones. Of the three models, only the original one is run using the GPU. The two variants only use the CPU. The TPU was not used with the Jetson Nano board.

For the STM32MP157C-DK2 board, the results show that the device is not powerful enough to run the *tflite* model using only the CPU, whether it be quantized or not, and fit the requirements. The quantization process does allow for a slight decrease in the inference time, of a factor of 1.1 only. This improvement is far from enough to satisfy the real-time condition that was set. The only viable solution is to use the TPU accelerator in which case the inference time is reduced by a factor of 13 when comparing it with the same model without the use of the

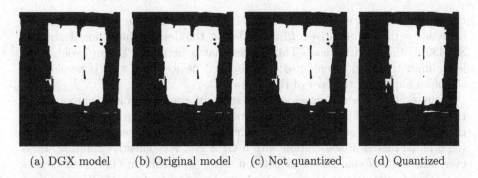

(a) DGX model   (b) Original model   (c) Not quantized   (d) Quantized

Fig. 5. Examples of the output of the different models on the Jetson board.

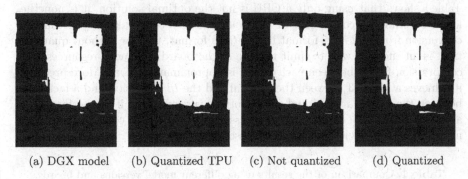

(a) DGX model   (b) Quantized TPU   (c) Not quantized   (d) Quantized

Fig. 6. Examples of the output of the different models on the STM board.

accelerator. Only in this case is the real-time condition met for this board. However, using the accelerator does require the model to be quantized which results in a degradation of the performances as shown by the relative IOU score of 0.93. Considering the major decrease in the inference time, the slight deterioration of the performances is justified, especially since it is the only scenario that fills the real-time requirements. It is interesting to note, however, that since the IOU score is 1 for the non-quantized model, the conversion from the *hdf5* format to the *tflite* does not impact its performances and the only effect is to reduce its overall size.

The results obtained with the Jetson Nano board show that there are two possibilities that respect the real-time constraint, either by using the *hdf5* model with the GPU or by using the quantized model with the CPU. The most efficient solution is to use the original model as there is no deterioration in the performances due to the quantization process. Similarly, to the other board, the quantization of the *tflite* model decreases the inference time, in this case by a factor two. This shows that the speed increase is also related to the hardware and not just dependent on the conversion and quantization.

The *tflite* models, whether it is the quantized version or the non-quantized one, allow for the comparison of the hardware of the boards, and more specifically the CPUs. There is more than a factor 10 between the time needed to run the inference with the quantized *tflite* model on the Jetson Nano board and the STM32MP157C-DK2 board. This proves that a better CPU can avoid, or at least limit, the need to enhance an embedded device with a TPU accelerator, therefore impacting the cost of the solution.

The results in Table 1 provides interesting information on key components of the boards. More importantly, it gives insight on elements to look out for when trying to deploy AI models on smaller devices. The first takeaway is that using the original model in association with a GPU is a very effective solution. However, this kind of component is not commonly available on embedded devices and can be relatively expensive. Moreover, the quality of the CPU conditions the need for supplemental hardware such as a TPU accelerator. Even though Table 1 shows that using only a CPU is not the optimal solution, it is nonetheless a determining component of the boards. The second takeaway is that the conversion from the *hdf5* format to the *tflite* format, with or without quantization, is an effective way to limit the use of the board's memory resources. The compression factor between each model is approximately three. More precisely, it achieves a factor 3 between the original and the *tflite* version and a factor 3.6 between the non-quantized and the quantized version. Even if the performances are impacted by the quantization process, it still allows for complex and heavy model to run on devices with limited resources.

Table 1. Comparison of the results using different model versions and boards.

	Inference time	IOU score	Model size
Baseline	0.4 s	N/A	93 MB
STM *tflite* not quantized	2 m 11 s	1	31 MB
STM *tflite* quantized without TPU	1 m 57 s	0.93	8.7 MB
STM *tflite* quantized with TPU	9 s	0.93	8.7 MB
Jetson *hdf5*	6 s	1	93 MB
Jetson *tflite* not quantized	22 s	1	31 MB
Jetson *tflite* quantized	11 s	0.93	8.7 MB

5   Conclusion and Future Work

Deep neural networks require large amounts of resources to operate. This is not a problem when they are deployed on various servers with powerful GPUs; however, this impedes on deploying trained models on embedded devices with limited capabilities. To tackle this problem and avoid having to rewrite models in programming languages that are better suited for smaller devices such a C or C++, different converters exist to reduce the size and the necessary resources for the models to run. These converters allow models that were developed using high end APIs such as TensorFlow to be easily deployed on boards such as the STM32MP157C-DK2 or the Jetson Nano 2 GB.

In this paper, a deep neural network with a UNet architecture for semantic segmentation was converted to the *tflite* format using the TensorFlow tools, allowing it to run on two small devices. The evaluation of the boards proposed in this paper was based on the comparison of three criteria: the inference time, the IOU score relative to the non-converted model, and the model size. The obtained results are very encouraging as they show that it is possible to deploy the converted model in a real-time context while limiting the performance losses due to its conversion. The time constraints at the wine press are relatively light which allows the exploration of model architectures that are not necessarily conceived for real-time applications, such as the original UNet architecture that was used in this case study. However, different architectures will be explored in the future that are lighter and can provide similar performances. Nonetheless, this paper gives some insight into the trade-off between performances and inference time when deploying models to smaller devices.

Still, other alternative converters have not been studied here. For instance, NVIDIA promotes its optimizer and runtime TensorRT [1] to be used in conjunction with Jetson Nano 2GB boards. Also, the N2D2 platform [2] developed by the CEA-List can convert models from an ONNX format to various targets, including the STM32MP157C-DK2 board. Using N2D2 would bypass the use of Python and TensorFlow Lite by creating a specifically designed project in C. These other converters may provide better inference time while maintaining the same performances and will be explored in the future.

Acknowledgments. This work has been performed in the project AI4DI: Artificial Intelligence for Digitizing Industry, under grant agreement No 826060. The project is co-funded by grants from Germany, Austria, Finland, France, Norway, Latvia, Belgium, Italy, Switzerland, and the Czech Republic and - Electronic Component Systems for European Leadership Joint Undertaking (ECSEL JU).

We also would like to thank the ROMEO Computing Center (https://romeo.univ-reims.fr) of the University of Reims Champagne-Ardenne, where part of the models were developed, and Vranken-Pommery Monopole, our partner in the AI4DI project, for allowing image collection in their vineyards and facilities.

References

1. NVIDIA TensorRT (2016). https://developer.nvidia.com/tensorrt
2. CEA-LIST/N2D2 (2021). https://github.com/CEA-LIST/N2D2. Original-date: 2017–01-06T13:01:02Z
3. Aquino, A., Barrio, I., Diago, M.P., Millan, B., Tardaguila, J.: vitisBerry: an android-smartphone application to early evaluate the number of grapevine berries by means of image analysis. Comput. Electron. Agric. **148**, 19–28 (2018)
4. Aquino, A., Millan, B., Diago, M.P., Tardaguila, J.: Automated early yield prediction in vineyards from on-the-go image acquisition. Comput. Electron. Agric. **144**, 26–36 (2018). https://doi.org/10.1016/j.compag.2017.11.026

5. Aquino, A., Millan, B., Gaston, D., Diago, M.P., Tardaguila, J.: vitisFlower®: development and testing of a novel android-smartphone application for assessing the number of grapevine flowers per inflorescence using artificial vision techniques. Sensors **15**(9), 21204–21218 (2015)
6. Behroozi-Khazaei, N., Maleki, M.R.: A robust algorithm based on color features for grape cluster segmentation. Comput. Electron. Agric. **142**, 41–49 (2017). https://doi.org/10.1016/j.compag.2017.08.025
7. Cecotti, H., Rivera, A., Farhadloo, M., Pedroza, M.A.: Grape detection with convolutional neural networks. Expert Syst. Appl. **159**, 113588 (2020). https://doi.org/10.1016/j.eswa.2020.113588
8. Chamelat, R., Rosso, E., Choksuriwong, A., Rosenberger, C., Laurent, H., Bro, P.: Grape detection by image processing. In: IECON 2006–32nd Annual Conference on IEEE Industrial Electronics, pp. 3697–3702 (2006). https://doi.org/10.1109/IECON.2006.347704
9. Dunn, G.M., Martin, S.R.: Yield prediction from digital image analysis: a technique with potential for vineyard assessments prior to harvest. Aust. J. Grape Wine Res. **10**(33), 196–198 (2004). https://doi.org/10.1111/j.1755-0238.2004.tb00022.x
10. Grimm, J., Herzog, K., Rist, F., Kicherer, A., Töpfer, R., Steinhage, V.: An adaptable approach to automated visual detection of plant organs with applications in grapevine breeding. Biosys. Eng. **183**, 170–183 (2019). https://doi.org/10.1016/j.biosystemseng.2019.04.018
11. Grossetete, M., Berthoumieu, Y., Da Costa, J.P., Germain, C., Lavialle, O., Grenier, G.: Early estimation of vineyard yield: site specific counting of berries by using a smartphone. In: International Conference on Agiculture Engineering (AgEng), pp. tabla137-C1915 (2012). https://hal.archives-ouvertes.fr/hal-00950298
12. Heinrich, K., Roth, A., Breithaupt, L., Möller, B., Maresch, J.: Yield prognosis for the agrarian management of vineyards using deep learning for object counting. In: Wirtschaftsinformatik 2019 Proceedings p. 15 (2019). https://aisel.aisnet.org/wi2019/track05/papers/3
13. Keresztes, B., Abdelghafour, F., Randriamanga, D., Da Costa, J.P., Germain, C.: Real-time fruit detection using deep neural networks. In: 14th International Conference on Precision Agriculture (2018). https://hal.archives-ouvertes.fr/hal-02518559
14. Liu, S., Marden, S., Whitty, M.: Towards automated yield estimation in viticulture. In: Proceedings of the Australasian Conference on Robotics and Automation, Sydney, Australia, p. 9 (2013)
15. Liu, S., Zeng, X., Whitty, M.: A vision-based robust grape berry counting algorithm for fast calibration-free bunch weight estimation in the field. Comput. Electron. Agric. **173**, 11 (2020). https://doi.org/10.1016/j.compag.2020.105360
16. Luo, L., Tang, Y., Zou, X., Wang, C., Zhang, P., Feng, W.: Robust grape cluster detection in a vineyard by combining the adaboost framework and multiple color components. Sensors (Basel, Switzerland) **16**(1212), 21 (2016)
17. Maldonado, W., Barbosa, J.C.: Automatic green fruit counting in orange trees using digital images. Comput. Electron. Agric. **127**, 572–581 (2016)
18. Nuske, S., Wilshusen, K., Achar, S., Yoder, L., Singh, S.: Automated visual yield estimation in vineyards. J. Field Robot. **31**(55), 837–860 (2014). https://doi.org/10.1002/rob.21541
19. Reis, M.J.C.S., et al.: Automatic detection of bunches of grapes in natural environment from color images. J. Appl. Logic **10**(44), 285–290 (2012). https://doi.org/10.1016/j.jal.2012.07.004

20. Ronneberger, O., Fischer, P., Brox, T.: U-Net: convolutional networks for biomedical image segmentation. In: Navab, N., Hornegger, J., Wells, W.M., Frangi, A.F. (eds.) MICCAI 2015. LNCS, vol. 9351, pp. 234–241. Springer, Cham (2015). https://doi.org/10.1007/978-3-319-24574-4_28
21. Rudolph, R., Herzog, K., Töpfer, R., Steinhage, V.: Efficient identification, localization and quantification of grapevine inflorescences in unprepared field images using fully convolutional networks. arXiv:1807.03770 [cs], pp. 95–104 (2018)
22. Santos, T.T., de Souza, L.L., dos Santos, A.A., Avila, S.: Grape detection, segmentation, and tracking using deep neural networks and three-dimensional association. Comput. Electron. Agric. 170, 105247 (2020). https://doi.org/10.1016/j.compag.2020.105247
23. Song, Y., Glasbey, C., Horgan, G., Polder, G., Dieleman, J., van der Heijden, G.: Automatic fruit recognition and counting from multiple images. Biosyst. Eng. 118, 203–215 (2014)
24. Yakubovskiy, P.: Segmentation models (2019). https://github.com/qubvel/segmentation_models
25. Zabawa, L., Kicherer, A., Klingbeil, L., Töpfer, R., Kuhlmann, H., Roscher, R.: Counting of grapevine berries in images via semantic segmentation using convolutional neural networks. ISPRS J. Photogramm. Remote. Sens. 164, 73–83 (2020). https://doi.org/10.1016/j.isprsjprs.2020.04.002

Abnormal Behavior Detection in Farming Stream Data

Juliet Chebet Moso[1,3]([✉]), Stéphane Cormier[1], Hacène Fouchal[1],
Cyril de Runz[2], and John M. Wandeto[3]

[1] CReSTIC EA 3804, Université de Reims Champagne-Ardenne, 51097 Reims, France
juliet-chebet.moso@etudiant.univ-reims.fr,
{stephane.cormier,hacene.fouchal}@univ-reims.fr
[2] BDTLN, LIFAT, University of Tours, Tours, France
cyril.derunz@univ-tours.fr
[3] Computer Science, Dedan Kimathi University of Technology, Nyeri, Kenya
john.wandeto@dkut.ac.ke

Abstract. Farmers have been able to detect, quantify, and respond to spatial and temporal variation in crops thanks to a variety of technological advancements in recent years. Precision farming aims to provide precise targeting of agricultural inputs while reducing waste and negative consequences. Precision agriculture technologies are effective instruments for increasing farm sustainability and production. These technologies provide ways to create more with less resources. Nowadays, improving agricultural production efficiency and crop yields is impossible without the use of contemporary digital technologies and smart machinery. The introduction of high-accuracy GPS technology into farm machinery, such as combine harvesters, has been a significant component of precision farming. In this paper, we present a streaming-based methodology for detecting anomalies in combine harvester GPS recordings. The key hypothesis is that, "similar points in a feature space have similar anomaly scores". We examine a data-driven strategy with the goal of applying unsupervised detection algorithms to find anomalies on the fly. Based on the results of the experiments, we can conclude that LSCP beats all other strategies when the number of base detectors is varied. The AUCPR performance of LSCP with two base detectors (HBOS and MCD) is 8.02% better than the second best technique MCD.

Keywords: Anomaly detection · Data streams · Precision farming · Unsupervised learning

1 Introduction

Smart Agriculture refers to the application of digital methods to innovate, control, and optimize agricultural production systems. Human intervention in agriculture is boosted by digital transformation, which aids in reducing effort, implementing particular measures, calibrating the use of chemical products on soil

© Springer Nature Switzerland AG 2021
S. Boumerdassi et al. (Eds.): SSA 2021, CCIS 1470, pp. 44–56, 2021.
https://doi.org/10.1007/978-3-030-88259-4_4

and crops, as well as ensuring and boosting yield. It also aids in the management of all procedures that permit or support agricultural output, such as economic and administrative ones. Smart Agriculture's goal is to provide solutions that can be used by all farmers, independent of farm size, location, or industry, while leveraging scale effects and keeping costs low. The benefits envisioned from the introduction and integration of technology processes in agriculture are now attributed to increased production and quality efficiency, cost reduction, input optimization, and environmental impact minimization.

The concept behind anomaly detection research is that exploitative behaviour differs quantitatively from normal system behavior. Anomalies are "patterns in data that do not conform to a well-defined notion of normal behaviour" [5]. These patterns reflect fresh, unexpected, or unknown data. Anomaly detection may be performed as a binary classification problem in the presence of labeled data using supervised learning approaches, with data labels being either normal or abnormal. This is seldom the case due to the lack of labeled data and the rarity of abnormal events. Unsupervised learning techniques are used in most anomaly detection systems since huge volumes of unlabeled data are available [5]. Intrusion detection, fraud detection, fault detection, system health monitoring, event detection in sensor networks, identifying ecological changes, and defect identification in images using machine vision are some of the examples of anomaly detection. Anomalies can be classified as erroneous data due to device failure/system failures or as odd data indicating rare/exceptional occurrences that occurred despite being abnormal [19]. Surprising data is unique to each instance, making it challenging to categorize these abnormalities using standard approaches.

This study examines anomaly detection in agricultural fields by analysing GPS logs generated by a combine harvester during wheat harvesting season. We utilize techniques based on hypothesis testing on the occurrence of an anomalous movement pattern during in-field harvesting. The primary assumption of our analysis is that, "Normal instances are far more frequent than anomalies". The key hypothesis is that, "similar points in a feature space have similar anomaly scores". When applied to grain harvesting: "If a combine harvester changes its speed rapidly at a particular point within the field, then it implies an anomaly has occurred". Our focus is on nonrecurring harvesting disruptions whose occurrence is usually unexpected and random.

We propose the following contributions:

1. We present a detailed state of the art on anomaly detection techniques with a focus on precision agriculture;
2. We define and investigate the issue of completely unsupervised anomaly ensemble construction.
3. We propose an ensemble based methodology for detection of anomalies from a data stream of combine harvester GPS logs;
4. We evaluate the methodology using a real data-set of GPS logs generated by a combine harvester during wheat harvesting and compare its performance with state of the art techniques under the streaming context.

The rest of this paper is structured as follows: Sect. 2 presents the state of the art investigation on Specialized Micro Transportation Systems, anomaly detection techniques and anomaly detection in agricultural data. Section 3 presents the problem statement. Section 4 presents the methodology. Section 5 presents the experimental evaluation of the proposed technique, and Sect. 6 presents the conclusion and future work.

2   Related Works

This section introduces works on Specialized Micro Transportation Systems, anomaly detection techniques, and application of anomaly detection to agricultural data.

2.1   Specialized Micro Transportation Systems

Intelligent Transportation Systems (ITS) offer substantial advances in transportation system safety, mobility, productivity and environmental conservation [7]. Specialized Micro Transportation Systems (SMTS) are a subset of ITS which comprise of a limited number of vehicles cooperating on a specialized job [23]. SMTS vehicles frequently follow predictable and recognized patterns of activity, which vary depending on the operation at hand. Due to the highly developed and mechanized state of agriculture, it is quite usual for farmers to use numerous vehicles in various essential agricultural operations in order to increase efficiency. Harvesting is perhaps one of the more engaging of these tasks, since it often involves three types of vehicles: combine harvesters, grain carts, and semi trucks. During grain harvesting a single combine harvester is sufficient for the majority of harvesting activities. However, due to due to its limited storage capacity and transport speed, a semi truck is generally needed to convey harvested grain from fields to a grain elevator for storage or sale. Since trucks are not adapted to the uneven field surfaces, grain carts are engaged to deliver the grain from the harvesters to the trucks at the edges of the fields. With good coordination between these three types of vehicles, a reasonable level of efficiency may be achieved in completing the work. ITS may be used to enhance SMTS management, monitoring, and efficiency.

2.2   Anomaly Detection Techniques

A lot of work has gone into developing a wide range of anomaly detection algorithms, which can be broadly classified as: Classification based, Nearest Neighbour based, Clustering based, Statistical methods, Information Theoretic based, Spectral and Graph based methods [5,18]. These categories are summarised in Fig. 1 together with the workflow followed in anomaly detection.

In the discovery of outliers in high-dimensional data, the isolation-based technique employs the Isolation Forest (IForest) anomaly detection algorithm [11]. IForest is an unsupervised method that does not require labelled data and does

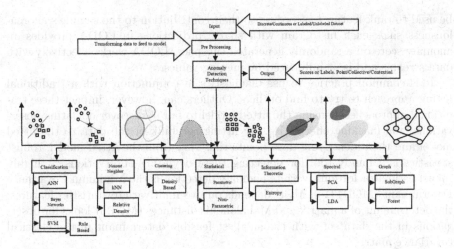

Fig. 1. Anomaly detection workflow and anomaly detection techniques [18]

not presume data distribution. It is also non-parametric and performs well on unbiased data with minimal noise points [2]. IForest is made up of a forest of randomly generated isolation trees (*itrees*). Because anomalies are uncommon and distinct from regular occurrences, a tree can be built to separate each one. At each tree, a determination is made as to whether or not an observation is normal. Anomalies are isolated closer to the tree's root due to their sensitivity to isolation, whereas normal points are isolated further down.

Locally Selective Combination in Parallel Outlier Ensembles (LSCP) [24] is an unsupervised anomaly detection algorithm that uses the consensus of a test instance's nearest neighbors in randomly selected feature subspaces to create a local area surrounding it. The Average of Maximum method is used to achieve LSCP, which involves fitting a homogeneous/heterogeneous list of base detectors to the training data, then picking the maximum outlier score to produce a pseudo ground truth for each instance. LSCP investigates both global and local data connections by training base detectors on the whole dataset and prioritizing data locality when combining detectors.

Histogram-based Outlier Score (HBOS) [9] is based on the assumption that features are independent, and hence computes outlier scores by creating histograms for each feature. Modeling the precise features of produced histograms and identifying deviations are used to identify anomalies. HBOS does not require data labeling and does not require any training or learning phase. With scoring-based detection, it also provides a quick computation time. A collection of k one-dimensional histograms is used by the Lightweight on-line detector of anomalies (LODA) [14] to identify anomalies. The probability density of input data projected onto a single projection vector is approximated by each histogram. Because LODA's output is proportional to the sample's negative log-likelihood, the greater the anomaly value, the less likely the sample is. This approach may be used to rank features according to their contribution to the sample's anomalousness since each histogram with sparse projections in LODA provides an anomaly score on a randomly generated subspace. LODA works effectively with data streams and isn't influenced by missing values.

It is common practice to use diagnostics in conjunction with a traditional fitting approach to try to find outliers. Outliers can, however, impact these traditional approaches, causing the fitted model to fail to discover deviating observations (the masking effect) [16]. By fitting the bulk of the data to the fitted model and then identifying data points that vary from the fitted model, robust statistics is a handy tool for detecting these deviating observations. A highly robust estimator for multivariate anomaly detection is the Minimum Covariance Determinant (MCD) [15]. MCD depends on two multivariate statistics features: the determinant of a matrix and Mahalanobis distances (MD). It looks for observations in the data set with the smallest feasible determinant in the classical covariance matrix.

2.3   Anomaly Detection in Agricultural Data

DeepAnomaly is proposed in [6] where a combination of background subtraction and Deep Learning is used for detection of obstacles and anomalies in an agricultural field. It takes advantage of the fact that agriculture field's visual features are homogeneous, and obstacles occur rarely. The main idea is to detect distant and heavily occluded objects and unknown object types. The detected obstacles included people, barrels, wells and a distant house. DeepAnomaly detects humans more accurately and in real time at larger distances as compared to state-of-the-art techniques. Anomaly detection of time series data by applying two machine learning models, Autoregressive Integrated Moving Average model (ARIMA) and Long Short-Term memory (LSTM) is presented in [1]. A temporal anomaly detection approach is developed that takes into account the temporal connections between digital farm sensor data. LSTM and ARIMA models are tested on real data collected from deployed agricultural sensors with the aim of identifying anomalous data readings. It was discovered that using LSTM results in improved anomaly detection prediction but requires more training time.

The automated identification of crop parcels with abnormal vegetation development is a current problem in precision agriculture. Detecting crop patches with significantly different phenological behaviors from the rest of the crop might aid users like farmers and agricultural cooperatives in improving agricultural practices, disease identification, and fertilizer management. In [13] Isolation forest unsupervised outlier detection algorithm is applied to synthetic aperture radar (SAR) and multispectral images acquired using Sentinel-1 (S1) and Sentinel-2 (S2) satellites to detect the most abnormal wheat and rapeseed crop parcels within a growing season. The four primary types of anomalies investigated were heterogeneity issues, growth anomalies, database errors, and non-agronomic outliers that were deemed irrelevant for crop monitoring. The results of the experiments showed that the use of both S1 and S1 features in anomaly detection resulted in more late growth anomalies and heterogeneous parcels being detected.

Detection of anomalous activity movement of combine harvesters was done in [20] using a Kalman filter and DBSCAN algorithm. The latitude and longitude values of GPS logs are converted to easting and northing coordinates and recursively applied to a Kalman filter that is based on a constant velocity (CV) dynamical model. Kalman filter residual is computed which gives the level of deviation of the filter estimates from the actual measurements. The Kalman filter residual is a measure for the smoothness of the combine harvester motion such that, sudden change in motion results in a higher residual value. The engine load, vehicle speed, and computed Kalman filter residual are then applied to DBSCAN algorithm which generates clusters indicative of the activity being carried out by the combine harvester. Based on the results, it was possible to identify clusters for uniform motion in field, uniform motion on road, stationary points and nonuniform motions (in-field turns, on-road turns, decelerating, accelerating).

3   Problem Statement

In typical combine harvester operation (whether harvesting or travelling between fields), the combine harvester travels in a straight path at a near constant pace. The behaviour of combine harvesters depend on whether they are harvesting in a field or traveling between fields. Changes in combine harvester speed, on the other hand, usually signal in-field or on-road actions such as turning and accelerating. During harvesting a combine harvester should operate at a maximum of 4mph for yield efficiency reasons and a maximum of 20mph on the road or when moving between fields [23]. Moving at high speed can result in grain being missed thus lowering the yield. The focus of this research is the identification of abnormal harvesting behaviour by focusing on local regions (i.e. local contextual anomalies). Detecting anomalies using GPS data logs is a multivariate task where the data is modelled as a data stream and applied to anomaly detection techniques using windowing concept. The primary assumption of the analysis is that, *"Normal instances are far more frequent than anomalies"*. Therefore, the key hypothesis is: *similar points in a feature space have similar anomaly scores*. Harvesting perspective: *"If vehicles change their speed rapidly at a particular point, then it implies an anomaly has occurred"*. A deviation based anomaly detection approach is applied with a focus on in-field harvesting data. To perform multivariate anomaly detection we will consider the following data attributes: latitude, longitude, altitude, speed, bearing and accuracy.

4   Methodology

A sliding window approach is employed in streaming anomaly detection, in which data samples inside a window are sorted by an outlier score, with highly ranked data samples being labeled anomalies. A pipeline framework was adopted where each incoming new instance x_t is passed through a pre-processor (unit norm scaler) which transforms x_t into a scaled feature vector without changing its dimensions. The scaled feature vector is then processed by the streaming anomaly detection model which predicts the label y_t for the instance. This predicted label is then passed to the running average post-processor which converts the score to the average of all previous scores in the current window. Figure 2 depicts the proposed anomaly detection framework.

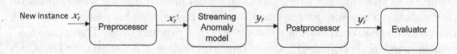

Fig. 2. Anomaly Detection framework

4.1 Data Pre-processing and Transformation

In this study we used a GPS data-set [21] collected using Nexus 7 tablets on a farm in Colorado U.S.A during 2017 wheat harvesting season. A GPS recorder app was kept running for each involved vehicle (combine harvesters, grain carts and trucks) during harvesting. In a typical harvesting scenario, there are more than one harvester working simultaneously in the field. This results in overlap of the trajectories of the vehicles. A single trajectory is considered as the consolidation of all GPS logs belonging to a single vehicle collected within a day. For the purpose of this study, we use the movement trajectory of a single combine harvester recorded in one day.

Definition: *Trajectory:* A raw trajectory consists of a sequence of n points $T = [p_1, p_2, \ldots, p_n]$, in which $p_i = x, y, z, t, A$, where x, y ,z represent the position (latitude, longitude and altitude) of the moving vehicle in space, t is the timestamp and A represents other attributes associated with the point (i.e. speed, bearing and accuracy).

Trajectory mining was done using Quantum GIS (QGIS) an open-source cross-platform desktop geographic information system application that supports viewing, editing and visualization of geospatial data. The key interest were the data points generated in the field during harvesting, therefore visualization and map matching was done using QGIS to ensure the GPS points were mapped to a field. The second step was to extract only those points within a specific field using a bounding box. The extracted data exhibited normal harvesting behaviour with all data points below 4 mph which is the maximum harvesting speed. To create an evaluation data-set, anomalies were introduced in the original data-set by varying the vehicle speed at specific points along the trajectory such that for specific sections of the trajectory a sequential number of points had their speed increased by a random number between a given range of values above 4 mph. Figure 3 presents the in-field trajectory of a combine harvester after introduction of anomalies with normal points in green, anomalies in red.

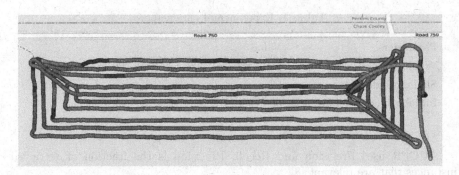

Fig. 3. Area of interest; in-field trajectory of a combine harvester showing normal points in green and anomalies in red (Color figure online)

Multivariate anomaly detection is performed by considering the latitude, longitude, altitude, speed, bearing and accuracy. The data is modelled as a data stream and applied to ensemble based technique for anomaly detection using windowing concept.

4.2 Performance Indicators

In order to evaluate the performance of the different approaches, we use the Area Under the Curve of the Receiver Operating Characteristic (AUC-ROC) [10] and the Area Under the Curve of Precision-Recall (AUCPR) [3]. Both indicators are based on the concepts of:

- True Positive (TP): True Positives are the correctly identified anomalies.
- False Positive (FP): False positive are incorrectly identified normal data.
- True Negative (TN): True negative are correctly identified normal data.
- False Negative (FN): False negative are incorrectly rejected anomalies.

The True Positive Rate (TPR), or Recall, is:

$$TPR = \frac{TP}{TP + FN}.$$

The False Positive Rate (TPR) is:

$$FPR = \frac{FP}{FP + TN}.$$

AUC-ROC receiver operating characteristics are TPR and FPR. The higher the AUC-ROC is, the better the detection is. AUC-ROC is the most popular evaluation measure for unsupervised outlier detection methods [4]. The AUCPR baseline is equivalent to the fraction of positives [17]:

$$AUCPR - baseline = \frac{TP}{TP + FP + FN + TN}$$

Table 1. Experimental parameters

Parameters	Values
Window sizes	100, 200, 300, 400, 500, 600, 700, 800, 900, 1000
Sliding window size	50
Initial window (training set)	500

AUCPR uses Precision and Recall. Precision is the fraction of retrieved instances that are relevant [8].

$$Precision = \frac{TP}{TP + FP}$$

5   Experimental Evaluation and Results

In this section, we present results obtained by experimenting anomaly detection techniques on GPS logs. The algorithms were implemented in Python programming language using PySAD framework [22] which allows us to integrate batch processing algorithms from PyOD [25] and to apply them to streaming data using sliding windows. HBOS, LODA, LSCP, MCD and IForest algorithms were implemented by adapting them to the streaming context using a reference window model. Since LSCP is an ensemble framework, we varied the number of base detectors in its implementation resulting in three models. LSCP_3 implements HBOS, MCD and IForest as the base detectors. LSCP_2 implements MCD and IForest as the base detectors. LSCP_1 implements MCD and HBOS as the base detectors. The reason for variation of base detectors was to attain unbiased overall detection accuracy with little variance by incorporating the capabilities of various base detectors while carefully combining their outputs to form a robust detector.

In the experiments we sort to find answers to the following questions:

– Which model best predicts anomalous cases given a streaming data set?
– Does the size of the window have an impact on how well models identify anomalies?
– What role does data association play in anomaly detection?

Multiple experiments with variation in the window size were carried out to establish the impact of the window size on the performance of the algorithms. Table 1 summarises the parameters used in the experiments.

AUC-ROC and AUCPR were utilized to investigate the algorithms' performance since they are suited for imbalanced data sets. The applied models output probabilities for each instance which are transformed into predicted labels using a decision threshold. These predicted labels are then used to compute the AUC-ROC and AUCPR values. Table 2 and 3 summarises the AUC-ROC and AUCPR results obtained from the experiments.

Table 2. AUC-ROC performance results for window size variation

Window size	LODA	HBOS	IForest	MCD	LSCP_1	LSCP_2	LSCP_3
100	0.5391	0.8851	0.9590	0.9913	0.9950	**0.9960**	0.9890
200	0.6529	0.8874	0.9739	**0.9948**	0.9926	0.9942	0.9891
300	0.7138	0.8950	0.9763	**0.9948**	0.9940	0.9924	0.9884
400	0.7719	0.9102	0.9788	0.9926	0.9905	**0.9938**	0.9907
500	0.7894	0.9208	0.9800	**0.9953**	0.9893	0.9932	0.9904
600	0.8067	0.9257	0.9783	**0.9955**	0.9911	0.9921	0.9889
700	0.8102	0.9328	0.9786	0.9923	0.9910	**0.9927**	0.9896
800	0.8168	0.9412	0.9800	0.9917	**0.9918**	0.9910	0.9899
900	0.8070	0.9502	0.9803	**0.9926**	0.9912	0.9911	0.9888
1000	0.8104	0.9560	0.9795	0.9900	**0.9920**	0.9902	0.9888
Average	0.7518	0.9204	0.9765	**0.9931**	0.9918	0.9927	0.9894

The experimental results reveal that the performance of LSCP with variation in the number of base detectors is very competitive. The performance is particularly notable in LSCP_1 which achieves a AUCPR value of 0.7661 which is 8.02% better than the second best technique MCD. Figure 4 and 5 shows that the performance of all algorithms in terms of AUC-ROC and AUCPR. The performance of LODA and HBOS in terms of AUC-ROC and AUCPR increases progressively with increase in window size. IForest, MCD and variants of LSCP show slight variation in AUC-ROC as the window sizes are varied.

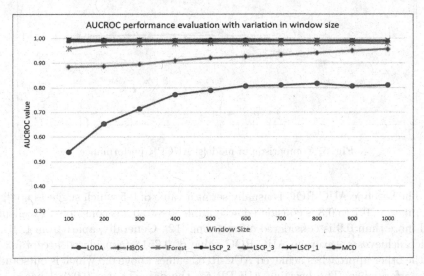

Fig. 4. Comparison of models' AUC-ROC performance

Table 3. AUCPR performance results for window size variation

Window size	LODA	HBOS	IForest	MCD	LSCP_1	LSCP_2	LSCP_3
100	0.0464	0.2162	0.4190	0.7072	0.8156	**0.8567**	0.7426
200	0.0563	0.2778	0.4853	0.7501	0.7730	**0.7914**	0.6989
300	0.1034	0.2936	0.4882	0.7398	**0.8081**	0.7538	0.7257
400	0.1283	0.3467	0.4937	0.6450	**0.7441**	0.7283	0.6844
500	0.2234	0.3626	0.5123	**0.7553**	0.7521	0.7408	0.7282
600	0.2026	0.3707	0.5079	**0.7591**	0.7500	0.7178	0.7085
700	0.2017	0.3956	0.5009	0.6404	**0.7477**	0.7328	0.7055
800	0.1994	0.4128	0.4974	0.6239	**0.7637**	0.7072	0.6913
900	0.1899	0.4364	0.5055	0.6516	**0.7470**	0.7229	0.6995
1000	0.1842	0.4662	0.4884	0.5867	**0.7602**	0.7099	0.7083
Average	0.1536	0.3578	0.4899	0.6859	**0.7661**	0.7462	0.7093

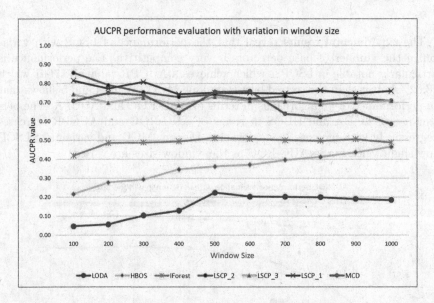

Fig. 5. Comparison of models' AUCPR performance

The baseline AUC-ROC is usually set at a value of 0.5 which suggests no discrimination, 0.7 to 0.8 is considered acceptable, 0.8 to 0.9 is considered excellent, and more than 0.9 is considered outstanding [12]. Generally, apart from LODA which achieves an average AUC-ROC value of 0.7518 (considered acceptable), all the other approaches achieved AUC-ROC values above 0.9 which is outstanding performance. The baseline AUCPR for the data-set was 0.0333 (based on a sample size of 7416 with 247 true positive anomalies). Based on the results obtained for AUCPR, it is safe to conclude that all the techniques are able to distinguish anomalies from normal instances.

6   Conclusion

Improving agricultural production efficiency and crop yields is impossible without the use of contemporary digital technologies and smart machinery. The introduction of high-accuracy GPS technology into farm machinery, such as combine harvesters, has been a significant component of precision farming. To address the issue of anomaly detection, several techniques have been developed. Anomaly detection has a wide range of applications that necessitate a dependable and precise solution. In this study we have considered the analysis of GPS logs collected from a combine harvester in order to detect anomalous behaviour during wheat harvesting. The implementation of the windowing concept facilitates the detection of anomalies on the fly. It is worth noting that, through the use of machine learning it is possible to detect deviating behaviour of combine harvesters. Also the application of ensemble techniques improves the precision and recall detection performance. Based on the obtained results, LSCP_1 with two base detectors (HBOS and MCD) is able to handle GPS logs and detect anomalies with efficiency and therefore can be used to detect anomalous behaviour during farm operations.

Our future work will focus on adjustments of the ensemble learning decision rules for efficiency improvement. It will also be interesting to perform anomaly detection in field production using yield values.

References

1. Abdallah, M., Lee, W.J., Raghunathan, N., Mousoulis, C., Sutherland, J.W., Bagchi, S.: Anomaly detection through transfer learning in agriculture and manufacturing IoT systems. arXiv preprint arXiv:2102.05814 (2021)
2. Aggarwal, C.C.: Outlier analysis. In: Aggarwal, C.C. (ed.) Data Mining, pp. 237–263. Springer, Cham (2015). https://doi.org/10.1007/978-3-319-14142-8_8
3. Boyd, K., Eng, K.H., Page, C.D.: Area under the precision-recall curve: point estimates and confidence intervals. In: Blockeel, H., Kersting, K., Nijssen, S., Železný, F. (eds.) ECML PKDD 2013. LNCS (LNAI), vol. 8190, pp. 451–466. Springer, Heidelberg (2013). https://doi.org/10.1007/978-3-642-40994-3_29
4. Campos, G.O., et al.: On the evaluation of unsupervised outlier detection: measures, datasets, and an empirical study. Data Min. Knowl. Disc. **30**(4), 891–927 (2016). https://doi.org/10.1007/s10618-015-0444-8
5. Chandola, V., Banerjee, A., Kumar, V.: Anomaly detection: a survey. ACM Comput. Surv. (CSUR) **41**(3), 1–58 (2009)
6. Christiansen, P., Nielsen, L.N., Steen, K.A., Jørgensen, R.N., Karstoft, H.: DeepAnomaly: combining background subtraction and deep learning for detecting obstacles and anomalies in an agricultural field. Sensors **16**(11), 1904 (2016)
7. Faezipour, M., Nourani, M., Saeed, A., Addepalli, S.: Progress and challenges in intelligent vehicle area networks. Commun. ACM **55**(2), 90–100 (2012)

8. Fawcett, T.: An introduction to ROC analysis. Pattern Recogn. Lett. **27**(8), 861–874 (2006)
9. Goldstein, M., Dengel, A.: Histogram-based outlier score (HBOS): a fast unsupervised anomaly detection algorithm. In: KI-2012: Poster and Demo Track, pp. 59–63 (2012)
10. Hanley, J.A., McNeil, B.J.: The meaning and use of the area under a receiver operating characteristic (ROC) curve. Radiology **143**(1), 29–36 (1982)
11. Liu, F.T., Ting, K.M., Zhou, Z.H.: Isolation forest. In: 2008 Eighth IEEE International Conference on Data Mining, pp. 413–422. IEEE (2008)
12. Mandrekar, J.N.: Receiver operating characteristic curve in diagnostic test assessment. J. Thorac. Oncol. **5**(9), 1315–1316 (2010)
13. Mouret, F., Albughdadi, M., Duthoit, S., Kouamé, D., Rieu, G., Tourneret, J.Y.: Outlier detection at the parcel-level in wheat and rapeseed crops using multispectral and SAR time series. Remote Sens. **13**(5), 956 (2021)
14. Pevný, T.: Loda: lightweight on-line detector of anomalies. Mach. Learn. **102**(2), 275–304 (2015). https://doi.org/10.1007/s10994-015-5521-0
15. Rousseeuw, P.J., Driessen, K.V.: A fast algorithm for the minimum covariance determinant estimator. Technometrics **41**(3), 212–223 (1999)
16. Rousseeuw, P.J., Hubert, M.: Anomaly detection by robust statistics. Wiley Interdiscip. Rev.: Data Min. Knowl. Discov. **8**(2), e1236 (2018)
17. Saito, T., Rehmsmeier, M.: The precision-recall plot is more informative than the ROC plot when evaluating binary classifiers on imbalanced datasets. PloS One **10**(3), e0118432 (2015)
18. Toshniwal, A., Mahesh, K., Jayashree, R.: Overview of anomaly detection techniques in machine learning. In: 2020 Fourth International Conference on I-SMAC (IoT in Social, Mobile, Analytics and Cloud)(I-SMAC), pp. 808–815. IEEE (2020)
19. Wang, X., Fagette, A., Sartelet, P., Sun, L.: A probabilistic tensor factorization approach to detect anomalies in spatiotemporal traffic activities. In: 2019 IEEE Intelligent Transportation Systems Conference (ITSC), pp. 1658–1663. IEEE (2019)
20. Wang, Y., Balmos, A., Krogmeier, J., Buckmaster, D.: Data-driven agricultural machinery activity anomaly detection and classification. In: Proceedings of the 14th International Conference on Precision Agriculture (2018)
21. Yaguang, Z., James, K.: Combine kart truck GPS data archive (2020)
22. Yilmaz, S.F., Kozat, S.S.: PySAD: a streaming anomaly detection framework in Python. arXiv preprint arXiv:2009.02572 (2020)
23. Zhang, Y., Balmos, A., Krogmeier, J.V., Buckmaster, D.: Working zone identification for specialized micro transportation systems using GPS tracks. In: 2015 IEEE 18th International Conference on Intelligent Transportation Systems, pp. 1779–1784. IEEE (2015)
24. Zhao, Y., Nasrullah, Z., Hryniewicki, M.K., Li, Z.: LSCP: locally selective combination in parallel outlier ensembles. In: Proceedings of the 2019 SIAM International Conference on Data Mining, pp. 585–593. SIAM (2019)
25. Zhao, Y., Nasrullah, Z., Li, Z.: PyOD: a Python toolbox for scalable outlier detection. J. Mach. Learn. Res. **20**(96), 1–7 (2019). http://jmlr.org/papers/v20/19-011.html

eWeightSmart - A Smart Approach to Beef Production Management

Rui Alves$^{(\boxtimes)}$, João Ascensão$^{(\boxtimes)}$, Diogo Camelo$^{(\boxtimes)}$, and Paulo Matos$^{(\boxtimes)}$

Polytechnic Institute of Bragança, Bragança, Portugal
{rui.alves,pmatos}@ipb.pt, {a34505,a36739}@alunos.ipb.pt

Abstract. The use of technologies related to the Internet of Things or Cloud Computing are presently becoming common in different activity sectors. The use of these concepts has allowed to create solutions to solve several social problems, optimizing some of the day-to-day tasks. The agricultural sector is no exception, where increasingly, "smart" solutions begin to emerge in an attempt to reduce the complexity of some tasks or, on a more conceptual level, to make it possible to exploit new markets. Beef production, an agricultural sub-sector, is in many world regions, the main source of income, however, this sub-sector is not always managed in the most optimized way. Cattle body weight management is an important aspect of this sub-sector, providing precious measures for food, health care, breeding and stock selection. For the farmers, the weight measurement when the animal is alive, allows a better commercialization of it, making possible a better management of feeding expenses, reducing waste. It's therefore necessary to find solutions to ensure a balance between beef production and the associated costs. This paper illustrates an approach to control the evolution of bovine animal's weight by means of automatic weighing and control of the food amount that is made available to each animal. Using a set of sensors, a mobile platform and using NB-IoT, a communication network, it was possible to devise an approach that can reduce costs in the sector and also enable the exploitation of new business models.

Keywords: Farmer · Weight · Cow · Beef · Production sensors

1 Introduction

Since ancient times, meat consumption has been common practice in society in general. Since it's often the only activity to generate wealth, beef production takes on extreme importance in some economies of the world [1]. Currently, beef production in the European Union ranks third in the world, with almost 64 million tonnes of meat consumed in 2018 [2]. The role of this sector is not only focused on food security and sustainable land use, but also on the socioeconomic well-being of rural communities and the gastronomic pleasure of urban and rural consumers around the world [3]. However, the beef industry is currently facing a small set of challenges.

S. Boumerdassi et al. (Eds.): SSA 2021, CCIS 1470, pp. 57–70, 2021.
https://doi.org/10.1007/978-3-030-88259-4_5

At the top of the list of this sector, the environmental issue appears, since cattle farms contribute significantly to the production of greenhouse gases. The large methane emissions, from nitrogen excreted, makes beef production one of the most polluting food production systems [4], leading some stables to reduce their emissions, by optimizing their processes, helping the ecological footprint. In addition to this challenge, the beef quality is increasingly important for the consumer. It's known that red meat contributes to some health problems (e.g., high cholesterol) [5,6], but also provides many important nutrients. In this way, issues of authenticity and food safety represents a challenge for the beef industry [7].

Another challenge facing the sector is the diversity of supply chains. There are different types of supply chains, but efficiency in operation can vary considerably between them. This diversity in efficiency, often creates problems of trust and understanding in the various parts of the supply chain, moreover, these problems also affect the mechanisms of generating value for the primary producer, since they aren't always transparent and clear. All these issues have a negative impact on the supply chain, but particularly on the farmer, as beef production is often of marginal profitability [8]. In this way, it's increasingly necessary to design tools that make this sector more efficient, trying to mitigate the challenges presented.

In this paper, an approach to control the evolution of the cattle weight is illustrated by means of automatic weighing and control of the food amount that is made available to each animal. Through a set of sensors, a mobile application and using NB-IoT, the presented approach contribute to reduce the operating costs of the sector and reduce the ecological footprint of the sector [9]. In short, it's intended with eWeightSmart optimize some of the processes involved in the beef production, allowing a better management of food resources and a reduction of waste generated. The remainder paper is organized as follows: Sect. 2 describes the technical details of the solution designed to respond the identified problem; Sect. 3 presents the conclusions of the work and guidelines for future work.

2   Architecture and Implementation

The design of the solution, facing the challenges presented in the Sect. 1 was not at all, a consensual task given the numerous existing actors in the context of the problem [10]. Thus, in order to respond to the illustrated challenges, several components have been added to the conventional feeding mechanism existing in most stables, optimizing the existing processes.

As referred previously, and visible in other sources [11], cattle are the primary agricultural source of greenhouse gases worldwide. Some of the most commonly known greenhouse gases are carbon dioxide (CO_2) and methane (CH_4), gases who over the last couple of centuries, are making the planet become warmer [12]. Within eWeightSmart, the use of IoT concepts introduces smart capabilities that otherwise wouldn't be possible. Inherent to this IoT concept, is the low fundamental cost, result of the diversity of devices that already exist and will continue to grow exponentially.

Having these problems, eWeightSmart, using a set of modern and smart technologies, will allow a better resource management in the sector, proving to be a viable solution to help to reduce the greenhouse gases.

A study by John Vidal in 2017 [13] determined that, without efficiency improvements, by 2025 all Information Technology and Communication industries (ICT) could use 20% of all world energy and emit up to 5.5% of global carbon emissions, thus hampering global attempts to meet climate change. These values are alarming and even though the growth of IoT devices is set to skyrocket, even increasing energy consumption, it is necessary to find ways of reducing it.

With this in mind, our solution is to use NB-IoT. Narrow Band-Internet of Things or (NB-IoT) is a communication technology designed so that IoT devices connect directly to the global network. This technology aim to connect "things" with the same easy and comprehensive connectivity of smartphones, but suited to the needs of IoT, namely ultra-low-consumption communications, causing the duration of energy means, like batteries, to be maximized to have greater efficiency energy, which can last for years without these means being replaced.

This technology is currently part of the LTE network and any place on the planet with network coverage, is fertile ground for NB-IoT that significantly improve IoT devices energy consumption. Currently expanding, NB-IoT was identified in 69 countries by 2019 [14,15]. Since NB-IoT is a mobile IoT network, security is not a problem as mobile operators ensure the encryption of customer/user data, or in some cases, VPNs with encrypted connections and APNs. Other security features are included, like Data over NAS (DoNAS), Non-IP Data Delivery (NIDD), or white-lists [16]. Resuming, NB-IoT uses licensed spectrum and secure communication channels, being this a vantage, as programmers or end users don't have to worry about.

2.1 Overview

In Fig. 1 it's possible to analyze the overview and high level of the built architecture, consisting of 5 elements:

- a web server that provides a set of endpoints, used by the mobile application to control the amount of food distributed to each animal and consult other parameters;
- a broker who will be responsible to manage the exchange of messages between the web server and the Arduino board MKR 1500 [17] (the first and unique from Arduino to be LTE Cat M1 and NB-IoT compatible [18,19]);
- a controller inserted into the food dispenser that will store the parameters associated with each animal and will contain the physical actuator to control the amount of food given to them;
- the feeder for animals, properly prepared to monitor what each animal should eat;
- a physical platform (not illustrated in Fig. 1 because it will be discussed in detail in Sect. 2.6) which will serve, using a set of sensors, to calculate the automatic weight of the animals.

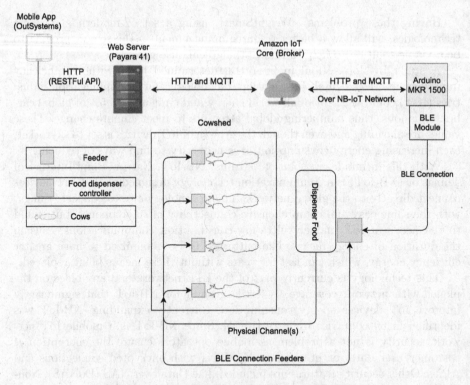

Fig. 1. Overview of eWeightSmart architecture.

Each of the components listed above has a specific functionality within the overall built architecture that will be explained and detailed in the next sections. It's important to note, that although only reference is made to a dispenser food, in more realistic scenarios (different from the development scenario) there may be more. However, the architecture presented in this paper does not yet contemplate this situation because it would be necessary to idealize the communication processes between the various components in a different way.

2.2 Web Server and Mobile Application

Due to the difficulty of installing computers in the stables, since it's an environment where there are many agents that destroy them quickly (e.g., dust) and in some cases the support to the internet is very weak, the solution makes use of a mobile application. Another advantage of using a mobile application instead of a web portal is the portability it offers. Using OutSystems technology [20], a mobile application (see Fig. 2) has been created that makes possible to: register new animals in the stable; consult the weight measurements of each animal; consult and update the amounts of food that are defined for each animal. In order to support all the operations described above, a set of web services (RESTfull) were implemented on a Java application server (Payara 41) [21]. This set of services supports the functionality of the application and, at the same time, acts as a point of connection with the controller placed in the animal feed tank in the stable.

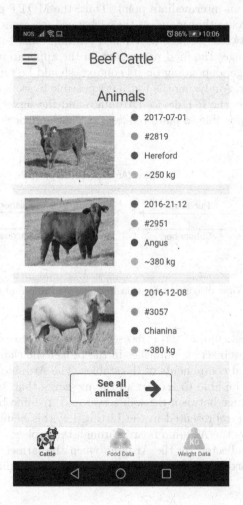

Fig. 2. Overview of eWeightSmart mobile application.

Additionally, it's also on the web server that are hosted the services that provides support for the automatic weighing mechanism, described in the Sect. 2.6. All communication between each mobile device and the server that provides the services is carried out using HTTP requests. The use of NB-IoT [22] communication technology is only restricted to communication between the Arduino MKR 1500 [23] and the broker which will be explained in the Sect. 2.3.

2.3   Broker (MQTT) and Arduino MKR 1500

Although Arduino has the ability to communicate directly with the web server, communication in the opposite direction isn't possible to be performed with the same ease without an intermediate point. Thus, the MQTT protocol was used, which through a broker that manages the exchanged messages, it guarantees the communication between the web server and Arduino board in both directions. When the user changes the food parameters in the application presented in the Sect. 2.2, this change, depending on its context, should be reflected in the food dispenser controller. Analyzing the Fig. 3 it's possible to see how the exchange of information between the IoT device (Arduino) and the server is realized. Inside the mobile app, is possible to place requests to view and/or change food-related data.

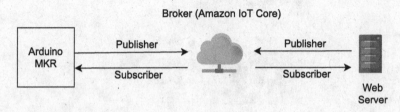

Fig. 3. Detailed view of communication between Arduino and the web server.

When the requests update data that set the state of the components installed in the stables, the web server publishes in the broker the change that has to be made in the physical components of the stables. The Arduino, after subscribing to the broker, will be able to receive all the messages that are intended for it. The message exchange between the web server and Arduino board is supported by the JSON string represented in the Listing 1.1, this being an example of a received message by the Arduino board through the broker.

This string is collected by the Arduino when the farmer modifies the food parameters of a particular animal, or simple, adds a new animal to the system to be controlled.

Listing 1.1. Example of JSON string received by Arduino board via broker

```
{
    "id_msg":123,
    "time":1623184918,
    "stable":1,
    "dispenser":1,
    "cow_identifier":
```

```
{
            "id":"PT012",
            "foodtype":0,
            "quantity":10,
            "place_food":"#12ER",
            "time_to_timer":10
    }
}
```

This message consists of 4 fields: id_msg, time, stable, and cow_identifier. The id_msg field corresponds to the received message identifier, the time field corresponds to the timestamp (Unix time) in which the message was subscribed to the broker and, additionally, the stable field identifies the message recipient. The dispenser field corresponds to the dispenser identifier to where the received message should be redirected, which, as mentioned, at the current stage of the project ends up being ignored, since there is only one dispenser per stable. Next, the time_to_timer (inside the field cow_identify) field corresponds to the time interval (in minutes) that exists between each replenishment of the cattle feed stations. Finally, the field cow_identifier contains the identifier of the animal in question, the amount (in kg) and type of food the system should assign to it and the identifier of the physical site where the animal should be fed. These messages, when forwarded to the food dispenser controller, will enable the construction of the data structure with the necessary information for the correct distribution of food to the various existing physical sites, as it's shown in the Sect. 2.4. The communication between Arduino and broker, hosted on the Amazon IoT core service [24], is done using NB-IoT.

As previous mentioned, analyzing the Fig. 1, it's easy to understand that the Arduino is the only point of communication with the web server, that is, the data exchanged between all the physical components installed in the stables and the web server are sent and/or received by Arduino. This board, in addition to this function, is also responsible, through the BLE module [25] that was added to it, for sending the received data to the food dispenser controller.

2.4   Food Dispenser Controller

The food stations that exists in the stable, as well as the amount of food that must be deposited in each one of them, are managed by the food controller dispenser. This component works by using an ESP32 chip [26] and a set of sensors, collecting from the Arduino, through BLE, all the information necessary for the management of animal feed. The Fig. 4 illustrates how the food dispenser controller works. As already mentioned, it's the ESP32 chip that manages the received information from the Arduino.

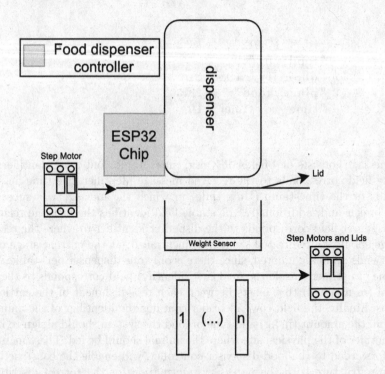

Fig. 4. Detailed view of the operation of the food dispenser controller.

Listing 1.2. Data dictionary in Food Dispenser Controller

```
[ {
        "cow_identifier":"PT122",
        "info_food":
        {
            "quantity":10,
            "place_food":"PT1234"
        }
    },
    {
        "cow_identifier":"PT162",
        "info_food":
        {
            "quantity":15,
            "place_food":"PT1245"
        }
    }
]
```

In the ESP32 memory, present in the food dispenser controller, a data dictionary is maintained, similar to the one illustrated in the Listing 1.2. It's through this dictionary that the mapping between the animal (cow_identify) and the physical site where it should be fed, (place_food) is performed. This dictionary is built on the basis of information arriving from the Arduino board.

In parallel to the construction of this dictionary, the ESP32 chip also receives from Arduino, the value of the timer that must be passed to each feeder that also contains an ESP32 chip. The transfer of this information is performed using BLE. Each feeder contains a BLE characteristic that the food dispenser controller must read after the pairing process. This reading makes possible to send the timeout time (represented in the Listing 1.1 by the time_to_timer field) to each feeder correctly. When a timeout is detected in one of the chips of the various existing feeders, the corresponding feeder, using BLE, sends a message to the food controller dispenser to warn that it needs to be replenished, passing on its identification the amount of existing food, avoiding food waste if there is still food, left by the animals, on the feeder.

In the food dispenser controller, the ESP32 chip activates the step motor [27] (actuator) (step motor left in Fig. 4) to open the barrier present in the dispenser. The defined food stations are supplied sequentially and not in parallel. This way, the ESP32 chip has access to the list of food stations and the amount that it should deposit in each of them. When the value read of the weight sensor (max: 30 kg), placed inside the box (see Fig. 4), corresponds to the value of the amount of food to be inserted into the station being fuelled, the ESP32 activates the step motor placed at the bottom of the valve to close it. This action is carried out in stages, avoiding that a quantity greater than that defined by the producer is deposited at the food station. The ESP32 chip will activate the step motor, and it will close the barrier when the values read from the weight sensor are close to the defined amount for that food station. After this task is complete, the food dispenser controller has a channel for each existing food station, each one related to an animal. The ESP32 chip will activate the step motor corresponding to the food station being supplied, so that the barrier is opened, and the food gets deposited in the correct place.

2.5 Feeder

To ensure that each animal eats the amount of food set by the producer, it was necessary to make changes to the food stations (see Fig. 5). An RFID tag [28] must be added to each animal, working as an identifier for that animal. Each food station is equipped with an ESP32 chip, an RFID reader [29], a presence sensor, a step motor and a protective barrier.

When an animal approaches the food station, and if its RFID tag matches to the station in question, the ESP32 chip activates the step motor so that the protective barrier is opened and the animal can have access to food. From that moment on, the ESP32 chip focuses on the values read by the presence sensor so when the animal moves away from the food station the step motor is activated

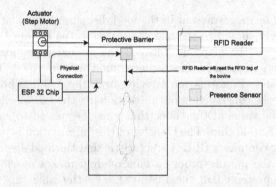

Fig. 5. Detailed view of the operation of the Feeder.

so that the protection barrier is closed. This ensures that each animal eats only the quantity defined by the producer and no more than that.

2.6   Automatic Weighing

Through the analysis of the literature of the area, it was possible to understand how far it has already been possible to arrive in the automatic weighing of cattle. The weight of the animals has to be thought efficiently in order to cause the least effort to the owners of the cattle and be as transparent as possible for them. Analyzing market solutions, it's possible to observe that some calculate the weight of cattle, based on mathematical formulas [30,31]. This paper follows the same line of thought as the last examples, starting from the following formula:

$$\frac{chest\_girth \ \times trunk\_length}{100} \times 2.5$$

To obtain these values, there are rudimentary possibilities, such as manual measurement, or the use of technologies such as cameras and sensors.

This paper illustrates an approach where Kinect [32] sensors are used to obtain 3D images, which will be processed to calculate the needed livestock measurements. This is also presented by Francesco Marinello [33], where through these sensors it's possible to obtain the Chest girth of the animal, necessary value for the formula. For the last value, the trunk length, it's possible to obtain it in the same way using these sensors [34], having with it, all the necessary values for the calculation of the weight. Similar sensors like Kinect are the LIDAR sensors [35,36], with which it's possible, equally, to calculate the body height. One of the reason about the preference of using Kinect sensors over LIDAR sensors is due to the price, since Kinect sensors are a low-cost solution, unlike LIDAR sensors. Other reason is due to the fact that Kinect sensors have RGB cameras, an infrared camera and an infrared laser emitter. In Fig. 6, it's present the automatic weighing architecture using these sensors.

This automatic weighing involves the use of 3 Microsoft Kinect Sensors to extract 3D images of the living animal. This 3D images after being post-processed

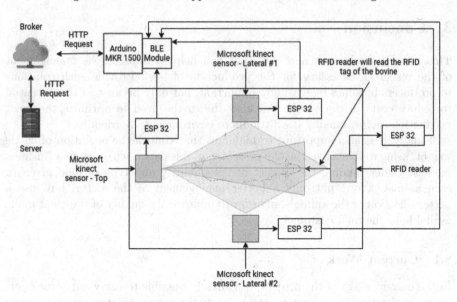

Fig. 6. Detailed view of the operation of the automatic weighing.

in the web server, will allow the extraction of various measurements of a certain bovine, such as, diagonal body length, chest girth, trunk length, etc. The animal should be weighted, e.g., once a week or once a month. The cattle owner have to conduct the animal into a compartment, where will be recognized and 3D scanned. In that compartment are installed three Kinect sensors, one RFID reader, four ESP32 chips and one Arduino MKR 1500 (already visible in Fig. 1). The three Kinect sensors and the RFID reader will be connected to their own ESP32 chip. These ESP32 chips will be connected to the Arduino board via BLE. When the animal enters the compartment where the equipment is installed, the RFID reader will recognize the bovine, and the ESP32 chip connected to the RFID reader will send a message to the microcontrollers (ESP32 chips) of the Kinect sensors to extract the 3D images of the animal. The obtaining of all 3D images of the animal needs to be done in the same time. Then to achieve that, a synchronization of the three ESP32 chips that are connected to the Kinect sensors needs to be assure. When the 3D images are obtained, the microcontrollers of the sensors will send these images to the Arduino board via BLE. Since each animal have a RFID Tag, and the Kinect sensors will not distinguish the animals, the ESP32 chip of the RFID reader will send the identifier of the bovine to the Arduino. After that, the Arduino will send to the web server, the 3D images and the identifier of the bovine. The web server will process the 3D images to extract the measures (chest girth and trunk length) needed to calculate the weight of the animal. The calculation of the weight of the bovine will be done by the server following the equation previously mentioned. After this process the value calculated will be updated to the application, where the cattle owner can observe the animal weight.

3   Conclusion

This paper introduces a new tool that will help to improve the management of the resources necessary for the production of beef. Provide such solutions to producers becomes increasingly important, not only because of the potential to reduce costs in the sector, but also due to the need to optimize the meat production sector, making it a little more environmentally friendly.

Finally, it is also important to highlight that control the evolution of cattle weight, using tools such as the one presented in this paper, will open new business models. Understanding the impact of the quantity and type of food given to each animal, allows not only a better management of the sector, but also a better selection of the animals, in order to improve the quality of the meat made available to the final customer.

3.1   Current Work

In the current stage of the project, it's already possible to carry out some operations in the mobile application and validate the entire message circuit between the web server and the other components, like Arduino and the set of ESP32 chips. However, although the remaining components have already been tested in isolated examples, it was not possible yet to complete the cycle, since the prototyping process of the presented architecture has suffered several delays. Finally, was not possible yet to install the architecture in a real context, since for the installation it's necessary more realistic equipment (different from the prototypes created).

3.2   Future Work

To future work, the main priority is to be able to build a prototype that is possible to install in a more realistic scenario. As already mentioned, after the installation of a more realistic version of the tool, one of the main objectives of this solution is to understand whether the quantity and type of food distributed to the animals has an impact on the quality of the meat that reaches the final customer. So, in summary form, despite the great potential presented, this solution still has a long way to go. Thus, the following points were left for future work:

- Understand the real impact of controlling the animals weight that this solution provides to producers.
- Allow more types of food to be added to the solution presented.
- Optimize the automatic weighing process.
- Analyze the possible positive effects of this solution on the ecological footprint of this sector.
- Change the current architecture so that it's possible to have several food dispensers in the same stable.

References

1. Hocquette, J.-F., Ellies-Oury, M.-P., Lherm, M., Pineau, C., Deblitz, C., Farmer, L.: Current situation and future prospects for beef production in Europe - a review. Asian-Aust. J. Anim. Sci. **31**, 1017 (2018)
2. Ritchie, H., Roser, M.: Meat and dairy production. Our World Data (2017)
3. Smith, S.B., Gotoh, T., Greenwood, P.L.: Current situation and future prospects for global beef production: overview of special issue. Asian-Aust. J. Anim. Sci. **31**, 927 (2018)
4. Place, S.E., Miller, A.M.: Beef production: what are the human and environmental impacts? Nutr. Today **55**(5), 227–233 (2020)
5. Bronzato, S., Durante, A.: A contemporary review of the relationship between red meat consumption and cardiovascular risk. Int. J. Prevent. Med. **8** (2017)
6. Pighin, D., et al.: A contribution of beef to human health: a review of the role of the animal production systems. Sci. World J. **2016** (2016)
7. Gordon, B.L.: Better beef quality drives stability in demand. https://www.beefmagazine.com/beef/better-beef-quality-drives-stability-demand. Accessed 08 May 2021
8. Koknaroglu, H., Loy, D.D., Wilson, D.E., Hoffman, M.P., Lawrence, J.: Factors affecting beef cattle performance and profitability. Prof. Anim. Sci. **21**, 286–296 (2005)
9. Solanki, A., Nayyar, A.: Green internet of things (G-IoT): ICT technologies, principles, applications, projects, and challenges, pp. 379–405, March 2019
10. Nayyar, A., Puri, V.: Smart farming: IoT based smart sensors agriculture stick for live temperature and moisture monitoring using arduino, cloud computing & solar technology, pp. 673–680 (2016)
11. Cows and climate change. https://www.ucdavis.edu/food/news/making-cattle-more-sustainable. Accessed 30 May 2021
12. Cows, methane, and climate change. https://letstalkscience.ca/educational-resources/stem-in-context/cows-methane-and-climate-change. Accessed 30 May 2021
13. Vidal, J.: 'tsunami of data' could consume one fifth of global electricity by 2025 (2017)
14. GSA. Narrow band IoT & M2M - global narrowband IoT - LTE-M networks, March 2019. https://gsacom.com/paper/global-narrowband-iot-lte-m-networks-march-2019/. Accessed 01 Mar 2021
15. GSMA. Mobile iot deployment map. https://www.gsma.com/iot/deployment-map/. Accessed 01 Mar 2021
16. GSMA. Security Features of LTE-M and NB-IoT Networks (2019). https://www.gsma.com/iot/wp-content/uploads/2019/09/Security-Features-of-LTE-M-and-NB-IoT-Networks.pdf. Accessed 07 Mar 2021
17. Nayyar, A., Puri, V.: An encyclopedia coverage of compiler's, programmer's & simulator's for 8051, PIC, AVR, ARM, Arduino embedded technologies. Int. J. Reconfigurable Embed. Syst. (IJRES) **5** (2016)
18. Arduino MKR NB 1500. https://dev.telstra.com/iot-marketplace/arduino-mkr-nb-1500. Accessed 05 June 2021
19. Mkr family. https://store.arduino.cc/arduino/mkr-family. Accessed 05 June 2021
20. Outsystems documentation. https://success.outsystems.com/Documentation/11/Developing_an_Application. Accessed 08 May 2021

21. Payara platform community. https://www.payara.fish/products/payara-platform-community/. Accessed 08 May 2021

22. GSMA. NarrowBand-Internet of Things (NB-IoT) (2020). https://www.gsma.com/iot/narrow-band-internet-of-things-nb-iot/. Accessed 29 Dec 2020

23. Arduino.CC. ARDUINO MKR NB 1500 (2020). https://store.arduino.cc/arduino-mkr-nb-1500-1413. Accessed 29 Dec 2020

24. What is AWS IoT core? https://aws.amazon.com/iot-core/. Accessed 08 May 2021

25. Pandit, A.: How to use HM-10 BLE module with arduino to control an LED using Android app (2020). https://circuitdigest.com/microcontroller-projects/how-to-use-arduino-and-hm-10-ble-module-to-control-led-with-android-app. Accessed 29 Dec 2020

26. Get started. https://docs.espressif.com/projects/esp-idf/en/latest/esp32/get-started/. Accessed 08 May 2021

27. What is a stepper motor? https://learn.adafruit.com/all-about-stepper-motors. Accessed 08 May 2021

28. Nicole Pontius in Industry Resources. What are RFID Tags? Learn How RFID Tags Work, What They're Used for, and Some of the Disadvantages of RFID Technology (2020). https://www.camcode.com/asset-tags/what-are-rfid-tags/. Accessed 29 Dec 2020

29. RFID Reader and Tag - Ultimate Guide on RFID Module (2021). https://www.circuitstoday.com/rfid-reader-tag. Accessed 29 Jan 2020

30. Pater, S.: How much do your animal weigh (2020). https://cals.arizona.edu/backyards/sites/cals.arizona.edu.backyards/files/p11-12.pdf. Accessed 29 Dec 2020

31. Rudenko, O., Megel, Y., Bezsonov, O., Rybalka, A.: Cattle breed identification and live weight evaluation on the basis of machine learning and computer vision. In: CMIS, pp. 939–954 (2020)

32. Zhang, Z.: Microsoft kinect sensor and its effect. IEEE Multimed. **19**(2), 4–10 (2012)

33. Marinello, F., Pezzuolo, A., Donato, C., Gasparini, F., Sartori, L.: Application of kinect-sensor for three-dimensional body measurements of cows, September 2015

34. Pezzuolo, F.M.A., Sartori, L.: Exploiting low-cost depth cameras for body measurement in the livestock sector (2020). https://ercim-news.ercim.eu/en113/special/exploiting-low-cost-depth-cameras-for-body-measurement-in-the-livestock-sector. Accessed 29 Dec 2020

35. What is lidar? https://oceanservice.noaa.gov/facts/lidar.html. Accessed 08 May 2021

36. Huang, L., Li, S., Zhu, A., Fan, X., Zhang, C., Wang, H.: Non-contact body measurement for qinchuan cattle with LiDAR sensor. Sensors **18**(9), 3014 (2018)

Gaia-AgStream: An Explainable AI Platform for Mining Complex Data Streams in Agriculture

Jan Schoenke[1]([✉]), Nils Aschenbruck[2], Roberto Interdonato[3],
Rushed Kanawati[4], Ann-Christin Meisener[1], Francois Thierart[5],
Guillaume Vial[5], and Martin Atzmueller[2]

[1] LMIS AG, Osnabrück, Germany
{Jan.Hendrik.Schoenke,Ann-Christin.Meisener}@lmis.de
[2] Osnabrück University, Osnabrück, Germany
{aschenbruck,atzmueller}@uni-osnabrueck.de
[3] Cirad, Montpellier, France
roberto.interdonato@cirad.fr
[4] University Sorbonne Paris Nord, Villetaneuse, France
rushed.kanawati@lipn.univ-paris13.fr
[5] MyEasyFarm, Bezannes, France
{fthierart,gvial}@myeasyfarm.com
http://www.lmis.de/
http://www.cs.uos.de/
http://www.cirad.fr/
http://lipn.univ-paris13.fr/
http://www.myeasyfarm.com/

Abstract. We present a position paper about our concept for an artificial intelligence (AI) and data streaming platform for the agricultural sector. The goal of our project is to support agroecology in terms of carbon farming and biodiversity protection by providing an AI and data streaming platform called *Gaia-AgStream* that accelerates the adoption of AI in agriculture and is directly usable by farmers as well as agricultural companies in general. The technical innovations we propose focus on smart sensor networks, unified uncertainty management, explainable AI, root cause analysis and hybrid AI approaches. Our AI and data streaming platform concept contributes to the European open data infrastructure project Gaia-X in terms of interoperability for data and AI models as well as data sovereignty and AI infrastructure.

Our envisioned platform and the developed AI components for carbon farming and biodiversity will enable farmers to adopt sustainable and resilient production methods while establishing new and diverse revenue streams by monetizing carbon sequestration and *AI ready* data streams. The open and federated platform concept allows to bring together research, industry, agricultural start-ups and farmers in order to form sustainable innovation networks. We describe core concepts and architecture of our proposed approach in these contexts, outline practical use cases for our platform and finally outline challenges and future prospects.

© Springer Nature Switzerland AG 2021
S. Boumerdassi et al. (Eds.): SSA 2021, CCIS 1470, pp. 71–83, 2021.
https://doi.org/10.1007/978-3-030-88259-4_6

Keywords: Explainable AI · Sensor networks · Distributed systems · Uncertainty management · Complex networks · Machine learning · Anomaly detection · Root cause analysis · Knowledge graph · Data quality · Agroecology · Carbon farming · Biodiversity · Data fusion

1   Introduction

In order to adapt to climate change and preserve biodiversity, the agricultural sector and in particular farmers can do a lot by changing their practices, but they need support on decision making for strategic aspects as well as in their daily business. Today, farmers do not aim to increase the physical productivity but rather try to preserve, or even increase, the economic productivity of their work. To achieve this goal, they embarked on the path of agroecology as a holistic ecological concept which aims to maximize biodiversity on a functional level in order to strengthen biological self-regulations rather than resorting to external inputs and management activities. This is based on a number of key principles:

1. Increasing the recycling of biomass and achieve a balance in the flow of mineral elements.
2. Providing the most favorable soil conditions w.r.t. growth of plants, by maintaining a level of organic matter and high biological regulation mechanisms.
3. Minimizing the loss of nutrients from the circuit system and form relatively closed loops rather than open streams.
4. Improving the functional biodiversity of plants and animals, natural and domestic, cultivated or raised, above and in the ground, in order to strengthen the *immune system* of agricultural systems.

Thus, agroecology as a holistic approach requires contributions from farmers, contractors, consultants, research, education and so forth. We focus on carbon farming and biodiversity as the most important aspects in order to fight and adapt to climate change and contribute to the preservation of biodiversity. We need to strengthen the resilience of our agricultural economy and accelerate the adoption of sustainable production methods.

On a technical level, we already see Gaia-X (https://www.gaia-x.eu/) [12] as a perfect fit to our vision of a federated learning platform. However, the Sovereign Cloud Stack (SCS) that is currently developed by the 22 founding members of the AISBL only covers the interoperability on infrastructure level. Even though we have massive amounts of satellite images, farm management data, drone videos and other sensor readings, which all contribute to the big data treasure in agriculture, there is still too little utilization of such data in terms of modern AI components which find their way into software and hardware products for farmers and farm equipment manufactures as well as agricultural software companies.

In this position paper, we present a concept for an AI and data streaming platform for the agricultural sector. The goal of our proposal is to support agroecology in terms of carbon farming and biodiversity protection by providing an AI and data streaming platform called *Gaia-AgStream* that accelerates the adoption of AI in agriculture and is directly usable by farmers as well as agricultural companies in general. The technical innovations we propose focus on smart sensor networks, unified uncertainty management, explainable AI, root cause analysis and hybrid AI approaches. With this, biodiversity and other complex information can be monitored in real-time – to be utilized for guiding agronomic decisions farmers have to take in their daily business as well as for strategic planning.

The rest of the paper is structured as follows: Sect. 2 discusses related work. After that, Sect. 3 presents our Gaia-AgStream approach as well as the targeted use cases. Finally, we conclude in Sect. 4.

2   Related Work

Below, we first present related projects, before discussing sensor networks and explainable AI as core concepts for our proposed approach.

2.1   Related Projects

As our proposal brings together AI and data streams in agriculture, there are different related open source projects which focus on one or several of these aspects and we can only list some of them. Recently, the Linux foundation has launched the open source agriculture infrastructure project *AgStack*[1] in order to offer a secure digital operating system for the agricultural industry. *farmOS*[2] is an open farm management software which offers a web-based application for management and planning.

There is a widely used open-source technology stack for handling data streams, e. g., Apache Kafka, Apache Spark, RabbitMQ, etc. Approaches like Kafka or Apache Flink not only allow to manage data streams at scale, but also support data stream processing and together with common AI frameworks like TensorFlow or PyTorch build a solid technological foundation for state-of-the-art AI projects for data streams. In particular, Kafka-ML aims to fit TensorFlow and Kafka streams into one user-frienly web interface and River merges creme and scikit-multiflow into a single python library for machine learning on data streams.

None of these frameworks includes a seamless uncertainty management from initial data generation to AI output consumption by users. Approaches like MLOps help to emphasise the importance of data for AI applications during training and operation by keeping track of every artefact. Projects like Kube-Flow or MLFlow help to automate pipelines for training and deployment of AI models in multi-cloud and edge-computing scenarios.

Unfortunately, none of these efforts has changed the fact that still about 80% of the time it takes to bring an AI model to production is spent on working with the data due to data quality issues. Thus, even initiatives like Gaia-X which contribute to the accessibility of data may have a limited impact on the adoption to AI without focusing on data quality.

---

[1] https://agstack.org/.

[2] https://farmos.org/.

Gaia-X is a European initiative for fostering the digital sovereignty in Europe. The most important aspect related to our proposal is the aim to establish sovereign data exchange for all companies, organizations and citizens within the Gaia-X framework. This overall goal is realized in many different domain specific projects which cover basic building block for data exchange like interoperability and the harmonization of standards.

A highly visible project within Gaia-X is Agri-Gaia which aims to build an AI platform for the agricultural industry, in order to make AI accessible for the all participants in the domain, especially small and medium enterprises. Agri-Gaia and its consortium has founded the agriculture domain within the German Gaia-X hub. Another project related to Gaia-X is NalamKI which focuses on fostering sustainable production methods by means of AI and the aggregation of sensor and machinery data in one central platform. A core aspect here is data sharing along the value chain in order to create new innovation networks. Further contributions to Gaia-X originate from Soil-X which focuses on soil data with respect to accumulation, harmonization and utilization of such data.

One key aspect of Agri-Gaia with respect to providing data for AI at scale is the generation of synthetic data for training AI models in order to leverage existing high-quality real data. Here, we want to complement this line of work by developing a uniform uncertainty management embedded in the proposed AI and data streaming platform to support the generation of 'AI ready data' and find an application-agnostic data quality indication, cf., [13,14,28] for according related work about uncertainty estimation, architecture concepts and robust self-optimization. The importance of handling uncertain data is inherent to AI applications, but the current balance between the effort for handling data and tuning the model puts a disproportional weight on data handling. This includes standard tasks like data collection, analytic, harmonization, aggregation and versioning. The goal of all of these activities is to ensure and enrich the quality of the data which is ultimately used for training AI models. This need for high quality data is especially hard to meet in applications which include federated or distributed learning, e.g. in edge computing scenarios with limited or only partial connectivity. In such cases, there is no human operator or observer who maintains the edge unit and thus, the systems needs to operate fully autonomous including all aspects of data preparation. But even in cloud computing scenarios the automation of data processing is the best lever to foster AI applications.

2.2   Sensor Networks

Wireless Sensor Networks (WSN) consist of a large number of small, cheap, resource - and power-constrained devices. Depending on their sensing task, they are equipped with one or multiple sensors [2]. These devices form automatically a local wireless network that collects the data at one or multiple sinks. A sink is typically connected to the Internet. The purpose of the devices in such a distributed system is the environmental sensing of physically measurable phenomena, like temperature, relative humidity, or soil moisture. Sometimes more powerful nodes even perform audio and video sensing. However, the applied devices are typically low-cost and thus resource constrained. However, this makes them suitable for large-scale and long-term deployments. The sensing accuracy of each single device is usually limited. However, this limitation is compensated by multiple collaborating devices. Thus, WSNs allow for continuous monitoring, providing sensor information at high temporal as well as spatial resolution.

WSNs in agriculture have been a research topic for more than one decade now, cf. [26]. Here, technological advancements continuously reduced the physical size and costs of the devices. Nowadays, WSNs complement existing monitoring systems in the context of precision agriculture with ground-based information advancing productivity and sustainability. Possible applications range from site-specific irrigation, fertilization, and crop treatment, to disease control as well as horticulture and animal monitoring [27]. WSNs are usually integrated into Farm Management and Information System (FMIS) and IoT platforms (cf. e. g., [32]).

For a large-scale environmental monitoring, often a large number of sensors is required. From an economic perspective, the price of the individual sensors is crucial for the Return on Invest (ROI). Thus, there is a trend to reduce the number of devices in sensor networks in real deployments and complement them by remote sensing, e. g., based on satellites or drones. The WSN provides in-situ data to calibrate the remote sensing data. In addition, information gained in-situ via a WSN can be transferred to larger areas using remote sensing data.

2.3 Explainable AI and Decision Support

Recently, the area of explainable AI [17] (XAI) has emerged as a prominent paradigm to enhance decision support, which is particularly relevant in economically and environmentally sensitive applications and the use cases we target in Gaia-AgStream [3]. While there are several solutions providing AI and machine learning in agricultural contexts, typically black-box models are applied, which make it difficult to validate their analytics insights, predictions, recommendations, and root causes those are based on. In general, intransparent methods and models make it more difficult to spot mistakes, as algorithmic methods can potentially learn "bad habits" from improper data. If the data used for constructing AI models, e. g., contains misleading or wrongly classified examples, then it is highly likely that the resulting model incorporates specific biases and data artefacts which can lead to wrong conclusions. In addition, in the case of black box models the applied models and their decisions are then not understandable for humans, which can lead to wrong and/or bad decisions. Essentially, those can then not be considered as actionable. XAI aims at providing explanations for the models, their analytics insights or their predictions and recommendations.

In the case of Gaia-AgStream we target this regarding monitoring and anomaly detection, e. g., by adapting and building on interpretable models and detailed root cause analysis methods, e. g., [1,6,10]. For recommendation, e. g., specific (historic) example cases can be provided for justification, or interpretable patterns summarizing typical (causal) influence factors can be presented. This also relates to, in particular, explanation-awareness [5,8] and XAI in such contexts [17,29,31], recommendation methods on complex feature-rich data, modeled as complex networks, e. g., [16,21,25,30], and interpretable models for deep anomaly analytics, covering anomaly detection, explanation and providing interpretable models cf., [4, 7, 15, 34].

In addition, we furthermore aim at proposing deep learning approaches able to leverage heterogeneous information sources (multi-source satellite images, sensors, and more) in order to produce accurate estimations regarding the soil carbon and the biodiversity of a certain area, cf., [20, 23]. The eventual use of sensors also opens up to the use of advanced geometric deep learning techniques, i.e., graph convolutional networks able to exploit non-euclidean structures in the data, such as network graphs, e.g., [9, 33]. Note that the use of advanced deep learning techniques allows to work on data fusion at a feature level. Classic data fusion approaches generally include early fusion (i.e., integrating the different sources of information at the beginning of the process, in order to obtain a single dataset that can be used as input for the machine learning algorithm) and late fusion (i.e., aggregating the predictions from models associated with each data source into a global prediction). Devising advanced deep learning architectures, e.g., [18, 19, 22, 29] able to deal with multi-source data allows to extract an optimized data representation for each source (e.g., representation learning on multi-branch architectures, where each branch deals with a data source), producing optimized features that are then used as input of the final step of the process, e.g., classification or regression.

3   The Gaia-AgStream Approach

The scope of the problem we tackle can be highlighted using biodiversity as an example. The measurements for biodiversity are getting better and better, still further improvements need to be done in order to get AI ready and actionable data which leverage the existing data sources in order to get reliable long-term predictions and near real-time data for day-to-day recommendations. These recommendations need to be based on trustworthy data and explainable AI in order to get the acceptance of farmers, farm equipment manufactures and other partners in the agricultural domain like consultants and contractors. Thus, our goal is to foster trust and transparency along data processing pipelines and in complex innovation networks.

3.1   Proposed Approach

Gaia-AgStream provides an AI data stream processing platform as an infrastructure component within Gaia-X and demonstrates the benefits of the platform in an agroecology use case that comprises the development of ready to use AI components together with a smart sensor network management. The proposed approach, connected to exemplary case studies and services provided is depicted in Fig. 1. The center of our activities is the farmer and his need to master carbon farming and support biodiversity. Our platform provides smart sensor networks for farmers as well as explainable AI recommender systems. Overall, the platform builds an innovation network by connecting traditional agriculture companies, AI startups and farmers in order to share and exchange data and AI-models.

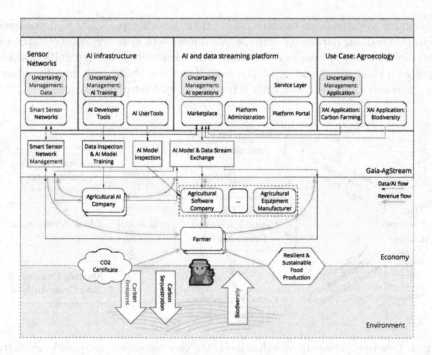

Fig. 1. Overview: schematic visualization of the overall technical and economic solution, and the respective case studies/application areas.

The core innovation and knowledge distribution detailing the technical foundation of Gaia-AgStream is depicted in Fig. 2 – focusing on the dynamic, uncertain causal knowledge graph model which integrates dynamic and uncertain data, and enables AI-based recommenders and analytics.

Our platform is in line with the currently founded project Agri-Gaia and aims to extend this AI infrastructure project by providing capabilities for data stream processing and the corresponding AI components for learning from data streams. Data streams are inherently different to handle than data set as data needs to be prepared and used for learning incrementally and in production. In the hybrid on-line and off-line connection scenarios we are facing in agriculture, this rises the need for IoT solutions that allow to learn on the edge or on device in order to minimize the data traffic and build economically viable solutions. Learning from data stream on the edge or device requires a holistic approach to data analysis, preparation and monitoring as there is no operator which can observe and handle the learning process as it is common in cloud computing. Edge computing here may apply to individual sites of a larger farm, machinery or small farms as they usually have limited computing resources. The challenge here is to allow for an easy deployment and mostly independent learning of the edge units while at the same time support farms by means of centralized monitoring and reasoning capabilities offered by the platform. This requires the edge units to provide meta data about their learning processes and consume appropriate data, parameter or hyperparameter sets in order to accelerate and steer the learning process in a federated way where different edge units working together in the same field or at the same farm can share their insights about e. g., anomalies, and validate each other's data and learning outcomes.

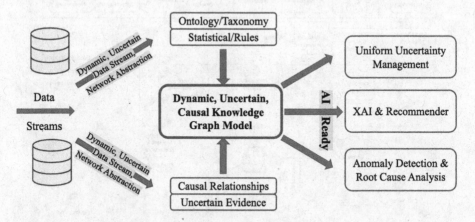

Fig. 2. Overview: schematic visualization of the core innovation and knowledge distribution for the technical foundation of Gaia-AgStream

Validating data from different sources like satellite, machinery and field sensors for building useful recommendations to farmers is only possible by understanding how the farmer plans his activities, executes the plans and reflects about the outcome of his work. The practices on each farm tend to be unique although best practices spread word and become adopted by a community. Therefore, one contribution of our project will be an AI component capable of building a knowledge graph which reflects the options and practices for individual farms by analyzing the farm management data and fuse this data with existing databases and meta data models, e. g., within the Agricultural Data Space.

In order to get to useful recommendations for farmers trust and transparency are of paramount importance. From a platform point of view the core aspects we can provide here are explainable AI components which get trained and evaluated on high quality data. Data quality is one of the most important topics in any machine learning project, but the systematic to assure data quality in every step of the processing pipeline is still poorly supported by standard tools. Our goal is to make data quality a cornerstone of the platform by ensuring a transparent and unified uncertainty handling from measurement to recommendation, prediction or any other kind of AI application. Networks of smart sensors are best to showcase this capability of the platform as we can cover the whole data flow from measurement where data quality is rated based on physical properties of the signal, over to preprocessing and analysis on the device or edge where data quality becomes more influenced by master data about expected operating conditions as well as complex analysis e. g., to detect certain species in pictures or from audio recordings and the corresponding model uncertainties. For federated learning approaches, this uncertainty modeling is essential meta data which allows to fuse data based on relevance rather than mass and make informed deep dives into individual decisions from models and AI components.

Hence, the sensor network management system we are going to build as part of the platform will not only allow for an easy deployment of complex algorithms to sensor nodes, but also ensure the data quality monitoring from an application agnostic point of view, i. e., via sensor health monitoring, signal to noise estimations, intra network validation of data with sufficient redundancy etc. The goal is to generate data which is 'AI ready' and therefore can directly be used for AI components in training and evaluation.

3.2   Agroecology Use Cases

For Gaia-AgStream the focus is on defining requirements for the overall platform development including the relevant basic AI components and services as well as the preparation and start of the field tests. In addition to that, we foresee a blended iterative approach for the development of the XAI components for carbon farming and biodiversity. This allows us to validate and refine the requirements from the technical perspective based on the insights from carbon farming and biodiversity. Further, stemming from the experience gained in working on carbon farming and biodiversity we add the use case level perspective to our unified uncertainty management. The hybrid XAI approach we follow allows to easily integrate prior knowledge of individual farmers about their fields, practices or crops. This will help us to interact with the community we build and get a common understanding about how the XAI components need to behave when integrated into end-user products. The application of the platform is exemplified via two use cases, which address those two of the most urgent topics of our time.

Carbon Farming. Carbon farming refers to agricultural methods that aim at reducing the amount of atmospheric carbon by capturing carbon in the biomass within the soil and/or favoring stocking carbon in crop roots and leaves. In addition to carbon emission reduction, which already is a main target for sustainable agriculture, this can favor both plant growth and reducing use of fertilizers. Thus, this contributes to enhancing or at least preserving biodiversity in target fields.

The goal of this first use case of our proposal is to learn new rules that can help farmers in enhancing their carbon farming approaches. Personalized recommendations based on background knowledge but also on processing heterogeneous data collected form target fields will be provided. These rules allow farmers to change their practices not only with respect to capturing carbon in the soil, but also for process optimization and thus, the reduction of carbon emissions (e. g., reducing fuel consumption, change crop rotation, change soil preparation steps, etc.).

Biodiversity. Our planet is losing biodiversity at an unprecedented high rate [24]. Thus, there is an urgent need to measure the impact of agriculture on biodiversity. By doing so, biodiversity can be one factor in the decision process of individual farmers about their fields, practices or crops.

There are different methods for determining biodiversity [11]. These methods include measuring bird richness, mammal richness, keystone species, etc. WSNs using audio and video sensing can measure the raw data to derive these parameters using sophisticated AI based data fusion. In the end, we need to identify and count the different animals. The AI components developed within Gaia-AgStream will enable us to do this and, thus, measure the biodiversity. Based on these measurements we can support continuous improvement cycles which include XAI recommender systems and enable the farmers to seamlessly integrate biodiversity considerations into their strategic planning and daily routines.

4   Conclusion

In this position paper, we presented Gaia-AgStream – an explainable AI platform for mining complex data streams in agriculture; it integrates explainable AI on complex data as a core approach, enabling smart analytics and decision support – being exemplified via two uses cases in agroecology. We discussed the relevant core concepts, and outlined the platform by sketching its technical architecture.

Our platform and sensor network management address key success factors for the agricultural domain in Europe which is dominated by SMEs which cannot afford to invest in AI capabilities on a large scale or have no inhouse AI resources at all. We provide the means to simplify the development and deployment of AI components and have a special focus on data streams as they are key to build recommendations based on near real time data and act accordingly. The crisis prevention mechanisms to fight climate change and biodiversity will become effective on larger time scales, but need the continuous monitoring and care taking in every action we take. Thus, the technology we are providing for our agroecology use case can seamlessly be applied to other scenarios which pose similar requirements.

The sensor network management system offers farmers the ability to create value for their own practices and further commercialize their data by sharing it with AI technology providers which use the data to build and refine their AI components. Ultimately, the platform is going to build a sustainable innovation and data cycle between farmers, AI providers and other stakeholders. The application of IoT and Edge computing in agriculture is a growing market with excellent perspectives for AI applications.

References

1. Abele, L., Anic, M., Gutmann, T., Folmer, J., Kleinsteuber, M., Vogel-Heuser, B.: Combining knowledge modeling and machine learning for alarm root cause analysis. IFAC Proc. Vol. **46**(9), 1843–1848 (2013)

2. Akyildiz, I.F., Su, W., Sankarasubramaniam, Y., Cayirci, E.: Wireless sensor networks: a survey. Comput. Netw. **38**(4), 393–422 (2002)
3. Arrieta, A.B., et al.: Explainable artificial intelligence (XAI): concepts, taxonomies, opportunities and challenges toward responsible AI. Inf. Fusion **58**, 82–115 (2020)
4. Atzmueller, M., Arnu, D., Schmidt, A.: Anomaly detection and structural analysis in industrial production environments. In: Data Science – Analytics and Applications, pp. 91–95. Springer, Wiesbaden (2017). https://doi.org/10.1007/978-3-658-19287-7_13
5. Atzmueller, M., Hayat, N., Schmidt, A., Klöpper, B.: Explanation-aware feature selection using symbolic time series abstraction: approaches and experiences in a petro-chemical production context. In: Proceedings of INDIN, pp. 799–804. IEEE (2017)
6. Atzmueller, M., et al.: Big data analytics for proactive industrial decision support. atp **58**(9), 62–74 (2016)
7. Atzmueller, M., Mollenhauer, D., Schmidt, A.: Big data analytics using local exceptionality detection. In: Enterprise Big Data Engineering, Analytics, and Management. IGI Global, Hershey (2016)
8. Atzmueller, M., Roth-Berghofer, T.: The mining and analysis continuum of explaining uncovered. In: Bramer, M., Petridis, M., Hopgood, A. (eds.) SGAI 2010, pp. 273–278. Springer, London (2011). https://doi.org/10.1007/978-0-85729-130-1_20
9. Bloemheuvel, S., van den Hoogen, J., Atzmueller, M.: Graph signal processing on complex networks for structural health monitoring. In: Benito, R.M., Cherifi, C., Cherifi, H., Moro, E., Rocha, L.M., Sales-Pardo, M. (eds.) COMPLEX NETWORKS 2020. Studies in Computational Intelligence, vol. 943, pp. 249–261. Springer, Cham (2021). https://doi.org/10.1007/978-3-030-65347-7_21
10. Bloemheuvel, S., Kloepper, B., Atzmueller, M.: Graph summarization for computational sensemaking on complex industrial event logs. In: Di Francescomarino, C., Dijkman, R., Zdun, U. (eds.) BPM 2019. LNBIP, vol. 362, pp. 417–429. Springer, Cham (2019). https://doi.org/10.1007/978-3-030-37453-2_34
11. Boykin, K.G., Harings, N.M., Seamster, V.A., East, N.F., Guy, R.K., Andersen, M.C.: Methods for determining biodiversity metrics, focal species, and conservation practices for multi-scale analysis in support of the conservation effects assessment project (CEAP). United States Department of Agriculture - Natural Resources Conservation Service (2016)
12. Braud, A., Fromentoux, G., Radier, B., Grand, O.L.: The road to European digital sovereignty with Gaia-X and IDSA. IEEE Netw. **35**(2), 4–5 (2021)
13. Brockmann, W., Buschermöhle, A., Schoenke, J.H.: Cobra-a generic architecture for robust treatment of uncertain information. INFORMATIK 2013-Informatik angepasst an Mensch, Organisation und Umwelt (2013)
14. Buschermöhle, A., Schoenke, J., Brockmann, W.: Uncertainty and trust estimation in incrementally learning function approximation. In: Greco, S., Bouchon-Meunier, B., Coletti, G., Fedrizzi, M., Matarazzo, B., Yager, R.R. (eds.) IPMU 2012. CCIS, vol. 297, pp. 32–41. Springer, Heidelberg (2012). https://doi.org/10.1007/978-3-642-31709-5_4
15. Deng, A., Hooi, B.: Graph neural network-based anomaly detection in multivariate time series. In: Proc. AAAI Conference on Artificial Intelligence (2021)
16. Falih, I., Grozavu, N., Kanawati, R., Bennani, Y.: A recommendation system based on unsupervised topological learning. In: Arik, S., Huang, T., Lai, W.K., Liu, Q. (eds.) ICONIP 2015. LNCS, vol. 9490, pp. 224–232. Springer, Cham (2015). https://doi.org/10.1007/978-3-319-26535-3_26

17. Gade, K., Geyik, S., Kenthapadi, K., Mithal, V., Taly, A.: Explainable AI in industry: Practical challenges and lessons learned. In: Companion Proceedings of the Web Conference 2020, pp. 303–304 (2020)
18. Gbodjo, Y.J.E., Ienco, D., Leroux, L., Interdonato, R., Gaetano, R.: Fine grained classification for multi-source land cover mapping. arXiv:2004.01963 (2020)
19. van den Hoogen, J., Bloemheuvel, S., Atzmueller, M.: An Improved wide-kernel CNN for classifying multivariate signals in fault diagnosis. In: Proceedings of 2020 IEEE International Conference on Data Mining Workshops (ICDMW). IEEE (2020)
20. Ienco, D., Interdonato, R., Gaetano, R., Minh, D.H.T.: Combining sentinel-1 and sentinel-2 satellite image time series for land cover mapping via a multi-source deep learning architecture. ISPRS J. Photogramm. Remote. Sens. **158**, 11–22 (2019)
21. Interdonato, R., Atzmueller, M., Gaito, S., Kanawati, R., Largeron, C., Sala, A.: Feature-rich networks: going beyond complex network topologies. Appl. Netw. Sci. **4**(1), 1–13 (2019). https://doi.org/10.1007/s41109-019-0111-x
22. Interdonato, R., Ienco, D., Gaetano, R., Ose, K.: Duplo: a dual view point deep learning architecture for time series classification. ISPRS J. Photogramm. Remote. Sens. **149**, 91–104 (2019)
23. Interdonato, R., Magnani, M., Perna, D., Tagarelli, A., Vega, D.: Multilayer network simplification: approaches, models and methods. Comput. Sci. Rev. **36**, 100246 (2020)
24. IPBES: The global assessment report on biodiversity and ecosystem services - summary for policymakers (2019). https://doi.org/10.5281/zenodo.3553579
25. Kanawati, R., Atzmueller, M.: Modeling and mining feature-rich networks. In: Proceedings of WWW 2019 (Companion). IW3C2/ACM (2019)
26. Langendoen, K., Baggio, A., Visser, O.: Murphy loves potatoes: experiences from a pilot sensor network deployment in precision agriculture. In: Proceedings of of 20th International Parallel and Distributed Processing Symposium (IPDPS), pp. 1–8. Rhodes Island, Greece (2006). https://doi.org/10.1109/IPDPS.2006.1639412
27. Rehman, A.U., Abbasi, A.Z., Islam, N., Shaikh, Z.A.: A review of wireless sensors and networks' applications in agriculture. Comput. Stand. Interfaces **36**(2), 263–270 (2014). https://doi.org/10.1016/j.csi.2011.03.004
28. Schoenke, J.H., Brockmann, W.: Robustification of self-optimising systems via explicit treatment of uncertain information. In: 2015 Conference of the International Fuzzy Systems Association and the European Society for Fuzzy Logic and Technology (IFSA-EUSFLAT-15), pp. 152–161. Atlantis Press (2015)
29. Schwenke, L., Atzmueller, M.: Show me what you're looking for: visualizing abstracted transformer attention for enhancing their local interpretability on time series data. In: Proceedings of 34th International Florida Artificial Intelligence Research Society Conference. FLAIRS, North Miami Beach (2021)
30. Trousse, B., Jaczynski, M., Kanawati, R.: Using user behaviour similarity for recommendation computation: the broadway approach. In: HCI (2), pp. 85–89 (1999)
31. Tsakiridis, N.L., et al.: Versatile internet of things for agriculture: an eXplainable AI approach. In: Maglogiannis, I., Iliadis, L., Pimenidis, E. (eds.) AIAI 2020. IAICT, vol. 584, pp. 180–191. Springer, Cham (2020). https://doi.org/10.1007/978-3-030-49186-4_16
32. Vasisht, D., et al.: FarmBeats: an IoT platform for data-driven agriculture. In: Proceedings of of the 14th USENIX Conference on Networked Systems Design and Implementation (NSDI), Boston, MA, USA, pp. 515–528 (2017)

33. Wu, Z., Pan, S., Chen, F., Long, G., Zhang, C., Philip, S.Y.: A comprehensive survey on graph neural networks. IEEE Trans. Neural Netw. Learn. Syst. **32**, 4–24 (2020)
34. Zimek, A., Schubert, E., Kriegel, H.P.: A survey on unsupervised outlier detection in high-dimensional numerical data. Stat. Anal. Data Min.: ASA Data Sci. J. **5**(5), 363–387 (2012)

Comparison of Machine Learning and Deep Learning Methods for Grape Cluster Segmentation

Lucas Mohimont[1,2]($\boxtimes$) , Mathias Roesler[1] , Marine Rondeau[2] ,
Nathalie Gaveau[2] , François Alin[1] , and Luiz Angelo Steffenel[1]

[1] Université de Reims Champagne Ardenne, Laboratoire LICIIS - LRC CEA DIGIT,
51687 Reims Cedex 2, France
{lucas.mohimont,mathias.roesler,francois.alin,
angelo.steffenel}@univ-reims.fr
[2] Université de Reims Champagne Ardenne, RIBP - EA4707 - USC - INRAE1488,
51687 Reims Cedex 2, France
{marine.rondeau,nathalie.gaveau}@univ-reims.fr

Abstract. Automatic grape detection is one of the first steps towards automatic yield estimation. This step is often performed with a computer vision algorithm using the classic feature extraction and classification approach. Many grape bunch detection algorithms have been proposed in the last decade and most of them follow this standard approach. An alternative is semantic segmentation with deep learning models. The main objective of this work is to compare existing algorithms based on machine learning to encoder-decoder segmentation models (UNet and PSPNet). The comparison was performed on two challenging datasets of white grape varieties in natural lighting conditions. The UNet model reached better performances on both datasets with up-to 0.76 IoU score (compared to 0.59 IoU for the second best model). UNet was combined to a linear model to estimate the total number of grape bunches in 200 plants and reached 86% counting accuracy. The results show that deep learning models are more robust to white grape detection compared to classic segmentation techniques. This is an important property for early yield estimation before veraison.

Keywords: Grape detection · Precision viticulture · Deep learning · Semantic segmentation

1 Introduction

Viticulture is highly demanding in manual labor. Some tasks, like visual inspection for disease recognition, are repetitive and time-consuming because of the large scale of vineyards (thousands of vine plants) and the parcels divisions (the size of the parcels can vary). Another important step that requires manual labor is yield estimation. This estimation is necessary to organize the harvest's logistics and to respect the quality norms (i.e., yield quota). A classic estimation

© Springer Nature Switzerland AG 2021
S. Boumerdassi et al. (Eds.): SSA 2021, CCIS 1470, pp. 84–102, 2021.
https://doi.org/10.1007/978-3-030-88259-4_7

approach uses random grape bunch sampling. This is necessary to assess yield components like the number of bunches per vines, the number of berries per bunch, and the weight of the berries [11]. However, this random sampling is limited because it is destructive and because yield is highly variable (as high as a 10-fold difference in the same vineyard) [6].

Better methods are necessary to lower the estimation error rates and in the pursuit of this goal, better sampling strategies have been proposed to include the intra-field variability in the modelization steps [3].

A possible solution is to automate the process with computer vision algorithms. Automatic grape bunch detection and counting would allow for large-scale processing and better modelization. Grape detection was first proposed by Dunn et Martin [14] to measure the potential of computer-vision based yield estimation. Computer vision has been applied to yield estimation by Nuske et al., Aquino et al., Millan et al. and Liu et al. [2,26,28,29]. A classic approach to computer vision was used in these articles, with subjective criteria to select detection algorithms, feature extractors, and classifiers. The development of specific algorithms can be tedious and time-consuming, requiring image calibration with artificial lighting at night (or with an artificial background) and a high-quality camera. A more recent approach is deep learning with convolutional neural networks (CNNs). Deep learning models use several stacked convolutional, pooling, and fully connected layers to perform both feature extraction and classification (or segmentation). End-to-end learning can replace a complex algorithm by learning robust feature representations. It has been the state-of-the-art approach for image classification since a CNN model won the ImageNet Large Scale Visual Recognition Challenge in 2012 [13,23]. Deep learning has also been adapted to semantic segmentation with the Fully Convolutional Network [35].

This work presents a comparative study of machine learning and deep learning methods for grape bunch segmentation and offers the following contributions:

- Multiple existing segmentation algorithms based on machine learning are reproduced, fine-tuned and evaluated on two challenging datasets with white grape varieties in natural conditions [4,5,27,44,45].
- The classic methods were compared to semantic segmentation models: UNet and PSPNet [31,43].
- The performances of the UNet model was evaluated on grape bunch counting and reached an accuracy of 86%.

While we were able to reach 86% accuracy on grape bunch counting, the nature of the data impacts the performance of visible detection, and the nature of the models (morphology and linear regression) still requires additional work to perform a sufficiently accurate yield estimation.

The first part of this paper presents related work for grape bunch segmentation, while Sect. 3 presents the data sources and methods used for this study. Section 4 presents the results and discusses them, while Sect. 5 concludes this study and describes future works.

2   Related Works

Many grape detection methods have been proposed. The most straightforward method uses color-based thresholding to detect red grapes [14] in cropped images. It has also been used for red and white grape detection at night with artificial lighting [30]. Color-based thresholding has many limitations: it is too sensitive to lighting and color variation to be practical in a natural environment. This sensitivity can make it hard to separate the background from the fruit area in the foreground. Artificial lighting at night, or artificial backgrounds, can be employed but reduces the practicality of this method.

Grape detection can also be achieved by detecting individual berries. This is the approach used by Nuske et al. and Aquino et al. [2,29]. Berry candidates can be easily selected because the light produces a specular reflection pattern on the surface of the berries. This pattern follows a Gaussian distribution that can be detected with a filter [18], with circle detectors as the Hough transform or the fast radial symmetry transform [21,29] or with a local maxima detector [2]. Filtering rules and classifiers, like the multi-layer perceptron, are then used to remove the false positives. The performances can vary depending on the feature extraction techniques and classifiers selected by the researchers. This can be automated by training a CNN for this purpose [21,44]. This approach gave good yield estimation results as low as a 2% error rate [29]. Nonetheless, it has some limitations: artificial lighting and high-quality cameras are needed, and the detection is limited to the fruits only.

A classic approach to grape segmentation uses pixel-wise, or patch-wise, classification with a sliding window as input. The feature extraction is performed on a small neighborhood around the pixel, and the classifier's output is applied to the central pixel of the input (or the whole patch). This approach can be helpful when few images are available because pixel neighborhoods can be extracted easily to create balanced datasets like the one published by Škrabánek et al. [45]. This method was first studied with Zernike moments and Support Vector Machine (SVM) for patch-wise segmentation of red grapes [9], and many other methods have been proposed since then. In the work of Luo et al. [27], color features with an AdaBoost classifier were considered for red grapes in natural conditions. In the work of Behroozi-Khazaei and Maleki [4], the color features and the MLP size were both selected with a genetic algorithm for white grapes in natural conditions. Finally, a local structure tensor with Bayesian classification for vine segmentation with artificial lighting (flash) was proposed by Abdelghafour et al. [1]. Although good performances were achieved, they present some drawbacks: (1) the segmentation accuracy can be limited by the small input size, (2) pixel-wise classification can be slow and needs further optimization, (3) the researcher must select the appropriate feature extractor.

The feature extractor selection can be automated with a CNN that will learn the best representation from the raw images. Many classic CNN architectures have been studied for this purpose [8]. Pre-trained models are often used to compensate for the lack of data, and many models trained on the ImageNet dataset are freely available. However, there are some limitations to the evaluation of this kind of model. Both models presented by Behroozi-Khazaei and Maleki, and Cecotti et al. [4,8] were only evaluated on the extracted pixel's neighborhood. Therefore, the high performances are not representative of the actual segmentation performance because the dataset has a limited size (due to class balancing or manual selection of pixel neighborhoods). Better deep learning models have been studied for grape bunch detection: Mask R-CNN [34], Faster R-CNN, R-FCN, and SSD [20]. They were limited to grape bunch segmentation or detection with bounding boxes. Semantic segmentation models were applied to individual berry detection [17,41] and inflorescence detection [32].

In this work, semantic segmentation models are compared to pixel-wise classifiers on images that are harder to process. This comparison is limited to binary segmentation (grape bunch and background classes only). We argue that semantic segmentation models are adapted to this task because of the following reasons:

- Machine learning models use balanced datasets, constructed manually from the images, during training. The unbalanced classes problem is not addressed during the prediction. This problem and the small input size leads to noisy segmentation. Deep learning avoids these problems by performing the training on the raw images.
- Deep learning is able to construct good feature representations from the raw images. This could be useful for white grape varieties segmentation because yield estimation should be performed early (before the veraison).

3   Methods

3.1   Datasets, Tools, and Resources

Two datasets were used in the grape segmentation evaluation presented here. The first one is the dataset proposed by Berenstein et al. [5], which contains 129 RGB images with a size of 800×600 pixels. These images correspond to white grapes taken in natural conditions (the variety is not mentioned), and the images are labeled with binary masks (grape or background). Also, the camera's position limits the direct sun exposure, and the plant-camera distance remains constant throughout the dataset. These elements make it an interesting dataset for prototyping and evaluating grape segmentation methods.

The second dataset was collected by our team in July 2019 at a Vranken-Pommery parcel located in Reims, France. Three consumer-grade cameras (Nikon D7200, Samsung DV 150F, and Sony DSC-W310) with variable resolutions were used to take images of Chardonnay in natural lighting and background conditions. The whole dataset is uncalibrated (natural lighting, variable fruit-camera distances). Its purpose is to evaluate the grape segmentation methods in a challenging setting. The dataset contains 386 high-resolution images (at least 4000×3000 pixels) with binary masks corresponding to the fruit area. The images were manually labeled with bounding polygons (with the LabelMe tool [39]). An image and the associate ground truth mask are illustrated in Fig. 1.

Both datasets were used to evaluate the different methods described in the following subsections.

Three other datasets were used to assess the potential transferability of the model for other detection tasks. Hence, we explored red grape detection over a dataset composed of 31 images of the Pinot Noir variety. Another experiment was performed on inflorescence detection, using a dataset composed of 32 images of the Chardonnay plants during the inflorescence phase. Finally, grape bunch counting was evaluated on 198 images of individual Chardonnay vines from 4 rows of 3 different parcels, crossing information with manual counting on the rows. These datasets were obtained using a GoPro Hero 7 camera.

The algorithms and models were developed and evaluated with multiple Python APIs: OpenCV and Numpy for image processing, Scikit-learn for machine learning, and Tensorflow with Keras for deep learning. A Python package was used to download pre-trained UNet and PSPNet models [40]. Training and evaluation were performed on the Nvidia DGX-1 workstation with 8 Nvidia Tesla V100 GPUs hosted by the ROMEO super computing center[1] from Université de Reims Champagne-Ardenne.

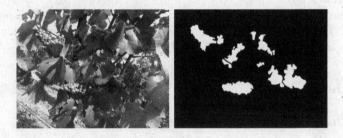

Fig. 1. Example of an image and its associated binary mask from our dataset.

3.2 Existing Grape Detection Algorithms

Multiple existing segmentation techniques for grape detection were selected and evaluated on the two datasets described in the previous section. The selected methods were based on pixel-wise classification. The method proposed by Luo et al. [27] uses average pixel values from the RGB, HSI, YCbCR, and Lab color spaces as training features. They selected multiple channels (R, G, B, H, Cb, and b*) with 7×7 pixel windows. The classification was performed with a strong AdaBoost classifier built with four linear classifiers [15]. Patches were selected manually: 400 for the grapes and 800 for the background. The method was evaluated on red grapes in natural conditions in both pixel-wise accuracy and object detection accuracy.

---

[1] https://romeo.univ-reims.fr.

A method to select the color features was proposed by Behroozi-Khazaei and Maleki [4]. It uses a genetic algorithm (GA) to select the color channels and the size of the MLP classifier [16]. The average values of the channels are then used as features. It was evaluated on the dataset published by Berenstein et al. [5]for segmentation of leaves, grapes, and background. Pixel-neighborhoods were manually selected (64 for each class) and the GA found that the best accuracy was obtained with a two-layer MLP with 15 and 35 neurons and with R-G, R-B, G-R, G-B, H, S, V, and b* channels.

The method proposed by Škrabánek et al. [45] uses Histogram of Oriented Gradients (HoG) [12] as features for an SVM classifier [7]. The claimed advantage of HoG is that it is not biased by color, being appropriate for white grape detection. However, the method was only evaluated on the extracted 40×40 pixel patches. The authors did not mention how their method was supposed to be applied. It can be used in two different ways: (1) grape filtering after a first detection [2,21,29] or (2) pixel-classification with a sliding window. The same authors compared this method to a CNN-based grape classifier [44].

Two pixel-wise classifiers were added as baselines. They have been chosen as the most straightforward machine-learning based segmentation models. The first baseline uses RGB average and standard deviation values as features, and the second baseline uses raw pixel values from a 3×3 window. The first baseline is inspired by the methods proposed by Luo et al. and Behroozi-Khazaei and Maleki [4,27] and the second baseline was used for grape disease detection in wine cellars by [37].

3.3 Semantic Segmentation for Grape Detection

Convolutional Neural Networks (CNN) were created by Yann LeCun in the late 1980s [24]. They were primarily designed for image classification, but they can also be adapted to time-series regression. CNNs are currently the state-of-the-art method for image classification because it is very effective for learning both the features and the classifier from the data. It was also applied to image segmentation with a sliding window for pixel-wise classification [10]. However, pixel-wise classification is highly inefficient because it only produces one output for the central pixel of the input. The output could be applied to the whole input patch, but it would lower the accuracy by producing a coarse segmentation. A solution was proposed by Shelhamer et al. [35] with a Fully Convolutional Neural Network (FCN). The dense layers of the CNN were replaced with transposed convolutions to produce an output that matches the input size. A FCN is, therefore, able to perform pixel-wise classification more efficiently. It also allows the processing of bigger input patches, hundreds of pixels wide, contributing to better segmentation performances. Indeed, bigger input processing is necessary to create robust object representations.

This kind of semantic segmentation model is known as an encoder-decoder architecture. The encoder is responsible for the automatic feature extraction. The decoder then uses its output to produce a dense pixel-wise prediction. Shortcut connections between the encoder and decoder layers are often used to compensate for the loss of information caused by the pooling layers. The encoder part can be achieved by any classification CNN (as long as the dense layers are removed). Generally, a backbone trained on ImageNet is used as an encoder (like VGG [36], ResNet [19], AlexNet [23], etc.).

In this study, two common architectures were trained on both datasets. The first one is UNet [31]. It is an FCN model with a symmetrical encoder-decoder and a shortcut connection for each pooling/upsampling block. Upsampling layers are used instead of transposed convolutions. The second one is PSPNet [43]. It uses a backbone followed by a pyramidal pooling module that processes the feature maps at different scales to produce a robust image representation. Both architectures were trained with different backbones and optimizers. The backbones were: (1) VGG-16 [36], a simple and popular CNN architecture, (2) ResNet-34 [19], a deep architecture with many skip-connections, and (3) MobileNetV2 [33], an optimized CNN architecture. The optimizers were: (1) SGD, the classic training algorithm with slow convergence but better generalization, (2) Adam [22], a good default optimizer, and (3) RAdam [25] with Look-Ahead [42], an optimizer that could provide both better generalization and convergence.

The default learning rate value was used for each training. A scheduled learning rate decrease strategy was used for the SGD optimizer, and the Jaccard Index was used as the loss function. The images of our dataset were resized to have the same size as Berenstein's dataset (800×600 pixels). Patches of 224×224 pixels were extracted for training and evaluation (240×240 for PSPNet). Each training was performed on a single Nvidia Tesla V100 GPU with mini-batches of 16 images. The best performing model was then trained on the images with their original resolution and with 512×512 patches. Data augmentation was not used during training.

3.4 Evaluation

Each method was evaluated on both datasets. The sliding-window based methods were first evaluated on patch classification with the accuracy metric (classes are balanced). Then each method was evaluated on the segmentation of the full images, using pixel-level metrics: recall, precision, F1-score, and Intersection Over Union. Metrics are described in Eqs. 1 through 5.

The existing methods were fine-tuned to maximize the patch classification accuracy before the evaluation of the whole images. The fine-tuning was performed for both datasets, by changing the classifier, the input size, and the number of patches. Training and validation patches were randomly selected from the labeled images, and a train-validation split of 70%/30% was used. Random patches were selected strictly inside the labeled grapes to lower possible errors due to labeling imprecision. The extracted datasets are balanced. Tables 1 and 2 present a summary of the different methods. The indicated samples correspond to the number of samples per class for sliding-window based methods and the total number of patches for semantic segmentation models.

The following formulas calculate the metrics, with TP, TN, FN, FP, which correspond respectively to the true positives, true negatives, false negatives, and false positives. Also, IoU (Intersection over Union) is computed with the ground truth mask (A) and the predicted mask (B).

$$Accuracy = \frac{TP + TN}{TP + FN + TN + FP} \tag{1}$$

$$Recall = \frac{TP}{TP + FP} \tag{2}$$

$$Precision = \frac{TP}{TP + FN} \tag{3}$$

$$F1score = \frac{2 \times Precision \times recall}{Precision + Recall} \tag{4}$$

$$IoU(A, B) = \frac{A \cap B}{A \cup B} \tag{5}$$

Table 1. Methods evaluated on the Berenstein et al. dataset

Method	Classifier	Features	Input size	Samples
Luo et al. [27]	MLP	Average values of R, G, B, H, Cb and b* channels	35 × 35	50 000
Behroozi-Khazaei et al. [4]	MLP	Average values of R-G, R-B, G-R, G-B, H, S, V and b* channels	35 × 35	50 000
Skrabanek et al. 2017 [45]	SVM	HoG	41 × 41	200
Skrabanek et al. 2018 [44]	CNN	CNN	31 × 31	10 000
RGB baseline	MLP	RGB average and standard deviation values	35 × 35	50 000
Raw baseline	MLP	Pixel values	3 × 3	100 000
UNet-ResNet-34 (ours)	UNet	UNet	224 × 224	3096

4   Results and Discussion

The performances are discussed in this section. Only validation metrics are reported because no sign of overfitting was found (3% maximum difference in the worst case). The two main approaches and the best performances are illustrated in Fig. 2.

4.1   Performances on the Berenstein Dataset

Performances for every method are shown in Table 4, where every sliding-window based method achieved over 80% accuracy on the randomly extracted pixel neighborhoods. The highest accuracy of 96% was achieved by the CNN, while the lowest accuracy of 86% was achieved by the HoG based method and the raw

Table 2. Methods evaluated on our dataset

Method	Classifier	Features	Input size	Samples
Luo et al. [27]	Adaboost	Average values of R, G, B, H, Cb and b* channels	31 × 31(resized to 7 × 7)	5000
Behroozi-Khazaei et al. [4]	MLP	Average values of R-G, R-B, G-R, G-B, H, S, V and b* channels	35 × 35	10 000
Skrabanek et al. 2017 [45]	MLP	HoG	31 × 31	10 000
Skrabanek et al. 2018 [44]	CNN	CNN	31 × 31	10 000
RGB baseline	SVM	RGB average and standard deviation values	21 × 21	2000
Raw baseline	MLP	Pixel values	3 × 3	10 000
UNet-ResNet-34 (ours, 800 × 600)	UNet	UNet	224 × 224	4632
UNet-VGG-16 (ours, original resolution)	UNet	UNet	512 × 512	24 318

pixels baseline. Similar performances were reported for the other methods with 92% for [27], 93% for [4], and 92% for the RGB baseline. However, these high accuracy scores do not always translate to high segmentation performances. The RGB baseline achieved the best performances with 74% F1 score and 0.59 IoU. The CNN follows it with slightly lower performances of 72% F1 and 0.56 IoU. The CNN achieved a higher recall rate with 87%, against 77%, but with 61% precision only (against 72% for the RGB baseline). An example of prediction is given in Fig. 3. The [27] and [4] methods achieved almost identical performances with, respectively, 69% F1 and 70% F1 (both methods obtained 0.54 IoU). Better performances were expected from the [4] method because it was originally evaluated on the same dataset and it was specifically fine-tuned for white grapes. Both methods have lower performances than the RGB baseline. The HoG based classifier achieved the lowest performances with only 44% F1 and 0.29 IoU. It is also lower than the raw baseline, which achieved 61% F1 and 0.45 IoU.

Overall, the best performances were achieved by deep learning semantic segmentation models. UNet models with VGG-16, ResNet34, or MobileNetV2 backbones, and with the SGD, optimizer achieved the same performances with 80% F1 and 0.69 IoU. Almost identical performances were achieved with PSPNet with VGG-16/Adam and ResNet-34/Radam-LookAhead with 80% F1 and 0.68 IoU. This is an improvement of 12 points for the F1 score and 17 points for the IoU, compared to the RGB baseline. This difference can be observed in the raw predicted masks. The sliding-window based methods produced noisy masks for two reasons: (1) the classification is performed with limited input, and (2) classes are heavily imbalanced in real images.

a) __Pixel-wise classification:__
- **74%** F1 score on calibrated images
- Example with RGB features for binary classification:

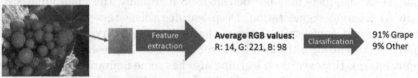

b) __Semantic segmentation with deep learning:__
- **86%** F1-score on calibrated images
- **72-80%** F1-score on uncalibrated images

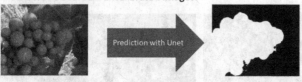

Fig. 2. The two main approaches for grape segmentation: a) pixel-wise classification with a sliding-window, b) semantic segmentation with deep learning

We were not able to reach the same patch-wise accuracy for most methods because different datasets were used. In the original paper, the method proposed by Luo et al. [27] reached 97.24% F1 score while our reproduction reached 92% accuracy. This difference was expected because this method was originally designed for red varieties. With the method of Behroozi-Khazaei and Maleki [4], we could not reach the same patch-wise accuracy, 93% against 99% in the original paper (the same dataset was used in both cases). This can be explained by the difference in the patch extraction step. We used automatic and random patch extraction, which can be used to create a training set of thousands of samples. We were also limited to binary classification while the authors of Behroozi-Khazaei and Maleki [4] added a third class for the leaves. The most significant difference was observed for the HoG based method, 86% accuracy against 99.4% F1 score in the original paper. Similar performances were observed for the CNN with 96% accuracy for our reproduction against 97% in the original work.

This limited input size with color-based features makes it hard to discriminate the white grapes from the leaves. HoG based features could be more appropriate because they are supposed to represent the pattern produced by the light reflection on the berries' surface. In practice, the window size and the distance between the camera and the fruits must be carefully selected to have the appropriate input. Therefore, it is unsuitable for segmentation and should be limited to grape candidate filtering after a first detection step. It should be noted that CNN achieves better performances because it can automatically learn the features from the data. However, in this simple case, the RGB baseline performs better.

The number of samples and the small input size are the two main limitations for several reasons. First, the number of samples is too small to represent the possible changes and variations found in natural images. Also, the training can not be performed on the whole dataset because it would be too time-consuming, and classic classifiers may not benefit from it. Finally, the small input size is a limit to coherent segmentation. Deep learning solves these limitations because it uses several convolutional layers that have the ability, with the stochastic gradient descent algorithm, to learn robust feature representations from bigger input images. However, deep learning also has some limitations because it needs many labeled images and expensive hardware (GPU) for training acceleration.

a)   b)

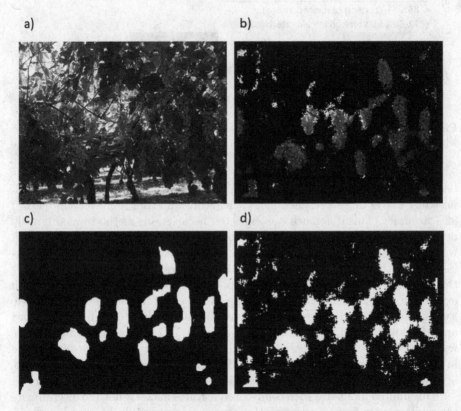

c)   d)

Fig. 3. CNN prediction: a) the original image, b) the segmented image, c) the labeled mask and d) the predicted mask

4.2   Performances on Our Dataset

Performances are shown in Table 5. Segmenting images from our dataset is a more difficult task because it is not calibrated: (1) natural lighting, (2) variable plant-camera distance, (3) variable angle of view, and (4) variable resolution. Nevertheless, the patch-wise accuracy was still over 70% for every sliding-window based method. In particular, the CNN achieved an impressive 98% accuracy. The second best performance was achieved by the RGB baseline, with 83% accuracy, and the [4] method with 81% accuracy. The other methods obtained an accuracy of 76% for the raw baseline, 74% for the HoG based method, and 73% for [27].

However, poor performances were observed when analyzing whole images. The CNN achieved the highest scores with 39% F1 and 0.27 IoU. Every other method achieved F1 scores lower than 30% and IoU lower than 0.2, this is an illustration of the limitation caused by the extraction of the pixel neighborhoods. The CNN performed poorly on the whole images despite the observed 98% accuracy on the extracted patches, which can be explained by the limited number of samples in the training and evaluation sets. Training is performed with a balanced dataset, but the classes are not balanced in the natural images. A solution could be to extract every patch, but this is quickly impractical on a big dataset or images of larger sizes. This limitation is most visible on this dataset because more variations are found in the non-calibrated images.

The best performances were obtained with UNet, with a VGG-16 backbone and the Adam optimizer, achieving 72% F1 score and 0.59 IoU. These metrics are less performant than UNet applied to the Berenstein dataset, which the non-calibrated nature of the images can easily explain. Also, the image resolution impacts the performances, with higher F1 and IoU scores for images keeping their original resolution. It achieved 80% F1 and 0.76 IoU (7% degradation compared to the Berenstein dataset) with 512×512 inputs. It should be noted that the model is able to detect grapes at different scales (background or foreground position of the fruit) and in some challenging conditions (shaded or over-exposed areas). An example of grape bunch segmentation is given in Fig. 4.

The application of the model to external images obtained from the Internet shows that the model is able to detect red grapes. The model is also able to segment, imperfectly, other spherical objects like cherries, plastic balls, or ray-tracing generated spheres. This implies that the model effectively learned robust and color-independent features. Therefore, transferring our model to different grape varieties is expected to yield good results. Also, the false positives and false negatives analysis shows that the main limitation is the lack of labeling precision (labeling error, misplaced edges).

The UNet-VGG-16 model was applied to inflorescences and red variety grapes. The model achieved 0.20 IoU on the inflorescences dataset and 0.37 IoU on the red variety dataset. Only a few false positives occur, and the main limitation of the performance is the low recall rate for the small objects like inflorescences and small grape bunches. Inflorescence segmentation is harder because the flowers have a green color almost identical to the foliage's color, and they are also smaller than berries. The model can detect red grapes when the lighting conditions are ideal (no shading caused by the leaves and no over-exposition). Better performances are expected with specific training. Examples for inflorescences and red variety segmentation are given in Figs. 5 and 6.

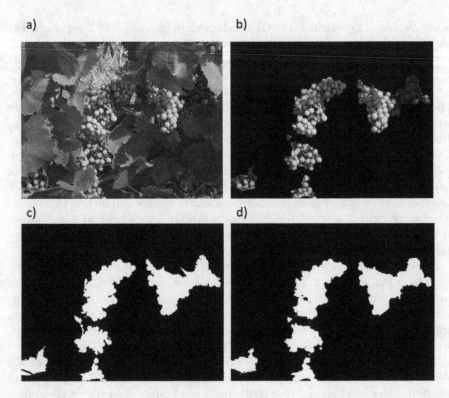

Fig. 4. Example of segmentation on white grapes: a) the original image, b) the segmented image, c) the labeled mask, and d) the predicted mask

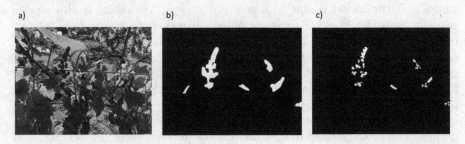

Fig. 5. Example of segmentation on inflorescences: a) the original image, b) the labeled mask, and c) the predicted mask

4.3   Evaluation for Counting Grape Bunches

The UNet model was applied to 198 images of individual vines to estimate the number of visible grape bunches. Morphology was applied to the predicted masks to remove the noise. A simple linear regression was used to predict the total number of grape bunches (visible and hidden) on four plant rows. Each row was modeled independently, and each model was later evaluated over the three

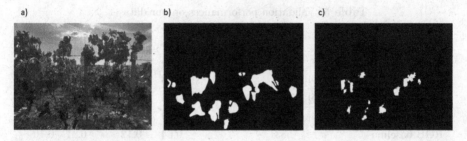

Fig. 6. Example of segmentation on red grapes: a) the original image, b) the labeled mask and c) the predicted mask

remaining rows. Error rates are shown in Table 3 The number of detected grape bunches was under-estimated with 1265 against 1998 manually counted grape bunches (37% error rate). This is due mainly to the morphology noise removal. Better performances were observed for the estimation of the total number of grape bunches with averages of 14.04% (depending on the model) and 11.28% (depending on the row). The error rate was higher for grape bunch counting at the individual plant level with 14.2%.

Table 3. Grape counting error

Type of counting:	Visible	Total	Total(individual)
Error rate:	37%	11.28–14%	14.2–14.27%

Table 4. Validation performances on the Berenstein et al. dataset

Method	Patch-wise accuracy	Recall	Precision	F1	IoU
Luo et al. [27]	0.92	0.82	0.61	0.69	0.54
Behroozi-Khazaei et al. [4]	0.93	0.81	0.63	0.70	0.54
Skrabanek et al. 2017 [45]	0.86	0.51	0.43	0.44	0.29
Skrabanek et al. 2018 [44]	**0.96**	0.87	0.61	0.72	0.56
RGB baseline	0.92	0.77	0.72	0.74	0.59
Raw baseline	0.86	0.81	0.51	0.61	0.45
UNet-ResNet-34(ours)	N/A	**0.92**	**0.82**	**0.86**	**0.76**

Table 5. Validation performances on our dataset

Method	Patch-wise accuracy	Recall	Precision	F1	IoU
Luo et al. [27]	0.73	0.66	0.10	0.15	0.09
Behroozi-Khazaei et al. [4]	0.81	0.63	0.13	0.20	0.11
Skrabanek et al. 2017 [45]	0.74	0.45	0.10	0.16	0.09
Skrabanek et al. 2018 [44]	**0.98**	0.49	0.36	0.39	0.27
RGB baseline	0.83	0.64	0.12	0.17	0.10
Raw baseline	0.76	0.36	0.32	0.27	0.17
UNet-ResNet-34(ours)	N/A	0.76	0.73	0.72	0.59
UNet-VGG-16(ours)	N/A	**0.87**	**0.78**	**0.80**	**0.69**

5   Conclusion and Future Works

Multiple existing algorithms for grape segmentation were compared to deep learning semantic segmentation models. The comparison was carried out on two datasets that are hard to process with white grapes and natural lighting conditions. In particular, our dataset was not calibrated, making it harder to process. The results have shown that classic algorithms have limited performances for multiple reasons: (1) the input size is too small, (2) the selected feature extractors may not be appropriate, and (3) they used limited datasets with balanced classes that are not representative of the whole images. A UNet model and a simple RGB classifier both performed better than existing methods [4,27,44,45] on the dataset published by Berenstein et al. [5]. These methods did not achieve good accuracy on the dataset that was not calibrated, while our UNet model also obtained the best performances.

The UNet model is able to detect white grapes in natural conditions with varying scales and angles. It was able to detect some spherical objects like red grapes, inflorescences, or cherries. Better performances are probably achievable on different grape varieties. However, deep learning has limitations because powerful hardware, like high-end GPU, is needed to train a model in a short time. It also needs large datasets of carefully labeled images. As mentioned earlier, the lack of labeling precision is the main limitation of the model performances.

Future work will be focused on berry counting-based yield estimation. This can be performed by counting the berries after grape segmentation [32] or by adapting the segmentation model for direct berry counting [17,41]. Efforts will also be carried on to add new classes, like the foliage, to the semantic segmentation model. It is a time consuming task because it requires manual image labeling. The addition of new classes could be useful for a more complex modelization part. For example, Victorino et al. proposed to use canopy porosity as variables for yield estimation [38]. Another estimation methods would use the automatic 3D reconstruction algorithm proposed by Liu et al. [26]. It has already been used for yield estimation but the problematic of background segmentation has not been adressed yet (artificial backgrounds were used during their experiments). Finally, efforts will be put towards deep learning implementation in low consumption hardware like the STM32MP157C-DK2 or Nvidia Jetson Nano 2 GB boards.

Acknowledgements. This work has been performed in the project AI4DI: Artificial Intelligence for Digitizing Industry, under grant agreement No 826060. The project is co-funded by grants from Germany, Austria, Finland, France, Norway, Latvia, Belgium, Italy, Switzerland, and the Czech Republic and - Electronic Component Systems for European Leadership Joint Undertaking (ECSEL JU).

We want to thank Vranken-Pommery Monopole, our partner in the AI4DI project, for allowing image collection in their vineyards. We also thank the ROMEO Computing Center (https://romeo.univ-reims.fr) of Université de Reims Champagne-Ardenne, whose Nvidia DGX-1 server allowed us to accelerate the training steps and compare several model approaches.

References

1. Abdelghafour, F., Rosu, R., Keresztes, B., Germain, C., Da Costa, J.P.: A bayesian framework for joint structure and colour based pixel-wise classification of grapevine proximal images. Comput. Electron. Agric. **158**, 345–357 (2019). https://doi.org/10.1016/j.compag.2019.02.017
2. Aquino, A., Millan, B., Diago, M.P., Tardaguila, J.: Automated early yield prediction in vineyards from on-the-go image acquisition. Comput. Electron. Agric. **144**, 26–36 (2018). https://doi.org/10.1016/j.compag.2017.11.026
3. Araya-Alman, M., et al.: A new localized sampling method to improve grape yield estimation of the current season using yield historical data. Precis. Agric. **20**(2), 445–459 (2019). https://doi.org/10.1007/s11119-019-09644-y
4. Behroozi-Khazaei, N., Maleki, M.R.: A robust algorithm based on color features for grape cluster segmentation. Comput. Electron. Agric. **142**, 41–49 (2017). https://doi.org/10.1016/j.compag.2017.08.025
5. Berenstein, R., Shahar, O.B., Shapiro, A., Edan, Y.: Grape clusters and foliage detection algorithms for autonomous selective vineyard sprayer. Intell. Serv. Robot. **3**(44), 233–243 (2010). https://doi.org/10.1007/s11370-010-0078-z
6. Bramley, R., Hamilton, R.: Understanding variability in winegrape production systems. Aust. J. Grape Wine Res. **10**(1), 32–45 (2004). https://doi.org/10.1111/j.1755-0238.2004.tb00006.x, https://onlinelibrary.wiley.com/doi/abs/10.1111/j.1755-0238.2004.tb00006.x
7. Burges, C.J.: A tutorial on support vector machines for pattern recognition. Data Min. Knowl. Discov. **2**(2), 121–167 (1998). https://doi.org/10.1023/A:1009715923555
8. Cecotti, H., Rivera, A., Farhadloo, M., Pedroza, M.A.: Grape detection with convolutional neural networks. Expert Syst. Appl. **159**, 113588 (2020). https://doi.org/10.1016/j.eswa.2020.113588
9. Chamelat, R., Rosso, E., Choksuriwong, A., Rosenberger, C., Laurent, H., Bro, P.: Grape detection by image processing. In: IECON 2006–32nd Annual Conference on IEEE Industrial Electronics, pp. 3697–3702 (2006). https://doi.org/10.1109/IECON.2006.347704

10. Cireşan, D.C., Giusti, A., Gambardella, L.M., Schmidhuber, J.: Deep neural networks segment neuronal membranes in electron microscopy images. In: Proceedings of the 25th International Conference on Neural Information Processing Systems - Volume 2, pp. 2843–2851. NIPS 2012, Curran Associates Inc., Red Hook, NY, USA (2012)

11. Clingeleffer, P.R., Martin, S.R., Dunn, G.M., Krstic, M.P.: Crop development, crop estimation and crop control to secure quality and production of major wine grape varieties : a national approach : final report to Grape and Wine Research and Development Corporation/principal investigator, Peter Clingeleffer; [prepared and edited by Steve Martin and Gregory Dunn]. Adelaide, Grape and Wine Research and Development Corporation (2001)

12. Dalal, N., Triggs, B.: Histograms of oriented gradients for human detection. In: 2005 IEEE Computer Society Conference on Computer Vision and Pattern Recognition (CVPR 2005), vol. 1, pp. 886–893 (2005). https://doi.org/10.1109/CVPR.2005.177

13. Deng, J., Dong, W., Socher, R., Li, L.J., Li, K., Fei-Fei, L.: Imagenet: a large-scale hierarchical image database. In: 2009 IEEE Conference on Computer Vision and Pattern Recognition, pp. 248–255 (2009)

14. Dunn, G.M., Martin, S.R.: Yield prediction from digital image analysis: a technique with potential for vineyard assessments prior to harvest. Aust. J. Grape Wine Res. **10**(33), 196–198 (2004). https://doi.org/10.1111/j.1755-0238.2004.tb00022.x

15. Freund, Y., Schapire, R.E.: A decision-theoretic generalization of on-line learning and an application to boosting. J. Comput. Syst. Sci. **55**(1), 119–139 (1997). https://doi.org/10.1006/jcss.1997.1504, https://www.sciencedirect.com/science/article/pii/S002200009791504X

16. Goldberg, D.E.: Genetic algorithms. Pearson Education India (2006)

17. Grimm, J., Herzog, K., Rist, F., Kicherer, A., Töpfer, R., Steinhage, V.: An adaptable approach to automated visual detection of plant organs with applications in grapevine breeding. Biosyst. Eng. **183**, 170–183 (2019). https://doi.org/10.1016/j.biosystemseng.2019.04.018

18. Grossetete, M., Berthoumieu, Y., Da Costa, J.P., Germain, C., Lavialle, O., Grenier, G.: Early estimation of vineyard yield: site specific counting of berries by using a smartphone. In: International Conference on Agiculture Engineering (AgEng), pp. tabla137-C1915 (July 2012). https://hal.archives-ouvertes.fr/hal-00950298

19. He, K., Zhang, X., Ren, S., Sun, J.: Deep residual learning for image recognition. In: 2016 IEEE Conference on Computer Vision and Pattern Recognition (CVPR), pp. 770–778 (2016). https://doi.org/10.1109/CVPR.2016.90

20. Heinrich, K., Roth, A., Breithaupt, L., Möller, B., Maresch, J.: Yield prognosis for the agrarian management of vineyards using deep learning for object counting. Wirtschaftsinformatik 2019 Proceedings, p. 15 (February 2019). https://aisel.aisnet.org/wi2019/track05/papers/3

21. Keresztes, B., Abdelghafour, F., Randriamanga, D., Da Costa, J.P., Germain, C.: Real-time fruit detection using deep neural networks. In: 14th International Conference on Precision Agriculture (2018). https://hal.archives-ouvertes.fr/hal-02518559

22. Kingma, D.P., Ba, J.: Adam: a method for stochastic optimization. In: Bengio, Y., LeCun, Y. (eds.) 3rd International Conference on Learning Representations, ICLR 2015, San Diego, CA, USA, 7–9 May 2015, Conference Track Proceedings (2015). http://arxiv.org/abs/1412.6980

23. Krizhevsky, A., Sutskever, I., Hinton, G.E.: Imagenet classification with deep convolutional neural networks. In: Proceedings of the 25th International Conference on Neural Information Processing Systems - Volume 1, pp. 1097–1105. NIPS 2012, Curran Associates Inc., Red Hook, NY, USA (2012)

24. LeCun, Y., Bengio, Y.: Convolutional Networks for Images, Speech, and Time Series, pp. 255–258. MIT Press, Cambridge, MA, USA (1998)

25. Liu, L., et al.: On the variance of the adaptive learning rate and beyond. CoRR abs/1908.03265 (2019). http://arxiv.org/abs/1908.03265

26. Liu, S., Zeng, X., Whitty, M.: A vision-based robust grape berry counting algorithm for fast calibration-free bunch weight estimation in the field. Comput. Electron. Agric. **173**, 11 (2020). https://doi.org/10.1016/j.compag.2020.105360

27. Luo, L., Tang, Y., Zou, X., Wang, C., Zhang, P., Feng, W.: Robust grape cluster detection in a vineyard by combining the adaboost framework and multiple color components. Sensors (Basel, Switzerland) **16**(1212), 21 (2016). https://doi.org/10.3390/s16122098, https://www.ncbi.nlm.nih.gov/pmc/articles/PMC5191078/

28. Millan, B., Velasco-Forero, S., Aquino, A., Tardaguila, J.: On-the-go grapevine yield estimation using image analysis and boolean model (December 2018). https://doi.org/10.1155/2018/9634752, https://www.hindawi.com/journals/js/2018/9634752/

29. Nuske, S., Wilshusen, K., Achar, S., Yoder, L., Singh, S.: Automated visual yield estimation in vineyards. J. Field Robot. **31**(55), 837–860 (2014). https://doi.org/10.1002/rob.21541

30. Reis, M.J.C.S., et al.: Automatic detection of bunches of grapes in natural environment from color images. J. Appl. Log. **10**(44), 285–290 (2012). https://doi.org/10.1016/j.jal.2012.07.004

31. Ronneberger, O., Fischer, P., Brox, T.: U-Net: convolutional networks for biomedical image segmentation. In: Navab, N., Hornegger, J., Wells, W.M., Frangi, A.F. (eds.) MICCAI 2015. LNCS, vol. 9351, pp. 234–241. Springer, Cham (2015). https://doi.org/10.1007/978-3-319-24574-4_28

32. Rudolph, R., Herzog, K., Töpfer, R., Steinhage, V.: Efficient identification, localization and quantification of grapevine inflorescences in unprepared field images using fully convolutional networks. arXiv:1807.03770 [cs] pp. 95–104 (July 2018). http://arxiv.org/abs/1807.03770, arXiv: 1807.03770

33. Sandler, M., Howard, A., Zhu, M., Zhmoginov, A., Chen, L.C.: Mobilenetv 2: inverted residuals and linear bottlenecks. In: Proceedings of the IEEE Conference on Computer Vision and Pattern Recognition (CVPR) (June 2018)

34. Santos, T.T., de Souza, L.L., dos Santos, A.A., Avila, S.: Grape detection, segmentation, and tracking using deep neural networks and three-dimensional association. Comput. Electron. Agric. **170**, 105247 (2020). https://doi.org/10.1016/j.compag.2020.105247

35. Shelhamer, E., Long, J., Darrell, T.: Fully convolutional networks for semantic segmentation. IEEE Trans. Pattern Anal. Mach. Intell. **39**(4), 640–651 (2017). https://doi.org/10.1109/TPAMI.2016.2572683

36. Simonyan, K., Zisserman, A.: Very deep convolutional networks for large-scale image recognition. In: Bengio, Y., LeCun, Y. (eds.) 3rd International Conference on Learning Representations, ICLR 2015, San Diego, CA, USA, 7–9 May 2015, Conference Track Proceedings (2015). http://arxiv.org/abs/1409.1556

37. Vazquez-Fernandez, E., Dacal-Nieto, A., Martin, F., Formella, A., Torres-Guijarro, S., Gonzalez-Jorge, H.: A computer vision system for visual grape grading in wine cellars. In: Fritz, M., Schiele, B., Piater, J.H. (eds.) ICVS 2009. LNCS, vol. 5815, pp.

335–344. Springer, Heidelberg (2009). https://doi.org/10.1007/978-3-642-04667-4_34

38. Victorino, G., Maia, G., Queiroz, J., Braga, R., Marques, J., Lopes, C.: Grapevine yield prediction using image analysis - improving the estimation of non-visible bunches. European Federation for Information Technology in Agriculture, Food and the Environment (EFITA), p. 6 (2019)

39. Wada, K., LabelMe, K.: Image Polygonal Annotation with Python (2016). https://github.com/wkentaro/labelme

40. Yakubovskiy, P.: Segmentation models (2019). https://github.com/qubvel/segmentation_models

41. Zabawa, L., Kicherer, A., Klingbeil, L., Töpfer, R., Kuhlmann, H., Roscher, R.: Counting of grapevine berries in images via semantic segmentation using convolutional neural networks. ISPRS J. Photogramm. Remote. Sens. **164**, 73–83 (2020). https://doi.org/10.1016/j.isprsjprs.2020.04.002

42. Zhang, M.R., Lucas, J., Hinton, G.E., Ba, J.: Lookahead optimizer: k steps forward, 1 step back. CoRR abs/1907.08610 (2019). http://arxiv.org/abs/1907.08610

43. Zhao, H., Shi, J., Qi, X., Wang, X., Jia, J.: Pyramid scene parsing network. arXiv:1612.01105 [cs] (December 2016). http://arxiv.org/abs/1612.01105, arXiv: 1612.01105

44. Škrabánek, P.: Deepgrapes: precise detection of grapes in low-resolution images. IFAC-PapersOnLine **51**(66), 185–189 (2018). https://doi.org/10.1016/j.ifacol.2018.07.151

45. Škrabánek, P., Doležel, P.: Robust grape detector based on svms and hog features. Comput. Intell. Neurosci. **2017**, 3478602 (2017). https://doi.org/10.1155/2017/3478602

Smart and Sustainable Agriculture
Machine Learning Behind This (R)evolution

Christophe Maudoux[✉] and Selma Boumerdassi

Cnam Paris – Cedric Lab, Paris, France
{christophe.maudoux,selma.boumerdassi}@cnam.fr

Abstract. Last decade has seen the emerging concept of Smart and Sustainable Agriculture that makes farming more efficient by minimizing environmental impacts. Behind this evolution, we find the scientific concept of Machine Learning. Nowadays, machine learning is everywhere throughout the whole growing and harvesting cycle.

Many algorithms are used for predicting when seeds must be planted. Then, data analyses are conducted to prepare soils and determine seeds breeding and how much water is required. Finally, fully automated harvest is planned and performed by robots or unmanned vehicles with the help of computer vision. To reach these amazing results, many algorithms have been developed and implemented.

This paper presents how machine learning helps farmers to increase performances, reduce costs and limit environmental impacts of human activities. Then, we describe basic concepts and the algorithms that compose the underlying engine of machine learning techniques. In the last parts we explore datasets and tools used in researches to provide cutting-edge solutions.

Keywords: Smart and sustainable agriculture · Machine learning · Datasets · Supervised and unsupervised algorithms · Practical applications

1 Introduction

Smart farming is a concept of agriculture management based on information and communication technologies implemented to increase products quantity and quality [1]. Different kind of technologies can be found behind this concept: *(i)* Sensors to scan soils or scale water, light, humidity or temperature *(ii)* Software for specific farm applications *(iii)* Communication technologies like cellular network *(iv)* Positioning by GPS *(v)* Hardware and software systems that enable IoT-based solutions and automation like drones [2] *(vi)* Data analytics to make decision and predict outcomes.

All these technologies integrated on farms allow farm-holders making farming processes data-driven and data-enabled. This emerging concept makes agriculture more efficient. Next step is now to reach a sustainable agriculture with

© Springer Nature Switzerland AG 2021
S. Boumerdassi et al. (Eds.): SSA 2021, CCIS 1470, pp. 103–121, 2021.
https://doi.org/10.1007/978-3-030-88259-4_8

the help of high-precision algorithms. The mechanism that drives it is *machine learning* which is the scientific approach that provides machines the ability to learn by themselves [3]. It has emerged with the help of data sciences, computing progresses and the ability to collect then store more and more data.

The rest of this article is organized as follows. Section 2 presents an overview of ML applications employed by smart agriculture. In Sect. 3, we expose main concepts behind machine learning. Sections 4 and 5 describe with details some supervised and unsupervised algorithms respectively. In Sect. 7, we present some widely employed tools and detail `Weka`. Then, some common metrics for evaluating approach performances are defined. Section 8 concludes this paper.

2 Applications

From *smart farming* to *sustainable agriculture*, Machine Learning Algorithms or MLAs are mechanisms behind this evolution. The most popular models deployed in agriculture are ANN which stands for Artificial Neural Networks and Support Vector Machines (SVM).

2.1 Crop Management

Yield Prediction. ML can help to determine the best yield mapping or crop type to match supply with demand. Furthermore, an early and reliable estimation of crop yield is essential in quantitative and financial evaluation at the field level for determining strategic plans in agricultural commodities for import-export policies and increasing farmer's incomes [4].

Crop Quality. The accurate detection and classification of crops can increase gain and reduce waste. ML can analyse interconnections to highlight new features biasing crops quality [5].

Disease Detection. To control diseases, farmers spread pesticides over the cropping areas. To be effective, this method requires significant amounts. ML can be used here for limiting financial costs and environmental impacts [6].

Weed Fighting. Weeds are harmful for crop production and it can be a boring and difficult task to get rid of this threat. Main problem in weed fighting is that they are difficult to highlight and discriminate from crops. MLAs can overcome these difficulties by minimizing cost and side effects [7].

2.2 Species Management

Species Breeding. Species selection is a tedious process. It requires identifying and selecting specific genes that determine adaptation to climate change, protect plants against diseases, provide a better taste, and so on .... MLAs take huge amount of data to analyse crops performance and build a model to determine which genes will increase a specific feature to a plant [8].

Species Classification. Classical approach consists in comparing colour and leaves shape. ML can provide more accurate and faster results by analysing the leaf vein morphology which expresses more information [9].

Species Reproduction. Pollination is the process in which pollen is taken from one plant to another so that it can reproduce. This task is essentially done by bees and insects. Problem is that bee number is dramatically decreasing. ML can help to detect the most fertile plants or select the most suitable time period when fertilization can happen and deploy drones to help in reproduction process [10].

2.3 Fields Management

Water Management. Water management in agriculture impacts environment balance. ML-based applications are connected with weather forecasting and evaporation estimations for a more effective use of irrigation systems [11].

Soil Management. Soil is a complex resource with many outside interactions. MLAs study evaporation processes, soil moisture and temperature to understand the dynamics of ecosystems and consequences [12].

2.4 Livestock Management

Livestock Production. ML predicts outcome or evolution to optimize economic efficiency of livestock production allowing farmers to modify feeding or life conditions [13].

Animal Welfare. Diseases, promiscuity, boredom can lead to lethal consequences for cattle. ML classifiers can detect behaviour changes to determine stress, unhappiness or weariness and alert that a problem could occur [14].

3 Main Concepts

All applications presented above are based on ML. This part introduces underlying concepts and describes algorithms mainly deployed in agriculture.

3.1 Definitions

MLAs are programs that can learn from data and improve from experience. Learning tasks may include defining the best function that maps input to output, finding out the hidden structure of unlabelled data or grouping samples such that objects within the same cluster are more similar to each other than to the objects from another cluster.

The most common type of machine learning process is to learn the mapping function: $Y = f(X) + e$ to make predictions of Y for new X with an irreducible error e based on the lack of attributes to sufficiently characterize the best mapping. This is called predictive modelling. The goal here is to make the most accurate possible predictions, irrespective of the function form.

3.2   Assumptions

MLAs make different assumptions about the shape and structure of the function and how best to optimize a representation to approximate it. Due to this reason, it is very important to try out different algorithms on a machine learning problem.

Assumptions are used for optimizing learning process, but can restrict what can be learned. Algorithms using strong assumptions are named *parametric* MLAs. Algorithms with weak assumptions about the mapping function form are classified as *non-parametric* MLAs. By not making assumptions, they can learn any functional shape from the training data. *Decision Trees, Naive Bayes* or *Neural Networks* are non-parametric MLAs.

To summarize, *parametric* methods make large assumptions about the mapping function and are faster to train, require less data but may not be as powerful. *Non-parametric* methods make few or no assumptions about the target function and in turn require a lot more data, are slower to train and have a higher model complexity, but can result in more powerful models [15, 16].

4   Supervised Algorithms

Input and output variables are available and an algorithm is used to learn the mapping function from the input to the output. It is called *supervised* learning because the learning process is based on a training dataset where the correct answers are already known. The algorithm iteratively makes predictions on the training data and is corrected by the "teacher". Learning stops when the algorithm achieves an acceptable level of performance. Supervised learning tasks can be used for resolving *classification* (output variable is a real value) or *regression* (value is a category) problems. The aims of supervised algorithm are make machines learn explicitly, predict outcomes or direct feedback.

4.1   K-Nearest Neighbour

KNN does not require to pre-process the training dataset. KNN predicts new data by searching into all the data for the K most similar means named neighbours and summarizing the output variable for those instances. For *regression* the mean output variable is used, in *classification* it is the most common class value. A distance measurement, commonly the *Euclidean* one, is computed to define which of the K instances in the training dataset are most similar to a new entry.

$$\text{EuclideanDistance}(a, b) = \sqrt{\sum_{i=1}^{n}(a_i - b_i)^2} \tag{1}$$

Other distance measures are existing like *Mahalanobis*, *Hamming*, ... The best distance metric to use depends on data properties. *Euclidean* suits if input data are close. Prefer the *Manhattan* one if not. The computational complexity of KNN increases with the amount of the training dataset. For huge dataset, KNN can be optimized by using stochastic approach. A snippet is cut out from the training dataset and the K-most similar instances are computed from it. For regression problems, the prediction is based on the median value. For classification, it is the highest frequency class from the K-most similar instances (Fig. 1).

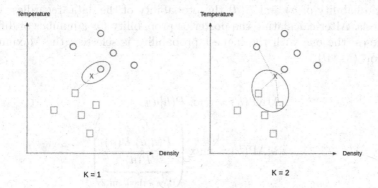

Fig. 1. KNN example

4.2 Linear Discriminant Analysis

LDA is a dimensionality reduction algorithm used for multi-class classification. It aims to split the samples in a training dataset by their class value. The algorithm try to find out a linear combination of input variables that achieves the maximum separation for means between classes d^2 and the minimum variation of means within each class, the scatter s^2. LDA creates an axis and projects the data onto this axis in a way to maximize the separation of categories (Fig. 2).

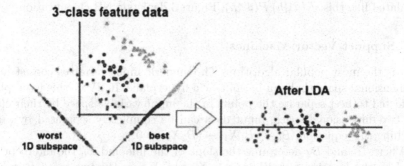

Fig. 2. LDA example

4.3 Naive Bayes

NB is based on eponymic theorem Eq. (2) that provides a way to calculate the probability of a hypothesis given prior knowledge:

$$P(h|d) = \frac{P(d|h)\,P(h)}{P(d)} \tag{2}$$

where $P(h|d)$ is the probability of hypothesis h given the data d (posterior probability), $P(d|h)$ the probability of data d given that the hypothesis h was true, $P(h)$ the probability of hypothesis h being true regardless of the data (prior probability of h) and $P(d)$ the probability of the data, regardless of the hypothesis. After calculating the posterior probability for a number of different hypotheses, the one with the highest probability is selected: the Maximum A Posteriori (MAP).

$$\text{MAP}(h) = \max[P(h|d)] \tag{3}$$

$$\Leftrightarrow \text{MAP}(h) = \max \left(\underbrace{\frac{P(d|h)\,P(h)}{P(d)}}_{\text{Bayes theorem 2}} \right) \tag{4}$$

$$\Leftrightarrow \text{MAP}(h) = \max[P(d|h)] \tag{5}$$

Equation (4) is obtained by substituting in Eq. (3) the Eq. (2) result. Then we find Eq. (5) after removing constants $P(d)$ and $P(h)$ in Eq. (4) because we are interested in the most probable hypothesis. Furthermore, we have an even number of instances in each class also the probability of each class will be the same.

It is named *Naive Bayes* because probabilities computation for each hypothesis are simplified and assumed to be conditionally independent. It requires a rigid independence assumption between input variables. Therefore, it is more proper to call "Simple Bayes" or "Independence Bayes". Rather than attempting to calculate the values of each attribute value $P(d1, d2, d3|h)$, they are separately calculated like this: $P(d1|h)\,P(d2|h)$. Figure 3 depicts a NB classification.

4.4 Support Vector Machines

SVM is the most popular algorithm. The numeric input variables consist in an n-dimensional space that can be split by a hyperplane. In SVM, this hyperplane is selected to best separate the points in the input variable space by their class. In a two-dimensional space, input data can be completely separated by a line matching this equation: $B_0 + (B_1 X_1) + (B_2 X_2) = 0$.

Where B_1 and B_2 determine the slope of the line and B_0 the intercept are found by the learning algorithm with X_1 and X_2 are the two input variables. The distance between the line and the closest data points is referred to as the

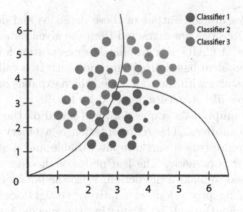

Fig. 3. NB example

margin. The optimal separation line is the one with the largest margin named the *Maximal-Margin hyperplane*. The margin is defined as the perpendicular distance from the line to only the closest points. Only these points are used for defining the line and building the classifier. These points are called the *support vectors* and defined the hyperplane Fig. 4.

The hyperplane is learned from training data using an optimization procedure that maximizes the margin. Learning of the hyperplane in linear SVM is done by transforming the problem using some linear algebra. If the groups can not be easily split, values are transformed by a function to be able to separate them Fig. 5.

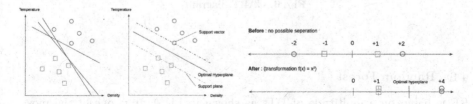

Fig. 4. SVM example   **Fig. 5.** Separation example

4.5 Decision Tree

DT or Classification and Regression Trees (CART) can be used for classification or regression predictive modelling problems but are better at solving classification ones. DT are composed of two nodes: *Decision* and *Leaf* nodes. It is a tree-structured classifier, where internal nodes represent the features of a dataset, branches are the decision rules and each leaf node represents the outcome. *Decision nodes* are used for selecting a branch (make a choice) and have multiple branches. *Leaf nodes* are the output of those decisions and do not contain any further branches. Decisions are extracted from the given dataset and depend on its intrinsic features. A CART is a graphical representation for getting all possible solutions to a problem based on given conditions. It is called a DT because, similar to a tree, it starts with the root node, which expands on further branches and constructs a tree-like structure depicted by Fig. 6.

A decision tree simply asks a question, and based on the answer, it further splits the tree into subtrees. The representation is a binary tree as shown by Fig. 6. Each node represents a single input variable and a split point on that variable assuming it is numeric. The leaf nodes of the tree contain an output variable which is used to make a prediction. With the binary tree representation of the CART, making predictions is relatively straightforward. Given a new input, the tree is gone through by evaluating the specific input started at the root node of the tree.

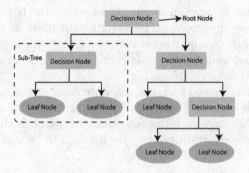

Fig. 6. CART diagram

4.6   Random Forest

RF is based on a multitude of DTs as shown in Fig. 7. It is one of the most popular and powerful MLAs. The problem with DTs is that they are greedy by nature. The variable which will be used to split the dataset is selected by using a greedy algorithm that minimizes error. Built DTs can have many structural similarities and so the same forecasting. By combining predictions from multiple models in ensembles works better if the forecasting from each sub-models are uncorrelated or weakly correlated. *Random Forest* changes the way the sub-trees are learned. With *Decision Trees*, when selecting a split point, the learning algorithm looks through all variables and all variable values in order to select the most optimal split-point. With *Random Forest*, the learning algorithm is limited to a random sample of features on which to search. Searched features at each decision node have to be passed to the algorithm.

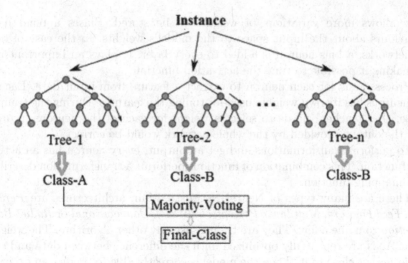

Fig. 7. Simplified RF

4.7   Artificial Neural Network

ANN is very often used in agriculture. It represents the structure of a human brain. It consists of neurons and synapses organized into layers (Fig. 8). ANN can have a huge number of neurons connected together, which makes it extremely efficient at analysing and memorizing various information.

There are different types of ANN but always composed of the same components: neurons, synapses, biases, weights and functions.

Neuron or node (Fig. 9) is the elementary component that receives information, performs basic computation task, and sends it to the next ones. *(i)* Input neurons receive information *(ii)* Hidden neurons process that information *(iii)* Output neurons perform result.

In large NN, neurons are stacked into layers: *(i)* An input layer to receive information *(ii)* Some hidden layers to compute intermediate calculation *(iii)* An output layer that provides valuable results.

Every neuron performs transformation on the input information. Neurons only operate numbers in the range [0, 1] or [−1, 1]. In order to transpose data into something that a neuron can handle, a normalization function like *Sigmoïd* is required. Neurons communicate each other through synapses.

Synapses are links that connect each neuron. Every synapse has a weight. The weights also add to the changes in the input information. The results of the neuron with the higher weight will be dominant in the next neuron, while low important information will not be passed over. The initialization phase consists in randomly assign weights which will be optimized later.

Bias allows more variations of weights to be stored. Biases append more behaviours about the input space to the model's weights. In the case of neural networks, a bias neuron is added to every layer. It plays an important role by making it possible to tune the activation function.

Process aims for each neuron to extract a feature from input data. Each of the neurons has its own weights used for tuning the features. During the training phase, the "teacher" needs to select a weight for each of the neurons in order that the output provided by the whole network would be correct.

To perform transformations and get an output, every neuron has an activation function. This combination of functions performs a transformation described by a mapping function.

There are many types of Neural Networks. Main architectures are *Perceptron, Feed Forward, Multilayer Perceptron (MLP), Convolutional* or *Radial Basis Function* to name a few. They are trained like any other algorithm. The weights of the ANN are repeatedly optimized until the difference between data and output is zero or close to it. Then the model is correctly able to predict an accurate output.

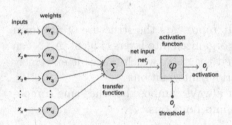
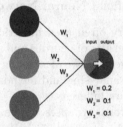

Fig. 8. ANN structure   **Fig. 9.** Neuron example

There are many types of ANN available or that might be in the development stage. They can be classified depending on their structure, data flow, neurons used and their density, number of layers and so on... Main architectures are Perceptron, Feed Forward, Multilayer Perceptron, Convolutional or Radial Basis Function for named a few.

5   Unsupervised Algorithms

Only input data are available and there is none corresponding output variables. The aim here is to model the underlying structure or distribution in the data in order to learn more about the data. This type of algorithms is called *unsupervised* learning because unlike *supervised* described above, there is no correct answers and no more "teacher".

Algorithms find out themselves and present the interesting structure in the data. Unsupervised learning problems can be split into *clustering problems* if you just want to group data and *association problems* if you try to define rules that describe large amount of data. Unsupervised algorithms can not be used for predicting results but are useful to identify patterns or structures.

5.1 Principle Component Analysis

PCA is a technique to build relevant features through linear or non-linear (kernel) combinations of the original variables. Relevant features are highlighted by linearly transforming correlated variables into a smaller number of uncorrelated variables. To do this, original data are projected into the reduced PCA space using the eigenvectors of the covariance matrix also known as the Principal Components (PCs). The resulting projected data are essentially linear combinations of the original data capturing most of the variance in the data. PCA can be defined as an orthogonal transformation of the data into a series of uncorrelated data.

Goals of PCA is to find linearly independent dimensions which can represent the data points and should allow to predict the original dimensions (Fig. 10).

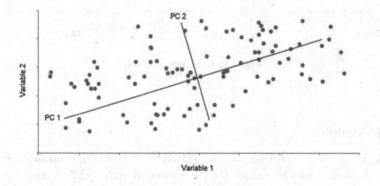

Fig. 10. PCA example

5.2 K-Means

Even if we do not know how the clusters will be constituted, the *K-Means* algorithm imposes to provide the expected number of clusters K. Some techniques exist to find the optimal K. Algorithm begins by randomly positioning center points named the *starter means*. Then it associates with the same clusters observations closest to these means. Next it calculates the average of the observations from each cluster and move corresponding means to computed position. After, the algorithm re-assign the observations to the nearest means and so on. To ensure the stability of found groups, the *starter means* selection is repeated several times because some initial draws may give a different configuration from the huge majority of cases.

Gathering the objects into well separated clusters K is performed by *K-Means* in such way that objects within each cluster are as close as possible to each other but as far as possible from objects in other clusters. Each cluster is characterized by its centre point named *centroid* which is the point whose coordinates are the average of the coordinates of points assigned to the clusters. In a dataset, *K-Means* algorithm tries to find the specified K number of clusters and their k centroids.

In following example, we suppose that dataset contains two variables and we expect to get two clusters (Fig. 11):

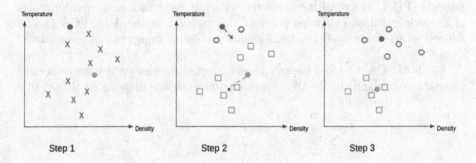

Fig. 11. K-Means example

5.3   K-Medoids

This algorithm is a clustering process related to *K-Means* and *medoidshift* algorithms. *K-Means* tries to reduce the total squared error, while k-medoids minimizes the sum of dissimilarities between points labelled to be in the same cluster and a point designated as the centre of that cluster. In contrast to *K-Means*, it chooses means as centres also known as *medoids*. A *medoid* is a data point of a dataset with the lowest average dissimilarity. It can be defined as the most centrally located dot in the dataset.

K-Medoids algorithm is less sensitive to noise and outliers than *K-Means* (Sect. 5.2) because it minimizes a sum of general pairwise dissimilarities instead of a sum of squared Euclidean distances. Choice of dissimilarity function is very wide. Main weak-point of the *K-means* algorithm is its sensitivity to outliers, because a mean can be easily biased by out-range values. To avoid this drawback, *K-Medoids* algorithm uses an actual point in the cluster to represent the centre of a cluster instead of the mean point. A *medoid* is the most centrally located object of the cluster, with minimum sum of distances to other points (Fig. 12).

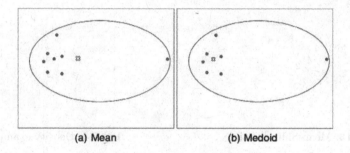

(a) Mean   (b) Medoid

Fig. 12. Mean versus Medoid

The group of points forms a cluster, while the rightmost point is an outlier. As mean can be biased, It could not represent the right cluster center. In the other hand, a medoid is robust to outliers and so correctly represents the cluster centre.

The most common implementation of *K-Medoid* clustering is the *Partitioning Around Medoids* algorithm. First, it randomly selects k of the n data points as the medoids. Secondly, the assignment step consists of associate each data point to the closest medoid. Then, for each medoid m and each data point o associated to m, it swaps m and o. Endlessly, the algorithm computes the total cost of the average dissimilarity of o to all the data points associated to m and select the medoid o with the lowest cost of the dissimilarity function. Steps 2 and 3 are repeated until there is no change in the assignments.

5.4   Mean Shift

It assigns the data points to the clusters iteratively by shifting points towards the highest density of data points in the region. Unlike *K-Means* (Sect. 5.2) clustering algorithm, *Mean Shift* does not require specifying the number of clusters in advance because it is determined by the algorithm with respect to the data. Main drawback to *Mean Shift* is its expensive computation time.

Mean Shift clustering algorithm required that data are mathematically represented because it is based on *Kernel Density Estimation*. KDE is a probability function used for estimating the underlying distribution by placing a kernel on each point in the data set. A kernel is a weighting function. Many types of kernels are existing but the most popular is the *Gaussian* one. Adding up all the individual kernels generates a probability surface example density function. The resultant density function will be different depending on the kernel bandwidth parameter (Figs. 13 and 14).

5.5   Density-Based Spatial Clustering of Applications with Noise

DBSCAN groups points that are close to each other based on a distance measurement like Euclidean distance Eq. (1) and a minimum number of points. Means

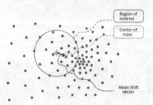

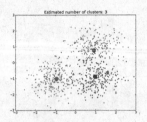

Fig. 13. Mean Shift principle   **Fig. 14.** Density example

in low-density regions are considered as outliers. The key idea here is that for each point of a cluster, the neighbourhood of a given radius *eps* has to contain at least a minimum number of points named *MinPts*. Partitioning methods like *K-Means* (Sect. 5.2) and hierarchical clustering are useful for finding compact and well-separated clusters with spherical or convex shapes.

But, real datasets contain arbitrary shape or noise. *DBSCAN* algorithm suits this kind of clusters better (Figs. 15 and 16).

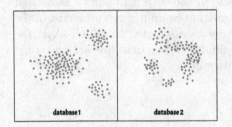

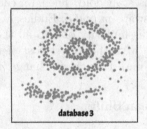

Fig. 15. Well-separated clusters   **Fig. 16.** Arbitrary shapes and noise example

6   Datasets

Provide a dataset is the main difficulty to deploy ML. Furthermore, labelled datasets are required to implement supervised approaches. Some smart agriculture data can be found but the majority of them are not on digital format. To perform researches, universities or scientists have built and provided a few datasets. This part describes a few ones that can be freely used.

6.1   Rice Leaf Diseases

This dataset is provided by UC Irvine Machine Learning Repository, and it is used for detecting and classifying rice plant diseases [17]. It has been created by manually separating infected leaves into different disease classes. There are three categories of disease: bacterial leaf blight, brown spot, and Leaf smut. Each one is composed of 40 jpg images. They were captured with a white background, in direct sunlight.

6.2   PlantVillage

PlantVillage is a not-for-profit project created by Penn State University in the USA and EPFL in Switzerland [18]. 10,000 images of diseased and healthy crops have been collected. The aim is to develop algorithms than can accurately diagnose a disease based on an image. The dataset is offering 38 classes and 54,305 images of 14 different plant species in total, 12 of which are healthy, 26 of which are diseased. The dataset also has one more class identifying 1143 background. Thus, total number of images is up to 55,000.

6.3   DeepWeeds

It is a multi-class weed species image dataset for deep learning [19]. It consists of 17,509 images capturing eight different weed species native to Australia with neighbouring plants.

6.4   PlantDoc

PlantDoc is a dataset for visual plant disease detection released by researchers at Indian Institute of Technology in 2019 [20]. Early detection of plant diseases is difficult due to the lack availability of sufficiently large-scale dataset. This dataset can be used for benchmarking classification models. It contains 2,598 data points in total across 13 plant species and up to 17 classes of diseases extracted from annotated internet images. Unlike similar dataset like *CropDeep*, this dataset is freely available to download for machine or deep learning.

6.5   CropDeep

It is a species classification and detection dataset, consisting of 31,147 images with over 49,000 annotated instances from 31 different classes. In contrast to existing vision datasets, images were collected with different cameras and equipment in greenhouses, captured in a wide variety of situations. It features visually similar species and periodic changes with more representative annotations, which have supported a stronger benchmark for deep-learning-based classification and detection.

7   Tools and Metrics

7.1   Machine Learning Implementation

Many tools and framework are existing to implement MLAs. We can cite four main tools: *(i)* Python with Jupyter is an interpreted high-level general-purpose programming language with many ML libraries. *(ii)* R with TensorFlow is a programming language provided with a free software environment named RStudio for statistical computing and graphics. The R language is widely used among statisticians and data miners. *(iii)* MatLab is a licenced proprietary multi-paradigm programming language and numeric computing environment developed by MathWorks. *(iv)* Weka a free, open-source and multiplatform collection of visualization tools and algorithms for ML.

7.2   The Workbench for Machine Learning

Waikato Environment for Knowledge Analysis is a freely available and commonly used open source software developed at the University of Waikato in New Zealand. The *Weka Toolbox*[1] is written using object-oriented language **Java**. It provides implementation of state-of-the-art data mining or MLAs [21]. It affords many functionalities as association, filtering, classification, clustering, visualization, regression, and so on.

Overall, data must be converted into an ARFF (Attribute-Relation File Format) file. This is an ASCII text file that describes a list of instances sharing a set of attributes. ARFF files have two distinct sections: *(i)* the Header which contains the name of the relation, a list of the attributes and their types, *(ii)* the Data:

```
%  Comment
@RELATION iris
@ATTRIBUTE sepallength    NUMERIC
@ATTRIBUTE sepalwidth     NUMERIC
@ATTRIBUTE petallength    NUMERIC
@ATTRIBUTE petalwidth     NUMERIC
@ATTRIBUTE class          {Iris-setosa,Iris-virginica}

@DATA
1,5,4,5,Iris-setosa
4,3,1,4,Iris-setosa
4,3,1,6,Iris-setosa
```

7.3   Basic Features

Algorithm performances can be evaluated by using multiple metrics defined and explained below. We can define the following four basic features:

True Positives (TP) correctly predicted to be true positives
    ⇒ correctly classified as malware
True Negatives (TN) correctly predicted to be false and really negatives
    ⇒ correctly classified as benign

---

[1] http://www.cs.waikato.ac.nz/ml/weka.

False Positives (FP) predicted to be true, but was incorrect, it was actually false

⇒ incorrectly classified as malware

False Negatives (FN) predicted to be false, but was incorrect., it was actually true

⇒ incorrectly classified as benign

7.4 Performance Metrics

Therefore, main performance metrics are calculated based-on the previous basic features:

Accuracy $\frac{TP+TN}{TP+FN+FP+TN}$ ⇒ gives the overall accuracy of the model, meaning the fraction of the total samples that were correctly classified

Misclassification rate or Classification Error $\frac{FP+FN}{TP+FN+FP+TN}$
⇒ tells what fraction of predictions were incorrect.

Precision $\frac{TP}{TP+FP}$ ⇒ expresses what fraction of predictions as a positive class were actually positive.

True-Positive Rate (TPR) or Recall or Sensitivity $\frac{TP}{TP+FN}$
⇒ fraction of all positive correctly predicted as positive

True-Negative Rate (TNR) or Specificity $\frac{TN}{TN+FP}$
⇒ fraction of negative cases correctly predicted as negative

False-Positive Rate (FPR) $\frac{FP}{TN+FP} = 1 - \text{TNR}$

False-Negative Rate (FNR) $\frac{FN}{TP+FN} = 1 - \text{TPR}$

F-Measure (FM) or F1 Score $2\frac{Recall.Precision}{Precision+Recall}$
⇒ is the harmonic mean of *Precision* and *Recall* (where 1 is 'good' and 0 is 'bad').

Matthews Correlation Coefficient (MCC)

$$\frac{TP.TN - FP.FN}{\sqrt{(TP+FP)(TP+FN)(TN+FP)(TN+FN)}}$$

Sensitivity and Specificity are inversely proportional to each other. So when we increase *Sensitivity*, *Specificity* decreases and vice versa.

8 Conclusion

Agriculture is more and more connected or automated. A huge amount of data is generated by all these smart and communicating devices. Collect then analyse them by machine learning techniques is probably the most suitable solution to evolve from a smart to a sustainable agriculture.

To provide and perform efficient answers to practical problems like weeds fighting, animals well-fare or diseases prevention, accurate algorithms must be developed. But to reach this goal, real or freely materials are required to be able to test proposed approaches or experiment new applications.

Help farmers to digitalize existing data could be a win-win solution to fill this data lake. Another way is to assist them in every way to deploy smart agriculture and in other hand, compile and broadcast collected information.

A smart and sustainable agriculture is the key to reach a better environment and provide the best one to our descent.

References

1. Sciforce. Smart Farming, or the Future of Agriculture. Medium, 14 January 2019. https://medium.com/sciforce/smart-farming-or-thefuture-of-agriculture-359f0089df69. Accessed 27 June 2021
2. 5 Top Harvest Automation Startups Impacting Agriculture. StartUs Insights, 14 October 2019. https://www.startus-insights.com/innovators-guide/5-top-harvest-automation-startups-impacting-agriculture/. Accessed 28 June 2021
3. Machine Learning in Agriculture: Applications and Techniques. KDnuggets. https://www.kdnuggets.com/2019/05/machine-learning-agriculture-applications-techniques.html/. Accessed 27 June 2021
4. Rashid, M., et al.: A comprehensive review of crop yield prediction using machine learning approaches with special emphasis on palm oil yield prediction. IEEE Access **9**, 63406–63439 (2021). ISSN 2169-3536. https://doi.org/10.1109/ACCESS.2021.3075159. https://ieeexplore.ieee.org/document/9410627/. Accessed 05 July 2021
5. Saha, A.K., et al.: IOT-based drone for improvement of crop quality in agricultural field. In: 2018 IEEE 8th Annual Computing and Communication Workshop and Conference (CCWC). 2018 IEEE 8th Annual Computing and Communication Workshop and Conference (CCWC), pp. 612–615. IEEE, Las Vegas, January 2018. ISBN 978-1-5386-4649-6. https://doi.org/10.1109/CCWC.2018.8301662. http://ieeexplore.ieee.org/document/8301662/. Accessed 05 July 2021
6. Sambasivam, G., Opiyo, G.D.: A predictive machine learning application in agriculture: cassava disease detection and classification with imbalanced dataset using convolutional neural networks. Egypt. Inf. J. **22**(1), 27–34 (2021). ISSN 11108665. https://doi.org/10.1016/j.eij.2020.02.007. https://linkinghub.elsevier.com/retrieve/pii/S1110866520301110. Accessed 05 July 2021
7. Sabzi, S., Abbaspour-Gilandeh, Y.: Using video processing to classify potato plant and three types of weed using hybrid of artificial neural network and partincle swarm algorithm. Measurement **126**, 22–36 (2018). ISSN 02632241. https://doi.org/10.1016/j.measurement.2018.05.037. https://linkinghub.elsevier.com/retrieve/pii/S026322411830424X. Accessed 05 July 2021
8. Thudi, M., et al.: Genomic resources in plant breeding for sustainable agriculture. J. Plant Physiol. **257**, 153351 (2021). ISSN 01761617. https://doi.org/10.1016/j.jplph.2020.153351. https://linkinghub.elsevier.com/retrieve/pii/S0176161720302418. Accessed 05 July 2021
9. Weiss, U., et al.: Plant species classification using a 3D LIDAR sensor and machine learning. In: 2010 Ninth International Conference on Machine Learning and Applications. 2010 International Conference on Machine Learning and Applications (ICMLA), pp. 339–345. IEEE, Washington, December 2010. ISBN 978-1-4244-9211-4. https://doi.org/10.1109/ICMLA.2010.57. http://ieeexplore.ieee.org/document/5708854/. Accessed 05 July 2021

10. Van Goethem, S., et al.: An IoT solution for measuring bee pollination efficacy. In: 2019 IEEE 5th World Forum on Internet of Things (WFIoT). 2019 IEEE 5th World Forum on Internet of Things (WF-IoT 2019), pp. 837–841. IEEE, Limerick, April 2019. ISBN 978-1-5386-4980-0. https://doi.org/10.1109/WF-IoT.2019. 8767298. https://ieeexplore.ieee.org/document/8767298/. Accessed 05 July 2021

11. Cardoso, J., Gloria, A., Sebastiao, P.: Improve irrigation timing decision for agriculture using real time data and machine learning. In: 2020 International Conference on Data Analytics for Business and Industry: Way Towards a Sustainable Economy (ICDABI). 2020 International Conference on Data Analytics for Business and Industry: Way Towards a Sustainable Economy (ICDABI), pp. 1–5. IEEE, Sakheer, 26 October 2020. ISBN 978-1-72819-675-6. https://doi.org/10.1109/ICDABI51230. 2020.9325680. https://ieeexplore.ieee.org/document/9325680/. Accessed 05 July 2021

12. Jain, P., et al.: Maximising value of frugal soil moisture sensors for precision agriculture applications. In: 2020 IEEE/ITU International Conference on Artificial Intelligence for Good (AI4G). 2020 IEEE/ITU International Conference on Artificial Intelligence for Good (AI4G), pp. 63–70. IEEE, Geneva, 21 September 2020. ISBN 978-1-72817-031-2. https://doi.org/10.1109/AI4G50087.2020.9311008. https://ieeexplore.ieee.org/document/9311008/. Accessed 05 July 2021

13. Nayeri, S., Sargolzaei, M., Tulpan, D.: A review of traditional and machine learning methods applied to animal breeding. In: Anim. Health. Res. Rev. 20(1), 31–46 (2019). ISSN 1466-2523, 1475-2654. https://doi.org/10.1017/S1466252319000148. https://www.cambridge.org/core/product/identifier/S1466252319000148/type/ journal_article. Accessed 05 July 2021

14. Salzer, Y., et al.: Towards on-site automatic detection of noxious events in dairy cows. Appl. Anim. Behav. Sci. 236, 105260 (2021). ISSN 01681591. https://doi.org/10.1016/j.applanim.2021.105260. https://linkinghub.elsevier.com/ retrieve/pii/S0168159121000472 (visited on 07/05/2021)

15. Brownlee, J.: Master Machine Learning Algorithms: Discover How They Work and Implement Them, 162 p. Machine Learning Mastery (2016)

16. Bonnardot, G.: 8 Machine Learning Algorithms Explained in Human Language. Datakeen (2017). https://datakeen.co/en/8-machine-learning-algorithms-explained-in-human-language/. Accessed 30 June 2020

17. Prajapati, H.B., Shah, J.P., Dabhi, V.K.: Detection and classification of rice plant diseases. IDT 11(3), 357–373 (2017). ISSN 18724981, 18758843. https://doi.org/10. 3233/IDT-170301. https://www.medra.org/servlet/aliasResolver?alias=iospress& doi=10.3233/IDT-170301. Accessed 27 June 2021

18. Hughes, D.P., Salathe, M.: An open access repository of images on plant health to enable the development of mobile disease diagnostics, 11 April 2016. arXiv: 1511.08060 [cs]. http://arxiv.org/abs/1511.08060. Accessed 28 June 2021

19. Olsen, A.: AlexOlsen/DeepWeeds, 21 June 2021. https://github.com/AlexOlsen/ DeepWeeds. Accessed 28 June 2021

20. Kayal, P.: Pratikkayal/PlantDoc-Dataset, 24 June 2021. https://github.com/ pratikkayal/PlantDoc-Dataset. Accessed 27 June 2021

21. Witten, I.H., et al.: Data Mining: Practical Machine Learning Tools and Techniques. Morgan Kaufmann Series in Data Management Systems, Morgan Kaufmann, San Diego (2016). 655 p. ISBN 978-0-12-804357-8

A Methodology for Early Detection of Plant Diseases Using Real Time Object Detection Algorithm

Ranjeet Walia[1(✉)], Shivam Sharma[1], and Swapnil Shrivastava[2]

[1] National Institute of Technology, Hamirpur, Anu, Himachal Pradesh 177005, India
[2] Centre for Development of Advanced Computing (CDAC), No. 1, Old Madras Road, Byappanahalli, Bangalore 560038, India
swapnil@cdac.in

Abstract. The convergence of Big Data Analytics, Deep Learning, Internet of Things (IoT) and Cloud Computing has catalyzed the emergence of novel applications in various domains. The growing need for Sustainable Agriculture and advancement in these emerging technologies has enabled applications like Precision Agriculture and Smart Farming. There are several such initiatives where agricultural data is being collected continuously by means of devices (e.g., sensors, cameras) and stored in a suitable Big Data Analytics platform. There is a need to generate actionable insights in real time for these applications using various analytical techniques including Deep Learning. Various techniques have been used for plant disease detection, pest detection, plant growth assessment, yield prediction and so on. As per the Food and Agriculture Organization of the United Nations, there is a growth in frequency of occurrences and complexity of plant diseases. In this work we have attempted to build a contemporary model with available resources for early detection of plant diseases. The freely available plant images dataset was collected from various sources followed by required pre-processing to prepare a large, assorted and robust plant disease dataset. The real time object detection algorithm is applied for efficient and timely plant disease detection. The detailed methodology for creation of material, building the detection model and inferring the result is discussed in this paper. The early detection of plant diseases would help in quick diagnosis and provisioning of remedial measures to the farmers for enabling timely preventive or curative actions.

Keywords: Plant disease detection · Yolo algorithm · Deep learning

1 Introduction

To ensure food security for the world population while facing serious environmental issues like climate change, depletion of natural resources and soil erosion is the grand challenge presently being faced by humanity. Sustainable Agriculture is being projected as the way forward in farming practices to meet the food needs of the growing world population in the 21st century [1]. The objective of this approach is to maximize crop

© Springer Nature Switzerland AG 2021
S. Boumerdassi et al. (Eds.): SSA 2021, CCIS 1470, pp. 122–139, 2021.
https://doi.org/10.1007/978-3-030-88259-4_9

productivity as well as profitability of farmers and at the same time minimize natural resource utilization and reduce negative impact on the environment. The National Research Council (NRC) defined Precision Agriculture as a management strategy that uses information technology to bring data from multiple sources to bear on decisions associated with crop production in a sustainable way [2]. Since 1980 Precision Agriculture has automated agricultural operations through the integration of Global Positioning System (GPS), Geographic Information System (GIS) and Remote Sensing technologies. Several methods have been devised to analyze agricultural data for Crop Growth Assessment, Weed Identification and Management, Pest and Disease Infestation, Crop yield and Production Forecasting as well as Nutrient and Water Status [3].

The Food and Agriculture Organization of the United Nations highlights the growing trend in the frequency of occurrences and complexity of plant diseases [4]. In a way, crop production is susceptible to uncontrolled occurrences and incidences of plant diseases. The periodic application of chemicals and pesticides is the conventional way of controlling the spread of diseases. On the flip side, this causes environmental pollution and excessive pesticide residue on plants that are harmful for human health [5]. The accurate and fast diagnosis of plant disease symptoms can act as an effective preventive measure of plant diseases. The traditional methods that include observation of growers and expert advice are slow, highly subjective, and lack a comprehensive approach. The convergence of Big Data Analytics, Deep Learning, Internet of Things (IoT) and Cloud Computing have catalyzed the emergence of various real time, efficient and affordable applications like Precision Agriculture, Smart Farming and Organic Farming in the agriculture domain to enable Sustainable Agriculture [6, 7]. These are real time applications which require real time processing and analysis of agricultural data collected from sensors and cameras installed in the field. The advancements in Deep Learning technologies have provided new methods and algorithms for efficient, high accuracy and cost-effective early detection of plant disease. The models belonging to the Convolutional Neural Network (CNN) sub branch of Deep Learning for image recognition are applicable for this task. The end-to-end automatic execution of these models overcomes the highly subjective and non-comprehensive limitations of traditional methods. This approach would save time and effort in disease detection as well as improve accuracy and efficiency of the results. The early detection of plant diseases would help in quick diagnosis and provisioning of remedial measures to the farmers for enabling timely preventive or curative actions. The Deep Learning research community is putting consistent efforts in improving efficiency and accuracy of neural networks for emerging real time applications. In this work we have attempted to build a real time plant disease detection model with available resources for early detection of plant diseases. We present a methodology to build a large, assorted and robust plant disease dataset from the freely available resources including the images collected in natural backdrop as well as plant disease detection using a real time object detection algorithm. The accuracy of the result is also discussed in this paper. The real time, accurate and efficient judgement on disease detection is the requirement in emerging applications for Sustainable Agriculture.

2 Related Works

The traditional manual methods for plant disease detection were time consuming and highly subjective. The advancements in Deep Learning technologies have enabled automation of plant disease detection using various image recognition models. These image recognition models are grouped under the Convolutional Neural Network (CNN) substream of Deep Learning. A number of CNN based image recognition models such as AlexNet [8], GoogleLeNet [9], VGGNet [10] and ResNet [11] were developed for image classification applications. The Deep Learning community is making continuous efforts in improving accuracy of these models. Several studies were conducted where CNN models were used for plant disease detection and pest detection [12–14] in crops like rice, apple and corn. The emergence of new applications requires object detection models. A massive breakthrough by the Deep Learning community was a shift in approach from image classification to object detection. The image classification models were trained to check for a certain pattern in an image and classify the image accordingly. Whereas, the object detection task involves detection and localization of multiple patterns in an image. The You Only Look Once (YOLO) [15] is a landmark algorithm developed for object detection. In this approach the image is annotated with bounding boxes and these boxes are detected as well as located in an image. The YOLO algorithm has found applications such as plant disease detection and pest detection in the agriculture domain. The CropDeep, a vision dataset comprises various crop images with precision agriculture domain specific annotations. The potential utility of the then version 3 of YOLO in agricultural detection tasks was also discussed in the paper [16]. In a separate study, tomato diseases and pests dataset consisting of images captured in natural settings was created. The then version 3 of YOLO was optimized using an image pyramid to achieve multi-scale feature detection for tomato diseases and pests detection. It was noted that this model detected the location and category of diseases and pests of tomato accurately and quickly [17].

R. Sahith et al. [18] employed UCI Machine learning repository rice leaf disease dataset. The features of the diseases were extracted by a colour layout filter available in WEKA. Decision tree-based machine learning methods like Random Forest were employed for classification. The maximum accuracy of all models was 76.19. S.P. Mohanty et al. [19] used a deep convolutional neural network trained on Plant Village Dataset for image-based plant disease detection. The training accuracy on a held-out dataset was 99.35%. However, when tested on images taken under different conditions, the accuracy fell to 31.4%. The authors thus concluded that a more diverse dataset is required for application in varying scenarios. In [20], authors created a non-lab extensive plant leaf disease dataset. Furthermore, they trained three models on the dataset and a maximum 31% accuracy was achieved.

To solve our problem statement discussed in the previous section there is a need for IoT applications specific plant disease dataset and disease detection techniques. A dataset customized by us for IoT based applications and implementation of YOLO on this dataset for faster crop disease classification done as part of our work is discussed next.

3   Material and Method

The early detection of plant diseases requires a large, assorted and robust image dataset of plant diseases. Here a real-world object detection algorithm is employed to solve multi-object detection problems by detecting the objects in the image and eventually labeling them to their respective category. The data flows at different steps for early plant disease detection viz. Data Source, Data Preprocessing, Feature Extraction, Object Detection, and Performance Evaluation is shown in Fig. 1.

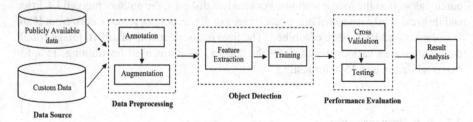

Fig. 1. Flowchart for early plant disease detection.

3.1   Data Collection

The key component for any image classification task is a proper dataset. One of the objectives was to use a dataset that was inclusive of the different scenarios. The scenarios which needed to be addressed were related to both image quality and the setting of the images. The training dataset with images of varying quality would improve the accuracy of the model. The different image settings which involve the non-uniformity pertaining to image background and leaf count in the image would make the model applicable in not only images with the uniform background but also in real-world scenarios like crop fields. Including these scenarios was of utmost importance in order to make the trained model apt for Precision Agriculture and other IoT applications in agriculture. Hence as part of this work, a new dataset that also included publicly available datasets was built. The details of publicly available datasets a newly created assorted dataset is discussed as follows:

Plant Village Dataset (PVD). PVD is a widely available dataset. The data records contain 54,309 images. The images span 14 crop species: Apple, Blueberry, Cherry, Corn, Grape, Orange, Peach, Bell Pepper, Potato, Raspberry, Soybean, Squash, Strawberry, Tomato. All the images are high quality, single leafed and captured in a controlled setting, which makes its use in real world scenarios limited.

Plant Doc Dataset. The dataset contains 2,598 images in total across 13 plant species and up to 17 classes of diseases. The images are in a non-controlled setting i.e., with varying backgrounds. Unlike PVD, the images have multiple leaves and are of varying quality.

UCI Rice Dataset. The dataset consists of 120 images across three different rice diseases (brown spot, bacterial leaf blight and leaf smut) with each consisting of 40 images. All the images are high quality and captured in a controlled setting.

Since the UCI dataset is in a controlled setting and its application in the real world is limited, the authors created a rice leaf dataset with the same diseases as UCI. The authors manually collected 187 images from various internet sources. All the images are in real-world scenarios with one or more leaves. All the datasets above address some key aspects which make our model suitable for different plant image based IoT applications. The datasets pairwise complement each other in terms of both the image quality as well as the image settings. For rice leaf diseases, the authors merged UCI rice and this real-world dataset. Then equal images of apple, potato, tomato, corn from Plant Doc dataset and PVD were combined. The final dataset consists of 14016 images of all the plants across various diseases. Of the dataset, 70% was used for training, 15% for cross-validation and 15% for testing.

3.2 Data Preprocessing

Annotation. Image annotation is the method that allows the computer systems to automatically assign metadata by captioning or labeling an image that has an object or multiple objects in it. This is very helpful in multiclass object detection or multiclass classification problems in computer vision. These labels are normally established in advance to the machine and are selected to provide the information to the computer vision model on objects portrayed in an image. Annotation specifically refers to the area where an object is located in the image. In the work discussed in this paper annotation of images has been done manually with the help of a toolkit. There are various techniques of image annotations in computer vision, and authors have used the bounding boxes technique for labeling the objects in the images.

Bounding boxes are simple and regularly used annotation technique in various object detection problems. In this technique, a rectangular shape box is specified in the target location where an object is located in the image. The rectangular box is represented by the pair of (x, y) coordinates of the top-left corner and the pair of (x, y) coordinates of the bottom-right corner of the rectangle.

There are various toolkits available for this task and authors of this paper have used the LabelImg [21] toolkit for annotation. The LabelImg is a software that helps in specifying the location of an object present in an image in terms of its minimum and maximum x, y coordinates (xmin, xmax, ymin, ymax) for top-left and bottom-right corners, occupied in the image. When a rectangular box is drawn at the location where the object is present in the image then LabelImg toolkit generates the XML files that contains the type of the object class, image location, height & width. The following examples show how annotation is done with LabelImg.

The metadata associated with the image shown in Fig. 2 is as follows:
xmin = 2, xmax = 768, ymin = 169, ymax = 392.
Object class = Rice Brown Spot.
Image width = 768, Image height = 514.

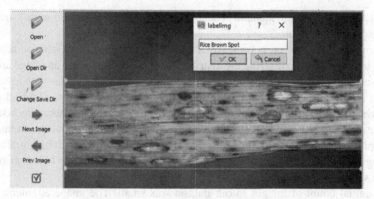

Fig. 2. Annotation of rice brown spot image.

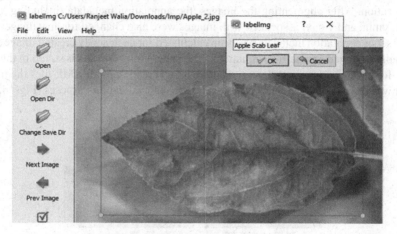

Fig. 3. Annotation of apple scab leaf.

Following is the metadata associated with the image shown in Fig. 3:
xmin = 41, xmax = 464, ymin = 41, ymax = 285.
Object class = Apple Scab Leaf.
Image width = 496, Image height = 348.

Augmentation. A large amount of data is essential for any Deep Learning model. For our plant disease detection, the assorted and customized dataset was not sufficient to train the model and produce good results. Image Augmentation is a technique that increases the number of instances in datasets by making a group of random changes to the images in the dataset. Thus, producing different image examples. In other ways, the image augmentation is randomly changing instances in a dataset to reduce a model's dependency on certain properties, and improve its capability for generalization. Image augmentation can be done in two ways, one way is artificially creating images by the combination of various processing mechanisms in the images through available tools or modules. Other ways are to manually rotate images, adjust brightness, contrast stretching or histogram equalization.

Histogram Equalization is basically a technique in image processing to adjust the contrast in images by recognizing the distribution of pixel densities in an image and plotting these pixel densities on a histogram. This enhances contrast of areas with lower local contrast. A limitation of this method is that it may increase the contrast of background noise, while decreasing the signal of necessary data in the image. Adaptive histogram equalization can be used as an alternative to normal histogram equalization, as it is a better option. It computes several histograms for an image, with each histogram corresponding to a distinct segment of the image, and uses that information to redistribute the contrast values of the image.

The initial count of images in our dataset was small. The image augmentation in our dataset has been done manually in different ways, by rotating the original image vertically along the x-axis, rotating at 180°, and by applying the adaptive histogram equalization. After augmenting the images, the annotation metadata (including xmin, xmax, ymin, and ymax) associated with images were also changed for new images. So, a new set of annotation metadata has been calculated for each newly created image from manually designed geometrical equations. The annotation metadata is stored in the new XML for each new image. After augmentation and creation of all XML files the image count was large enough and was used for training and validation purposes (Figs. 4, 5, 6 and 7).

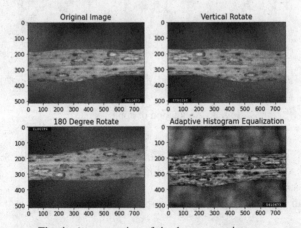

Fig. 4. Augmentation of rice brown spot image.

3.3 Feature Extraction

YOLOv4 Architecture. In the era of Computer Vision, the YOLO algorithm performs an important role in the detection of various objects in images. Object detection is a classic problem in computer vision to identify what object is shown and where it is located in the image. The detection of an object at a specific location in the image

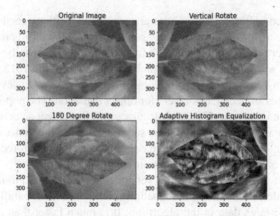

Fig. 5. Augmentation of apple scab leaf image.

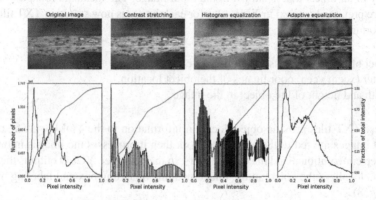

Fig. 6. Preprocessing rice brown spot image.

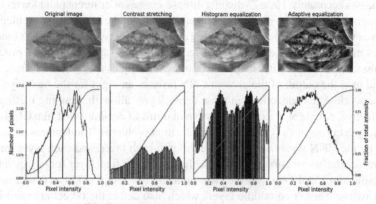

Fig. 7. Preprocessing apple scab leaf image.

is an extremely complicated task. There are various algorithms each with their own capabilities for recognizing objects in images. In YOLO, the aim is to predict a class of an object, where the bounding boxes in annotated images specify object location. YOLO algorithm was introduced by Joseph Redmon et al. [15] in 2015. YOLO is a fast algorithm and can be used for real-time object detection. YOLO uses Deep Learning with a large number of deep CNN layers for object detection. The popularity of YOLO in object detection is because of its high accuracy and fast object detection as compared to other detection algorithms. As the name suggests, it looks only once at an image and feeds the information to network layers in only one pass to make forecasts of the class of object present in the image with a bounding box.

The authors of YOLO released a new version 4 (YOLOv4) [22] to implement a fast system for object detection that has the capability of optimizing the parallel computations while training the large data in the algorithm. It is much faster than previous YOLO versions and is also very efficient in terms of accuracy and precision.

To understand how YOLOv4 works, it is important to know the objective class or category of an object that is shown in the input image. The metadata related to images that were previously stored in XML files for each image is now stored in TXT files with a new format as.

1. Label of the object class for multiclass classification,
2. center (xcen, ycen) coordinates of the object location,
3. width and height of the object in the image.

These TXT files provide object location information to the YOLOv4. The batches of input images are fed to the YOLO network then it processes the images in one pass with deep convolutional and max-pool layers. In the last layer, YOLO outputs the object class and localizes the object in the image with the bounding box and labeling over the box (Fig. 8).

Multiclass Feature Extraction. The objective of this paper is to detect the object in the image. All the objects belong to different classes and our aim is to distinguish those object classes accurately. Here 23 distinct disease-classes of different plant leaves images have been used that form a multiclass object detection and classification problem. This problem can be divided into object detection and then the classification of the object. The YOLOv4 model uses very dense CNN layers. Each CNN layer has its own processing mechanism, with distinct filter maps and pooling techniques to detect the features of the input and pass the output of the present CNN layer as an input for the next layer in the whole network. The connections in these dense layers allow the training method to be more effective, simple and more progressive in terms of accuracy just like CNN, which is also very accurate in various image classification problems. The features of an object learned by the CNN layers are processed through each layer, and each layer improves and increases the information related to the feature till the final layer for object detection and classification. YOLOv4 uses the layer number 139, 150, and 161 as detection layers in the network. These two middle layers which also detect the object are used here to check whether our model is doing well or not. With this architecture, YOLOv4 can easily learn complex features needed for our multiclass classification problem (Fig. 9).

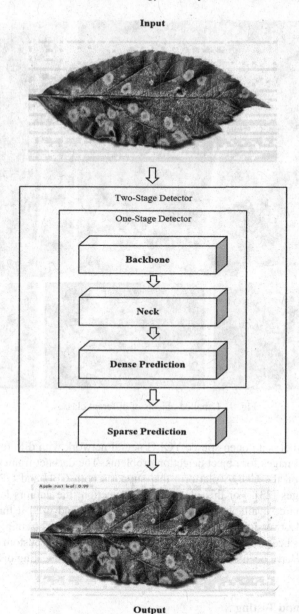

Fig. 8. YOLOv4 architecture.

Fig. 9. Labelled objects of different classes.

Darknet. Darknet is an open-source YOLO neural network with different versions of YOLO to train images for object detection problems. The darknet framework is coded in C language on the CUDA platform that supports both CPU and GPU variants to train input images [23]. For this plant disease detection, the authors have employed this Darknet source available on Github repository [24] and used it through Google Colab. The YOLO version 4 (YOLOv4) has been used for model training. A major file yolocvm.cfg has been updated with necessary changes to train the custom dataset. Other mandatory files have been created accordingly for training and testing of the dataset.

3.4 Training and Testing

Locating an object in an image requires lots of processing and time. Recent advancements in object detection algorithms have increased computational efficiency. YOLO is one of the state-of-the-art deep CNN-based object detection approaches with good performance in terms of both speed and accuracy. The applications of IoT in the agriculture field have also increased the useful data both in terms of quantity and quality. The YOLO network has high robustness for the detection of objects of varying sizes. It also features object localization with a high IoU (Intersection over Union) score which can meet the needs of plant diseases detection. The YOLO network has high detection and positioning accuracy, thus a strong capacity for detection of different plant diseases in complex environments and hence suitable for IoT based agriculture applications.

All the images of datasets used in this paper are of different sizes, so they are converted to a fixed size of 416 * 416. The available dataset was not enough for training YOLOv4. So, the images in the dataset are augmented. Although augmenting data with various techniques only provides a small amount of analytical information, it was useful as it increased data. All the images (original and augmented) are combined and annotated with bounding boxes. The metadata associated with each image is stored in an individual XML file. Now the input images are ready and the metadata in XML files should be converted into the format desired by YOLOv4. Therefore, metadata values are converted into a different set and stored in new TXT files. The data is distributed into the train set for training the YOLOv4, cross-validation set for evaluating the model, and the test set for predicting new labels of images. There are 23 different disease classes that are detected and classified with this object detection model. On testing, the model generates the labelled images where the label is specified on the top of the bounding boxes with a confidence score.

4 Result

The authors have used 70% of the data for training the model, 15% of the data for cross-validation, and the rest 15% data for testing. The results obtained from the performance analysis are in the below table, which shows the model's ability in plant disease classification (Fig. 10 and Table 1).

4.1 Performance Metric

The performance of YOLOv4 has been evaluated on cross-validation data which is derived from the same distribution as the training data set. The evaluation metrics F1-score, Mean Average Precision (mAP at 50% IoU), and intersection over union (IoU) have been used to check the effectiveness of the model. Images in the dataset are of different sizes, and the number of images in the cross-validation set is 2100 which is 15% of the dataset used. The predicted output from the classifier is divided into True Positive (TP), True Negative (TN), False Positive (FP), and False Negative (FN).

Precision checks the portion of predicted positive examples, and recall checks the portion of truly positive examples used from the dataset. For each target class, Average Precision (AP) has been calculated. The AP of an individual disease class can't be used as a performance metric, so mAP (mean of all APs) has been calculated and used as a performance metric.

$$Precision = \frac{TP}{TP + FP}$$

$$Recall = \frac{TP}{TP + FN}$$

$$F_1 Score = \frac{2 * Precision * Recall}{Precision + Recall}$$

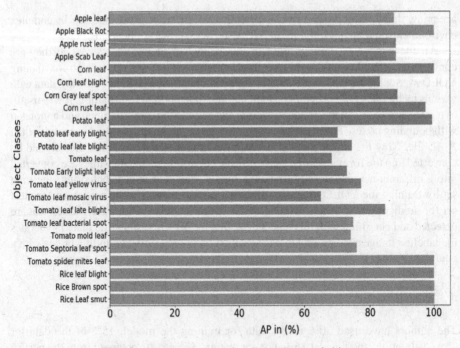

Fig. 10. Average precision for all the classes of objects.

F1-score is the harmonic mean of overall precision and recall. IoU is the ratio of the intersection area to the union area between the predicted bounding boxes and actually marked bounding boxes around the objects. If IoU is near to 1, the model will be more accurate to recognize the object in the input image (Table 2).

$$IoU = \frac{\text{Area of Intersection (Overlap)}}{\text{Area of Union}}$$

In Fig. 11(a), the accuracy (in %) of different performance metrics used, has been measured and it shows how YOLOv4 has performed on the dataset. Improvements in mAP (at 50% IoU) and IoU with increasing iterations in Figs. 11(b), and 12 illustrates the effectiveness of the proposed model on the dataset.

Table 3 depicts that the model discussed in this paper has performed significantly better in terms of mAP than the work in which [20] PlantDoc and PVD datasets with Faster CNN and InceptionResnetV2 were used. In comparison with [25], our model performed better both in terms of improved precision of results and application in real world scenarios, owing to our custom dataset and state of the art methodology.

4.2 Quantitative Analysis

In this section, the predicted output on the test set has been observed to guarantee the effectiveness of the model after evaluating on the cross-validation set. The predicted label

Table 1. Average precision of all output classes.

Plants classes	Average precision (AP)
Apple leaf	87.62
Apple black rot	100.00
Apple rust leaf	88.15
Apple scab leaf	88.15
Corn leaf	99.98
Corn leaf blight	83.25
Corn gray leaf spot	88.68
Corn rust leaf	97.33
Potato leaf	99.41
Potato leaf early blight	70.29
Potato leaf late blight	74.56
Tomato leaf	68.49
Tomato early blight leaf	73.09
Tomato leaf yellow virus	77.36
Tomato leaf mosaic virus	65.12
Tomato leaf late blight	84.80
Tomato leaf bacterial spot	74.95
Tomato mold leaf	74.20
Tomato septoria leaf spot	76.02
Tomato spider mites leaf	99.89
Rice leaf blight	99.85
Rice brown spot	100.00
Rice leaf smut	100.00

Table 2. Performance metrics results

Performance metrics	Result in (%)
Precision	73.00
Recall	78.00
F1 score	76.00
mAP (at 50% IoU)	85.57
Average IoU	87.65

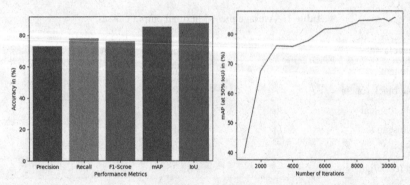

Fig. 11. (a) Performance Metrics. (b) Mean Average Precision (mAP at 50% IoU) is increasing with number of iterations.

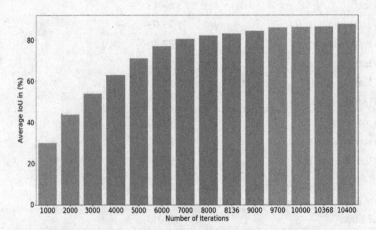

Fig. 12. Average IoU is increasing with number of iterations.

Table 3. Comparison with previous research.

Dataset	Model used	mAP (at 50% IoU) in (%)
PlantDoc [20]	Faster RCNN InceptionResnetV2	38.90
Customized dataset	YOLOv4	85.57

of objects above the bounding box with the confidence score indicates YOLOv4's ability to detect the object and predict the disease class of the object. Some random images have been selected and then tested with the model. The predicted label and confidence score above the bounding boxes in Fig. 13 shows the good performance of the model.

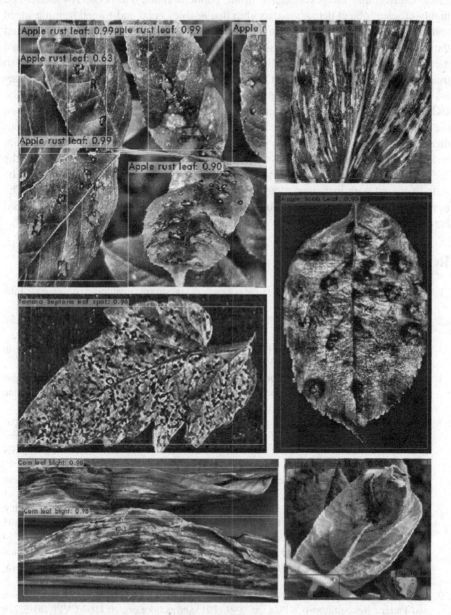

Fig. 13. Visual observation of YOLOv4 object detection results.

5 Conclusion

This paper proposes a real-time plant disease detection methodology using object-detection. A customized dataset is created as part of this work that includes crop diseases, datasets and images available in the public domain. The YOLOv4 model is a highly efficient object detection algorithm that enables great end-to-end training speed and real-time detection accuracy in this work. Experimental results have demonstrated the advantage of YOLOv4 on cross-validation and test data. This model has obtained a considerably better mAP (at 50% IoU) and F1 scores compared to [20] which also used PlantDoc and PVD datasets. Our research is more inclusive of real- world scenarios owing to custom dataset as compared to [25] and also has higher precision on the UCI Rice dataset. The manual annotation although time consuming greatly improved the results of our model. With an extremely fast algorithm and an extensive dataset, our methodology has enormous scope in real time applications like Precision Agriculture and Smart Farming. The accuracy of the proposed model can be improved with the addition of even more plants and improved image quality. The resulting classifier will be state-of-the-art with increased robustness in terms of diseases for different plants. The running time can be improved through faster versions of the algorithm and advanced hardware resources.

References

1. What is Sustainable Agriculture? https://sarep.ucdavis.edu/sustainable-ag. Accessed 9 June 2021
2. Bongiovanni, R., Lowenberg-Deboer, J.: Precision agriculture and sustainability. Precis. Agric. **5**, 359–387 (2004)
3. Shanmugapriya, P., Rathika, S., Ramesh, T., Janaki, P.: Applications of remote sensing in agriculture - a review. Int. J. Curr. Microbiol. App. Sci. **8**(01), 2270–2283 (2019)
4. Food and Agriculture Organization of the United Nations. Plant Diseases and Pests. http://www.fao.org/emergencies/emergency-types/plant-pests-and-diseases/en/. Accessed 9 June 2021
5. Ulberth, F.: Early warning systems for food safety and integrity need to be anticipative to be useful for preventing food crisis situations. Journal fur Verbraucherschutz und Lebensmittelsicherheit-J. Consum. Protect. Food Saf. **11**, 215–216 (2016). JRC102884. ISSN 1661-5751
6. Krintz, C., et al.: SmartFarm: improving agriculture sustainability using modern information technology (2016)
7. Roberts, D.P., Short, N.M., Sill, J., Lakshman, D.K., Hu, X., Buser, M.: Precision agriculture and geospatial techniques for sustainable disease control. Indian Phytopathol. **74**(2), 287–305 (2021). https://doi.org/10.1007/s42360-021-00334-2
8. Krizhevsky, A., Sutskever, I., Geoffrey, H.: ImageNet classification with deep convolutional neural networks. Neural Inf. Process. Syst. **25**, 1097–1105 (2012). https://doi.org/10.1145/3065386
9. Szegedy, C., et al.: Going deeper with convolutions. In: IEEE Conference on Computer Vision and Pattern Recognition (CVPR), pp. 1–9 (2015).https://doi.org/10.1109/CVPR.2015.7298594
10. Simonyan, K., Zisserman, A.: Very deep convolutional networks for large-scale image recognition. arXiv: arXiv:1409.1556 (2014)

11. Xie, S., Girshick, R., Dollár, P., Tu, Z., He, K.: Aggregated residual transformations for deep neural networks. In: IEEE Conference on Computer Vision and Pattern Recognition (CVPR), pp. 5987–5995 (2017). https://doi.org/10.1109/CVPR.2017.634
12. Chowdhury, R.R., et al.: Identification and recognition of rice diseases and pests using convolutional neural networks. Biosyst. Eng. **194**, 112–120 (2020). ISSN 1537-5110
13. Ferentinos, K.: Deep learning models for plant disease detection and diagnosis. Comput. Electron. Agric. **145**, 311–318 (2018). https://doi.org/10.1016/j.compag.2018.01.009
14. Sladojevic, S., Arsenovic, M., Anderla, A., Culibrk, D., Stefanovic, D.: Deep neural networks based recognition of plant diseases by leaf image classification. Comput. Intell. Neurosci., Article ID 3289801, 11 p. (2016)
15. Redmon, J., Divvala, S., Girshick, R., Farhadi, A.: You only look once: unified, real-time object detection. In: IEEE Conference on Computer Vision and Pattern Recognition (CVPR), pp. 779–788 (2016)
16. Zheng, Y.Y., Kong, J.L., Jin, X.B., Wang, X.Y., Zuo, M.: CropDeep: the crop vision dataset for deep-learning-based classification and detection in precision agriculture. Sens. (Basel, Switz.) **19**(5), 1058 (2019)
17. Liu, J., Wang, X.: Tomato diseases and pests detection based on improved Yolo V3 convolutional neural network. Front. Plant Sci. **11**, 898 (2020). ISSN 1664–462X
18. Sahith, R., Reddy, P.V.P., Nimmala, S.: Decision tree-based machine learning algorithms to classify rice plant diseases. Int. J. Innov. Technol. Explor. Eng. (IJITEE) **9**(1), (2019). ISSN: 2278-3075
19. Mohanty, S.P., Hughes, D.P., Salathe, M.: Using deep learning for image-based plant disease detection. Front. Plant Sci. **7**, article 1419 (2016)
20. Singh, D., et al.: PlantDoc: a dataset for visual plant disease detection. In: Proceedings of the 7th ACM IKDD CoDS and 25th COMAD, Hyderabad, India, 5–7 January 2020, pp. 249–253. Association for Computing Machinery, New York (2020)
21. Tzutalin, LabelImg, Git Code (2015). https://github.com/tzutalin/labelImg. Accessed 9 June 2021
22. Bochkovskiy, A., Wang, C.-Y., Liao, H.Y.M.: Yolov4: optimal speed and accuracy of object detection (2020). arXiv preprint arXiv:2004.10934
23. Redmon, J.: Darknet: open-source neural networks in C (2013–2016). http://pjreddie.com/darknet/. Accessed 9 June 2021
24. Redmon, J.: Darknet: open-source neural networks in C, Git Code (2018), https://github.com/pjreddie/darknet. Accessed 9 June 2021
25. Ahmed, K., Shahidi, T.R., Mohammad, S., Alam, I., Momen, S.: Rice leaf disease detection using machine learning techniques. In: International Conference on Sustainable Technologies for Industry 4.0 (STI), 24–25 December 2019 (2019)

Mathematical Modelling of Irrigation System Using Wireless Sensor Network

Abdelhak Benhamada[1]([✉]), Mounir Tahar Abbes[1]([✉]), Selma Boumerdassi[2]([✉]),
Elhassen Abdelouahed[1], Houari Boukhobza[1], and Mohamed Kherarba[1]([✉])

[1] Hassiba Ben Bouali University, FSEI, LME, Chlef, Algeria
{A.Benhamada,m.taharabbes,M.kherarba}@univ-chlef.dz
[2] CNAM/CEDRIC, Paris, France
selma.boumerdassi@inria.fr

Abstract. With the linear growth in demand for food, the need for smart and optimized agriculture is emerging as a primary solution in the modern economy. It is observed that farmers have to bear enormous financial losses due to poor forecasting of weather conditions (temperature, humidity, light, etc.) as well as imprecise irrigation for large-area crops. The evolution of wireless sensor network (WSN) technology has brought automatic irrigation to life in a different way in ever-growing agricultural fields. In this article, we propose a mathematical model for an automatic irrigation system that uses WSNs to optimize the use of water quantities and also maximize crop yield using combinatorial optimization tools like AMPL.

Keywords: WSN · Irrigation system · Combinational optimization · AMPL

1 Introduction

Currently, many systems require environmental parameters to be taken into account to measure physical phenomena in order to make the necessary decisions. The progress of recent years in microelectronics and micromechanics has made it possible to design sensors that are smaller and smaller, more and more efficient, autonomous and whose energy capacities have evolved over time. On the other hand, mobile network techniques make it possible to free up wires and therefore easily deploy sensor networks in places that are difficult to access them.

This new generation of networks makes it possible to revolutionize the way we live, and causes interaction with the environment around us. Thanks to their flexibility, low cost and ease of deployment, several areas of application are then considered. For example, we cite the forecasting identification and monitoring of natural event and disasters, environmental Monitor, smart building, biodiversity mapping, Sophisticated agriculture, recording and preventive maintenance are listed. Machinery, health and pharmacy, logistics and smart transport, etc. In addition, the use of wireless sensors is in increasing demand for supervision and

S. Boumerdassi et al. (Eds.): SSA 2021, CCIS 1470, pp. 140–152, 2021.
https://doi.org/10.1007/978-3-030-88259-4_10

security. Industries then offer wireless sensors that can inform the user about Multiple Data. These sensors can be linked, thus forming a wireless network based on protocols to communicate with each other and offer programs and on-board networks. Wireless Sensor Networks (WSN) are considered a specific type of ad hoc networks. They are made up of A large number of nodes for micro-sensors deployed in a dense manner within the phenomenon being captured or very Near to its surroundings. The position of the nodes used is not necessarily designed beforehand, which enables their random deployment in inaccessible terrain or during operations for disaster relief. The cooperative effort of the sensor nodes is another characteristic specific to this type of network, in fact, these nodes integrate on-board processors which allow them to perform simple calculation operations and subsequently to transmit only the data partially necessary. Processed, instead of sending all the collected information to processing operations intermediate nodes.

The consumption of water used in the irrigation of cultivated plants plays an important role in the field of agriculture, this technique has opened up new challenges in the field for this we offer a complete automatic solution for farmers to save water consumption by using WSN. The WSNs will be implanted in the ground in order to acquire environmental information and soil parameters, these parameters will be used to build a mathematical model that will serve as an input feature in the sensor node in order to detect whether or not we are starting intelligent irrigation of plants. Improving the management of water resources in the agricultural sector would make it possible to reduce the total over-consumption of water. The implementation of smart irrigation techniques and the use of wireless sensors that improve water use efficiency will help farmers to make more profitable their activities, at the same time as it will strengthen sustainability of agriculture as a whole, in order to significantly increase their yields. In this paper We propose an automatic watering system using WSN via mathematical model, with an irrigation technique suitable for plants grown in a type of soil with a type of climate. The rest of this paper is organized as follows. Sections 2 presents the related works. Sections 3 discuss the proposed solution. Section 4 details the software and hardware implementation. Section 5 analyze and discuss the obtained results. Finally, Sect. 6 concludes the paper.

2 Related Works

WSN have become an important tool in environmental monitoring and real time data. Precision Agriculture (PA) is one of them. Recently, the agriculture domain joined WSN to support its core surveillance operations. PA is the science of accurately understanding, estimating and evaluating crops for the purpose of determining the correct fertilizer use and actual irrigation needs with irrigation schedules, throughout the life of the crops. Several applications have been developed in PA, most of them making use of the IEEE 802.15.4 standard. For example, [1] developed a prototype of WSN with a two-part structure for greenhouses. In the first part, several sensor nodes were used to measure temperature, light and soil moisture. The other part consists of a GSM module and the management software based on a database operation on the remote PC. [2] presented a proposal for a distributed greenhouse monitoring and control system using Zig-Bee. [3] describes the results of the actual deployment of a WSN IEEE 802.15.4 compliant system to monitor and control the environment in greenhouses where melons and cabbages have been grown.

A recent work propopsed by [4] modeled mathematically and explored the wastewater treatment process. They recommend intelligent irrigation for the reuse of wastewater. Other wastewater treatment processes (WWTP) were compared to the one chosen to justify the choice and a detailed expiation of the general wastewater treatment process was provided.

In another study [5] authors try to anticipate the water demand of the crop, and give optimal irrigation scheduling with a significant reduction in water consumption based on climatology data of the Kingdom of Bahrain.

Authors in [6] investigate the problem of identification and control design for an irrigation process through an academic irrigation station (IS) system new optimal Takagi-Sugeno (T-S) fuzzy model of the IS process.

3   Proposed Solution

3.1   The Proposed Model

In this section, we proposed a mathematical model that models the irrigation system in agriculture and allows to limit the overconsumption of water. First we present the irrigation problem and describe it with a mathematical programming model. Then, we verify the model via the mathematical program software called AMPL. Finally we obtain an objective function that minimizes the amount of water allotted to a plant's irrigation (Fig. 1).

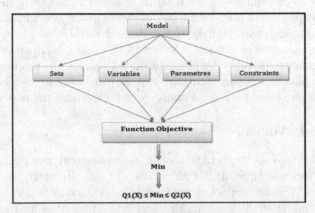

Fig. 1. Structure of mathematical models.

Before formalizing the model, we consider the following information:

– The type of the region where the crop is planted is (arid region and arid seedlings, etc.).

- The type of soil where the plant is planted, their useful water reserve and their humidity.
- The type of plant, their transpiration in a stage of development.
- The daily state of the climate, their precipitation, humidity and temperature.
- Each type of plant is planted in a specific soil type and climate.
- Each type of plant evaporates differently depending on their stages of development and the climate demand (temperature, humidity, etc.).
- Each type of soil has specific types of plant types.
- Each type of climate has specific types of soil.
- Each quantity of water (evaporated-transpired) must be recovered.
- Each type of plant wants a different amount of water for the stages of development.
- when the water stress reaches a particular level the crop cannot survive any further.
- It is possible for each stage of growth to consider a certain number of possible irrigation levels.
- Each amount of water (evaporated-transpired) depends on the temperature and relative humidity of the climate (Fig. 2).

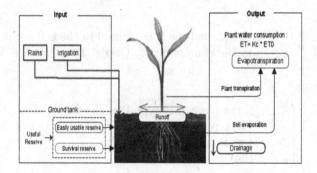

Fig. 2. Factors influencing water in irrigation.

3.2   Problem Formulation

There are three types of parameters required to implement the model:

- Soil-related parameters: soil moisture, useful water reserve, rooting depth.
- Climate-related parameters: temperature, humidity, wind speed, insolation.
- Parameters linked to the plant: type of plant, stage of development.

The objective function is to minimize the amount of water allocated for irrigation, in order to provide the plant with the actual amount of water it needs, denoted by min consumption(Total_consp).

$$min.\ Total\_consp = \sum_{i=1}^{n}(D_i - Q_i)^2.\ Z_{Ps}^i$$

The notations used in the model are described as bellows:

Sets:

- C Set of climates
- S Set of soils
- P Set of plants
- I Stages of development
- M Months of the year

Variable:

- ET Evapotranspiration of the culture at stage i [mm/day]
- PE Effective precipitation [mm]
- D Irrigation demand to be achieved at stage i [mm]
- Q Quantity of irrigation water (net irrigation dose) at stage i [mm]
- SW Soil water reserve at stage i [mm]
- DT Total irrigation demand that must be achieved during the life of the plant [mm]
- QT Quantity of irrigation water during the life of the plant [mm]

$$
Y_{ps}^c = \begin{cases} 1 & \text{If the plant type P is planted in the soil s type} \\ & \text{S in the climate c type C, } p \in P,\, s \in S,\, c \in C. \\ 0 & \text{Else.} \end{cases}
$$

$$
Z_{ps}^i = \begin{cases} 1 & \text{If the plant p of type P is chosen for the soil} \\ & \text{s of type S in stage i of type I, } p \in P,\, s \in S, \\ & i \in I. \\ 0 & \text{Else.} \end{cases}
$$

Parameters:

- DG Drainage [mm]
- ET_0 Reference evapotranspiration [mm /days]
- HR Average daily relative humidity of the air [%]
- Kc Crop coefficient
- P_m Average actual precipitation of minus m [mm]
- R Runoff [mm]
- Tm Average daily air temperature at a height of 2 m [°C]
- V Wind speed at a height of 2 m [m/s]
- N Number of developmental stages (N = 4)

Objective:

$$
min.\ Total\_consp = \sum_{i=1}^{n} (D_i - Q_i)^2 \cdot Z_{Ps}^i
$$

Constraints:

$$SW_i - SW_{i-1} = PE_i + Q_i - ET_i - R_i - DG_i \tag{1}$$

$$D_i = \sum_i^n (ET_i^p - PE_i) * Y_{ps}^c \tag{2}$$

$$D_t = \sum_i^n (D_i * Y_{ps}^c) \tag{3}$$

$$QT = \sum_i^n Q_i * Y_{ps}^c \tag{4}$$

$$0 \le Q_i \le D_i \tag{5}$$

$$\sum_c \sum_{ps} Y_{ps}^c \ge 1 \tag{6}$$

$$\sum_i Z_{ps}^i \ge 1 \tag{7}$$

The first constraint requires that the variation of the soil water reserve ($SW_i - SW_{i-1}$) in stage i is equal to the sum of the balance of the inputs (contributions) and the balance of the outputs (losses). The second constraint indicates that the irrigation demand in stage i is calculated based on the evapotranspiration of a crop and the effective rainfall contribution, and also depend on the variable Y_{ps}^c. The fourth constraint signifies that the total amount of irrigation is equal to the product of the sum of the amounts over the stages of development and the variable Y_{ps}^c. The fifth constraint expresses that the amount of irrigation water in stage i be less than the irrigation demand that must be achieved.

Efficient Precipitation (PE):
Effective precipitation refers to the portion of precipitation that can actually be used by plants. Several models for calculating effective rainfall which are detailed in [7].
$PE = Pm * (125 - 0.2 * Pm)/125 \quad for \ Pm \le 250 \, \mathrm{mm}$
$PE = 125 + 0.1 * Pm \qquad\qquad for \ Pm > 250 \, \mathrm{mm}$

Evapotranspiration (ET):
Crop evapotranspiration under standard conditions (ET) represents the evapotranspiration well-fertilized crop grown over a large area, under optimal water conditions and reaching its potential production under the given climatic conditions. According to the Crop Coefficient Approach, ET is calculated by multiplying the Reference Evapotranspiration (ET_0) determined by the FAO Penman-Monteith Method by the Crop Coefficient (Kc) [7].

$$ET = Kc * ET_0$$

$$ET_0 = \frac{0.48\Delta(R_n - G) + \delta \frac{900}{T_{mean}+273} U_2(e_s - e_a)}{\Delta + \delta(1 + 0.34U_2)}$$

where G is the soil heat flux density ($MJ\ m^{-2}d^{-1}$), R_n is the net radiation at the crop surface ($MJ\ m^{-2}d^{-1}$), U_2 is the wind speed at 2 m height (ms^{-1}),$T_{mean}$is the mean daily air temperature at a height of 2 m [°C] calculated based on maximum and minimum air temperature, $e_s - e_a$ represent the vapour pressure defici (VPD, kPa) measured from the saturation vapour pressure (e_s, KPa) and the actual vapour pressure (e_a, kPa), δ defines the psychrometric constant (kPa °C^{-1}), and Δ represent the slope of vapour pressure curve (kPa °C^{-1}).

Runoff (R):
Runoff is often neglected in the context of an irrigated plot ($R \approx 0$).

4   Hardware and Software Implementation

The components that are involved in th system are as follows:

Laptop: in which we create our application and it considered as adecision-making center, which aim to determine the amount of water needed by plants.

TelosB Sensor: is an ultra-low power wireless module for monitoring system and rapid application prototyping, that can detect temperature, humidity, and brightness. The TelosB performs properly between −40 and 123.8 °C, which is sufficient for severe weather conditions [8]. The TelosB mote will be collect data (humidity, temperature) and send it to the farmer computer. In TinyOS, the sensor motes were programmed [9] with the NesC [10].

Base Station: the base station is used to gather data from distributed nodes. The base station in this system consists of two components, the computer and the TelosB mote, represents the connection link between the application and the sensors.

The software development is Partitioned into 3 parts, i.e. ampl programming for the mathematical model, NesC programming for the TelosB sensor and Java programming in netbeans for the application.

nesC: a programming language used for networked embedded systems. The programming model supported by nesC includes competitiveness, environmental reactivity, and collaboration. With nesC we can Facilitate application development, minimize code size and eliminate several sources of bugs [11]. Where a set of nesC components construct a TinyOS program [12]. TinyOS is an operating system developed especially for embedded network systems, has a component-based programming model, codified by the NesC language [13].

AMPL: (A Mathematical Programming Language) [14] which, very similar to its mathematical nature, makes it possible to express an optimization problem in a declarative way. As show in Fig. 3. The definition of the AMPL problem typically consists of the model (which is a general type of the issue) and the data (values of the model parameters that make the model specific) [15].

First we use ampl for the resolution of the mathematical model, then we use nesc language for programming the sensors(humidity, temperature), and

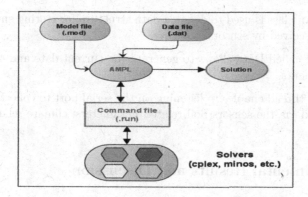

Fig. 3. AMPL files.

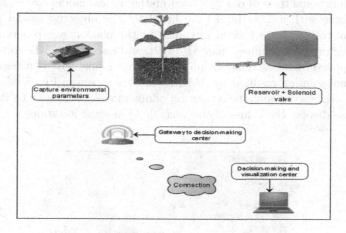

Fig. 4. Communication diagram in the platform.

create a Java/nesC graphical interface. This interface was developed to provide capabilities for two-way communications between a PC platform and a network of wireless sensor aims to communicate with the sensors and make the decision according to the values recorded by the sensors (Fig. 4).

Our platform called "IrriLog" and consists of the following elements:

Model.mod: represents the water mathematical model.

Model.dat: contains the data (climates, soil, vegetation ...) to solve the model.

TempHumidC.ns: this NesC code is a module file that reads from the TelosB sensor the temperature and humidity of the air. TempHumidAppC.ns: represents configuration file for the TelosB sensor that assembles the modules and interfaces used.

MainFrame: defines the graphical interface of the application.

Climate: Java class is used to define a data structure for storing environmental parameters received by sensors.

Date: thread called Date allows to generate the current date and time for irrigation treatments.

Read Data: thread enables to listening on the serial port to collect the parameters captured via the sensors(Soil-related parameters, climate-related parameters).

5   Experimental Results and Discussion

Computational Test Analysis

The computational tests of our proposed mathematical models were carried out on a machine with a 2.5G Intel Core i5 CPU. The objective model for minimization of the amount of water intended for the plant it was programed by a mathematic program language named AMPL and resolved by MIP solver Minos [10]. we applied MIP-based algorithm to verify our model based on the data file. The optimal solution resulted by AMPL/Minos is shown in Fig. 5, which equal = 0.06. It is observed that the resolution of our model go through 68 iterations. In Fig. 6 we display the values of the variable Q in some iterations.

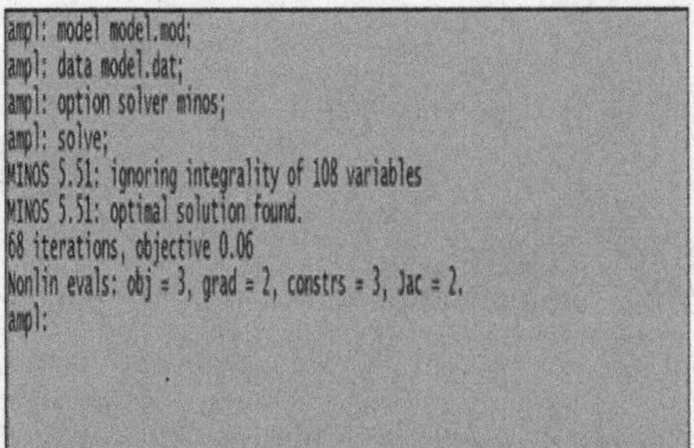

```
ampl: model model.mod;
ampl: data model.dat;
ampl: option solver minos;
ampl: solve;
MINOS 5.51: ignoring integrality of 108 variables
MINOS 5.51: optimal solution found.
68 iterations, objective 0.06
Nonlin evals: obj = 3, grad = 2, constrs = 3, Jac = 2.
ampl:
```

Fig. 5. The model execution result.

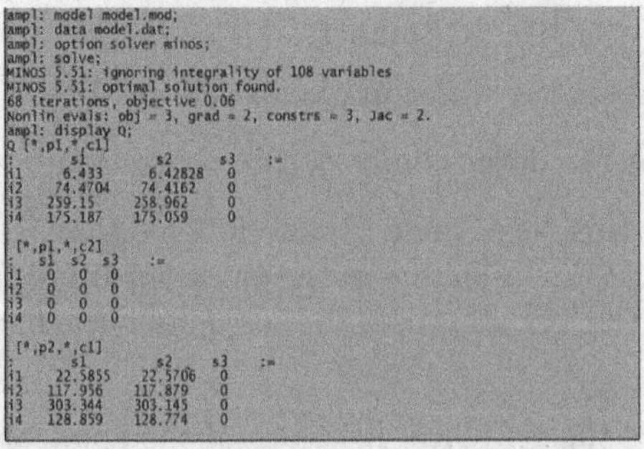

```
ampl: model model.mod;
ampl: data model.dat;
ampl: option solver minos;
ampl: solve;
MINOS 5.51: ignoring integrality of 108 variables
MINOS 5.51: optimal solution found.
68 iterations, objective 0.06
Nonlin evals: obj = 3, grad = 2, constrs = 3, Jac = 2.
ampl: display Q;
Q [*,p1,*,c1]
         s1         s2        s3    :=
i1     6.433      6.42828     0
i2    74.4704    74.4162      0
i3   259.15     258.962      0
i4   175.187    175.059      0

   [*,p1,*,c2]
       s1  s2  s3   :=
i1      0   0   0
i2      0   0   0
i3      0   0   0
i4      0   0   0

   [*,p2,*,c1]
         s1         s2        s3    :=
i1    22.5855    22.5706      0
i2   117.956    117.879      0
i3   303.344    303.145      0
i4   128.859    128.774      0
```

Fig. 6. The values of variable Q by the command display Q.

Result Analysis

To understand the system's behaviour facing climatic and analysis the results of water requirements of the selected crops, we have studied crops with different life cycles during the year. The crop-related data used are:

The crop coefficient (kc) which takes four values (initial, development, mid-season, late-season), we used standard and valid kc for the use of the Penman-Monteith formula [16]. Figure 7 summarizes the data related to the crops used, such as The duration of the developmental stages of each crop and their date of planting.

Duration of development phases (day)					Crop coefficient kc				Planting date
Cultures	int	dev	mid-sea	late-sea	cycle time	kc int	kc dev	kc mid	kc fin	
Tomato	30	40	45	30	145	0,45	0,75	1,15	0,8	02-march
Pepper	30	40	40	20	130	0,50	0,70	1,05	0,90	10-april
Carrot	30	40	60	20	150	0,45	0,75	1,05	0,90	20-sep

Fig. 7. Summary of crop-related data.

The irrigation needs of the main crops studied in the state of Chlef and Relizane, Algeria (climatic data since the year 2000 are considered from these stations) corresponding to planting dates we considered are presented in Figs. 8, 9 and 10.

Case 01: climate c1 = "CHLEF", soil s1 = "silty" and the plant p1 = "Tomato".

It can observed that the quantity of water consumed by the tomato planted in the silty soil and in the climate of chlef varies according to the temperature and the humidity rate and during each stage of development.

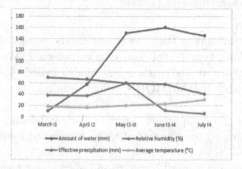

Fig. 8. Irrigation needs of tomato depending on climatic parameters.

Case 02: climate c1 = "Chlef", soil s2 = "clay" and the plant p2 = "Pepper".

Similarly, we can deduce that the amount of water consumed by the pepper planted in the clay soil and in the climate of Chlef region varies according to the temperature and the humidity rate and during each stage of development.

Case 03: climate c2 = "Relizane", soil s2 = "silty" and the plant p3 = "carrot".

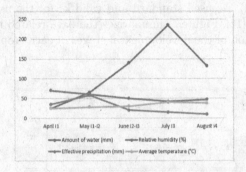

Fig. 9. Irrigation needs of Pepper depending on climatic parameters.

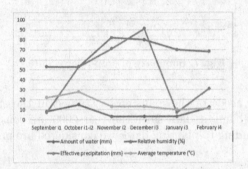

Fig. 10. Irrigation needs of carrot depending on climatic parameters.

we find that in each stage of development that the amount of water varies over time with temperature and humidity.

Model Validation
In order to attract attention that the water needs change depending on type of crop, planting date, type of soil and climate selected, We discuss and compare the results of our model with other model called A.AMMAR done by A.BOUDJELLAL and R.BAMMOUN, which studies the climate of Tipaza, Algeria.

Figure 11 shows the comparison between our model and the model named A.AMMAR according to the amount of water consumed by different crops.

Therefore, if we make a small comparison between our results and the results chosen for this purpose presented in Fig. 11, we note that the irrigation requirements of the first three crops assigned in our model are less than those of Model A.AMMAR

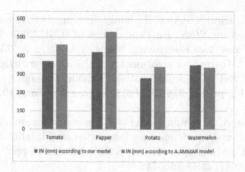

Fig. 11. Irrigation needs of carrot depending on climatic parameters.

It can observed that our model is more applicable in comparison with other results and other models. For this purpose, in order to realize our prototype by intelligent irrigation, we used a set of hardware instruments and software tools concerning the WSN networks.

6   Conclusion

In this paper, we have proposed a system that integrates a module for measuring and analyzing agricultural-meteorological data using real-time WSN with another mathematical optimization module to determine the optimal amount of water to apply in order to have an effective return. Our research shows that hybridization between a mathematical model and WSN is an effective monitoring technique in smart agriculture. This model has been used to study the optimal irrigation planning of various crops in semi-arid regions, that it is more applicable in agriculture and for the farmer himself. The evaluation of the mathematical model in comparison with the models of agronomists, it allowed us to deduce that the water model is more applicable in agriculture and for the farmer himself. However, improvement work is still necessary in order to consolidate the present system. They concern in particular the mathematical model which remains to be enriched with more parameters concerning the cost for example. The interest of such work is its great impact for applications related to WSN, especially those dedicated to the agricultural sector.

References

1. Liu, H., Meng, Z., Cui, S.: A wireless sensor network prototype for environmental monitoring in greenhouses. In: Proceedings of International Conference on Wireless Communications, Networking and Mobile Computing (WiCom 2007), Shangai, China, 21–25 September 2007 (2007)
2. Gonda, L., Cugnasca, C.E.: A proposal of greenhouse contral using wireless sensor networks. In: Proceedings of Computers in Agriculture and Natural Resources, 4th World Congress Conference, Orlando, FL, USA, 24–26 July 2006 (2006)

3. Yoo, S., Kim, J., Kim, T., Ahn, S., Sung, J., Kim, D.: A2S: automated agriculture system based on WSN. In: Proceedings of ICSE 2007. IEEE International Symposium on Consumer Electronics, Irving, TX, USA, 20–23 June 2007 (2007)
4. EL-Zemity, A.S.: Wastewater treatment model with smart irrigation utilizing PID control. In: 2020 2nd Novel Intelligent and Leading Emerging Sciences Conference (NILES), Giza, Egypt, pp. 374–379 (2020). https://doi.org/10.1109/NILES50944. 2020.9257882
5. Balbis, L., Jassim, A.: Dynamic model of soil moisture for smart irrigation systems. In: 2018 International Conference on Innovation and Intelligence for Informatics, Computing, and Technologies (3ICT), Sakhier, Bahrain, pp. 1–4 (2018). https:// doi.org/10.1109/3ICT.2018.8855748
6. Chrouta, J., Chakchouk, W., Zaafouri, A., Jemli, M.: Modeling and control of an irrigation station process using heterogeneous cuckoo search algorithm and fuzzy logic controller. IEEE Trans. Ind. Appl. **55**(1), 976–990 (2019). https://doi.org/ 10.1109/TIA.2018.2871392
7. AMPL home page. https://ampl.com/products/ampl/. Accessed November 2020
8. Júnior, L.C.V., et al.: Comparative assessment of modelled and empirical reference evapotranspiration methods for a Brazilian savanna. Agric. Water Manag. **232**, 106040 (2020)
9. Khriji, S., El Houssaini, D., Jmal, M.W., Viehweger, C., Abid, M., Kanoun, O.: Precision irrigation based on wireless sensor network. IET Sci. Meas. Technol. **8**(3), 98–106 (2014)
10. TinyOS home page. http://www.tinyos.net/. Accessed November 2020
11. NesC home page. http://nescc.sourceforge.net/
12. Gay, D., Levis, P., Von Behren, R., Welsh, M., Brewer, E., Culler, D.: The nesC language: a holistic approach to networked embedded systems. Acm Sigplan Not. **38**(5), 1–11 (2003)
13. Cheong, E., Lee, E.A., Zhao, Y.: Viptos: a graphical development and simulation environment for TinyOS-based wireless sensor networks. In: SenSys, vol. 5, p. 302, November 2005
14. Hill, J., Szewczyk, R., Woo, A., Hollar, S., Culler, D.E., Pister, K.S.J.: System architecture directions for networked sensors. In: Architectural Support for Programming Languages and Operating Systems, pp. 93–104 (2000). http://webs.cs. berkeley.edu
15. Zuo, X., Zhu, C., Huang, C., Xiao, Y.: Using AMPL/CPLEX to model and solve the electric vehicle routing problem (EVRP) with heterogeneous mixed fleet. In: 2017 29th Chinese Control And Decision Conference (CCDC), pp. 4666–4670. IEEE, May 2017
16. Fourer, R., Gay, D., Kernighan, B.: AMPL: A Modeling Language for Mathematical Programming. Scientific Press, San Francisco (1993)
17. Paredes, P., Pereira, L.S., Almorox, J., Darouich, H.: Reference grass evapotranspiration with reduced data sets: parameterization of the FAO Penman-Monteith temperature approach and the Hargeaves-Samani equation using local climatic variables. Agric. Water Manag. **240**, 106210 (2020)

Development of Soil Nitrogen Estimation System in Oil Palm Land with Sentinel-1 Image Analysis Approach

Rhavif Budiman[1]([✉]), Kudang Boro Seminar[2], and Sudradjat[3]

[1] Computer Science Department, IPB University, 16680 Bogor, Indonesia
[2] Mechanical and Biosystem Engineering Department, IPB University, 16680 Bogor, Indonesia
kseminar@apps.ipb.ac.id
[3] Agronomy and Horticulture Department IPB, IPB University, 16680 Bogor, Indonesia
sudradjat@apps.ipb.ac.id

Abstract. Oil palm is one of the plantation commodities that has an important role in the economy of Indonesia. The high demand for palm oil in the future must be supported by high productivity. Fertilization is one of the intensification methods to increase oil palm productivity. The main nutrient content in oil palm that helps the growth and development of oil palm is nitrogen. Soil samples and location coordinates were taken from oil palm plantations then adjusted to Sentinel-1 satellite images. The Sentinel-1 image obtained is then processed first to reduce the factors that aggravate the process afterward. The digital number value obtained from the reflection of the Sentinel-1 image was then used as an independent variable and the soil nitrogen results from the laboratory become the dependent variable. Data were trained and a model was built using Random Forest Regressor (RFR) and Multi Linear Regression (MLR). All models built were evaluated by the quality of the model using MAPE and the best model was determined by selecting the lowest MAPE. RFR model has 19.53% of MAPE and MLR has 22.41% of MAPE. The RFR is chosen to be the best model based on the lowest MAPE and based on interpretation, the RFR model has good accuracy for determining soil nitrogen nutrient content better than MLR model.

Keywords: Palm oil · Soil nutrition · Synthetic Aperture Radar

1 Introduction

Oil palm is one of the plantation commodities that has a very important role in the economy of Indonesia. Indonesia is the largest producer and exporter of palm oil in the world. Indonesia's palm oil production in 2016 reached 31.40 million tons. The increasing demand for oil palm causes the plantation area in Indonesia to expand. The area of oil palm plantations in Indonesia for the last five years has tended to show an increase, oil palm area increase from 10.75 million hectares in 2014 to 12.76 million hectares in 2018 [1]. The high demand for palm oil in the future must be supported by high productivity. Fertilization is one of the intensification methods to increase oil

© Springer Nature Switzerland AG 2021
S. Boumerdassi et al. (Eds.): SSA 2021, CCIS 1470, pp. 153–165, 2021.
https://doi.org/10.1007/978-3-030-88259-4_11

palm productivity. The objective of fertilization management is to provide oil palm with sufficient nutrient content in a balanced proportion to ensure the health and growth of the oil palm properly and with optimal yields. The benefits of good fertilization management are not only in the maintenance and healthy yield of oil palms, but also a prerequisite for sustainable palm oil [2]. In oil palm plantations, the costs used for fertilization range from 40% to 60% of the total cost of maintaining the crop or around 24% of the total production costs [3]. Therefore, the supply of fertilizer in large quantities is not very good, because the price of fertilizers is not cheap and many farmers who provide fertilizers are not following with the circumstances and recommendations. Various nutrients are found in the soil and these nutrients are needed for the development and growth of oil palm. Nitrogen is the most needed nutrient for plant metabolism and determining growth [4]. Research on soil conditions has been carried out using various methods such as laboratory, aerial, and satellite imagery [5]. Laboratory results to determine soil nitrogen content are indeed more precise and accurate but still have drawbacks, like it takes more time, costs, and manpower for large areas [6]. The use of aerial has the advantage that it has a high resolution and is more usable at any time, but it has the disadvantage of having an area coverage and is more expensive [7]. The use of satellites to determine soil nitrogen content has more advantages than lab results because the use of satellites can find out over a large area and can monitor developments regularly. The use of satellites has a problem, like a cloud interference, so obtaining data is more difficult than using aerial [8]. In this situation, the use of radar is chosen because it can collect data regardless of weather or light conditions [9].

Radar system satellite data is data that retrieves spatial information on earth and is not affected by weather conditions because the Synthetic Aperture Radar (SAR) is an active remote sensing system that uses microwaves. [10] stated that microwaves are longer than the light waves used by optical satellite systems in general. The longer the wavelength, the greater the ability to penetrate the clouds [11]. The most common algorithm that is most widely used today is Multiple Linear Regression or commonly called Multiple Linear Regression (MLR). Multi Linear Regression (MLR) is regression-based modeling that models the relationship between two or more independent variables and a dependent variable by adjusting a linear equation with the data obtained [12]. The Random Forest (RF) algorithm proposed by Breiman [13] is seen as the best algorithm for predictive cases of both regression and classification. RF in the regression case is called the Random Forest Regressor (RFR), while in the classification case it is called the Random Forest Classifier (RFC). The RF algorithm can model complex interactions between input variables and is resistant to outliers. The advantages of RF such as being able to work efficiently on large amounts of data, not being sensitive to bias and overfitting [14]. The purpose of this study is to create a model that can predict soil nitrogen, especially in oil palm land using Sentinel-1 radar satellite imagery, and decide which algorithm between random forest regressor algorithm and multiple linear regression has best predict performance. The benefit of this research is to facilitate the estimation of soil nitrogen content in oil palm plantations. This estimation used to recommend fertilization needed by oil palm plants and can quickly estimate the status of the land on oil palm plantations with a large coverage area.

2   Literature Review

2.1   Nitrogen in Oil Palm

Oil palm is highly dependent on environmental conditions and the treatment it provides. The environment is climate and soil. Soil is the main factor because the soil must be able to provide the nutrients needed by plants so that the soil must be fertilized. Fertilization is given to increase plant growth and production. Nitrogen, phosphorus, and potassium are the main nutrients of oil palm [15]. The function of plant nutrients cannot be replaced by other elements and if one of the plant nutrient contents cannot be fulfilled, it can inhibit plant metabolism. Nitrogen which is absorbed by plants is broken down into amino acids, which then forms proteins and nucleic acids. Nitrogen in plants is part of chlorophyll and is the main component of plants that absorbs the light needed in the photosynthesis process [16].

2.2   Synthetic Aperture Radar (SAR) Sentinel-1

The use of Synthetic Aperture Radar (SAR) for remote sensing has been widely used for agriculture such as estimating wheat biomass [14], soil moisture, soil salinity, organic matter, pH [17], and classification. plants [18]. The SAR sensor is influenced by the interaction of the microwave signal with the various components of the object it is exposed to. The Sentinel-1 includes a C-band Synthetic Aperture Radar (SAR) which operates at a center frequency of 5.405 GHz. The ability of this signal to penetrate plant and soil cover. Sentinel-1 was launched to provide continuous data with better enhancements such as return time, coverage, timeliness, and reliability. The above-ground (non-polar) observation mode is Wide Interferometric (IW) imaging which provides multiple polarization images (VV and VH) over 250 km plots at a spatial resolution of 5×20 m [19]. Polarization is the direction the waves are projected from the radar. Then the wave direction when returned after bouncing off an object, the waves leave the satellite and oscillate up and down vertically, and hits the ground, and return with the oscillating beam vertically [20].

2.3   Related Works

This section has purposes to review the related works or research that similar to this research but there is no similar research, especially in the implementation of machine learning to predict nitrogen in soil using SAR. On the other hand, example of research about the usage of SAR for remote sensing especially used for agriculture such as estimating soil moisture, soil salinity, organic matter, pH [17], crop classification [18], knowing the and identifying oil palm plantations [21]. Research about predicting nitrogen using various remote sensing method such as simultaneous determination of moisture, organic carbon, and total nitrogen by near infrared reflectance spectroscopy [22], carbon and nitrogen analysis of soil fractions using near-infrared reflectance spectroscopy [23] and NIR technique for rapid determination of soil mineral nitrogen [24]. Research about the application of MLR using satellites such as the temporal and spatial characteristics of plants [25] and prediction of leaf nutrition [26].

2.4 Multi Linear Regression

The dependent variable y represents the value of the dependent variable or variables to be predicted and x_1, x_2, x_3, and x_n are independent variables with the coefficients b_0, b_1, b_2, b_3, and b_n. MLR model development involves an assumption test process [27]. The assumptions are:

1. Linearity
    MLR requires a linear relationship between the independent and dependent variables. This is done to examine outliers because multiple linear regression is sensitive to the outlier effects. The assumption of linearity can best be tested with a scatterplot.
3. Little or no multicollinearity
    Multicollinearity occurs when the independent variables are not mutually independent. Variance Inflation Factor (VIF) is a multicollinearity examination method. VIF from linear regression is defined as VIF = 1/T. where T is the same tolerance as 1- R2. VIF > 10 indicates multicollinearity.
3. Normality
    MLR analysis requires all variables to be normal. These assumptions are best checked with a histogram and normality curve or Q-Q-Plot. When the data is not normally distributed for example on non-linearity it is biased to correct this problem using log transformations. However, it can cause multicollinearity effects.
4. Homoscedasticity
    The homoscedasticity assumption (homoscedasticity) is an assumption that the residual variations are similar at each point throughout the model. The spread of residuals must be fairly constant across each predictor variable point (or across a linear model. The test to determine homoscedasticity is the Breusch-Pagan test [28].

2.5 Random Forest Regressor

The random forest proposed by Breiman [13] is an ensemble learning method. Ensemble learning uses an approach using several algorithms and hypotheses (which can be called committees or ensembles) in predicting or classifying then a vote is given to the outcome data from the new data that is entered into the ensemble [29]. The two most widely known methods of ensemble learning are boosting and bagging. The boosting method in each successful decision tree will be given extra weight and adjust according to the bias ratio of the previous predictors and finally, only one model will be used, while in the bagging method, each decision tree will make a predictor and end with a majority vote taken according to the prediction data output. the closest to the original data output [30].

There are two types of random forest, namely the random forest regressor and the random forest classifier. The random forest adds an extra layer of randomness to the bagging process. The method of building a random forest is that each decision tree uses a different bootstrap sample from the data because this random forest changes the creation of a classification tree or a regression tree. The standard decision tree for each node is divided using the best separation among all variables, whereas, in a random forest, each node is divided using the best among the predictors randomly selected for that node. This somewhat counterintuitive strategy has been shown to perform very well in comparison to many other classification methods, including discriminant analysis, support vector machines and neural networks, and is strong against overfitting [13].

2.6 Model Performance Evaluation

The quality of the specified RFR and MLR models is determined by the extent to which bias results from the actual data. The smaller the better the forecast. For the model, the Mean Absolute Percentage Error (MAPE) method is used. MAPE is one of the most commonly used evaluation methods. MAPE has important features and is not included, absent, absent in the unit, no interpretation, clearer, capable of supporting statistical evaluations, and can use all biased information [31]. Mathematically the MAPE is expressed as follows:

$$MAPE = \frac{\sum_{t=1}^{n} \frac{|y_t - \hat{y}_t|}{y_t}}{n} \tag{1}$$

y_t in this study is the prediction result of the model that represents nitrogen nutrient content, $\hat{y}_t$ is the actual data on nitrogen nutrient content and n represents the amount of data used. Lewis [32] made a MAPE interpretation commonly used for industry and business which can be seen in Table 1.

Table 1. MAPE interpretation in business and industry

MAPE (%)	Interpretation
<10	High accuracy
10–20	Good accuracy
20–50	Reasonable accuracy
>50	Bad accuracy

Correctness is the inverse of MAPE which is used to facilitate interpretation of MAPE results. The correctness formula can be seen below.

$$Correctness = 100 - MAPE$$

The quality of the model data that has been obtained is then carried out by the K-Fold cross-validation process. K-Fold Cross-validation is a process of randomly dividing X data into K data which has the same number for each divided part. Then the training and test data are randomized and a model is built from each section K. The best model quality evaluation results selected to be the best model. This process is done to avoid overfitting the model [33].

3 Methodology

3.1 Data

347 soil sample data were taken in several places, namely at the location of the IPB-Cargill Jonggol Oil Palm Education and Research Garden, PT Bima Palma Nugraha

Kalimantan, PTPN 5 Riau, and PTPN 6 Jambi on various dates as well as Sentinel-1 radar image data according to the sampling date.

3.2 Research Design

This research begins with a data preparation stage consisting of soil sampling and the GPS coordinates of the sample location. Then the sample is analyzed in the Testing Laboratory of the Department of Agronomy and Horticulture. Sentinel-1 radar data is taken and adjusted to the GPS location of the sample and the Sentinel-1 data obtained must be carried out in the Sentinel-1 image processing stage according to what has been done by Filipponi [34] with slight modifications. This stage consists of applying the orbit file, calibration, speckle filtering, and range doppler terrain correction. The modification of the steps used in this study is the use of DEMNAS (National Digital Elevation Model). The processed Sentinel-1 image then be combined with the results of laboratory analysis according to the coordinates of the sample, after which the data obtained is then preprocessed. The data that has been processed then occurs two types of modeling, multiple linear regression and tuned random forest regressor. the prediction results of RFR and MLR were compared for deciding the best model for making the prediction map nitrogen content. The research procedure to be carried out can be seen in Fig. 1 as follows.

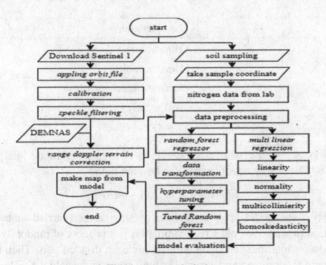

Fig. 1. Research design

3.3 Soil Sampling

Soil sampling is carried out using the SOP that has been made by SPKS [35] which is specifically carried out for fertilization recommendations. Soil sampling is done by digging the soil with a depth of 0–15 cm and 15–30 cm. After that the soil is composited.

Selection of the location of collection on the palm oil plate. Soil sample data that has been taken are also taken coordinate data using GPS to determine the location of the sampling and adjusted to the location of the Sentinel-1 radar data then the soil sample is given to the Testing Laboratory of the Department of Agronomy and Horticulture.

3.4   Sentinel-1 Imagery Preprocessing

The Sentinel-1 image that has been taken is processed first according to the data pre-processing steps in Fig. 1. The Sentinel-1 image has been processed using the SNAP ESA application and runs the functions applying orbit file, calibration, speckle filtering, and range doppler correction. The preprocessed Sentinel-1 image then the sample points that have been coordinated according to the soil sample are then extracted the parameter values based on the waves generated by the Sentinel-1 image. Extracting these values uses the point sampling tool function in the QGIS application using the average parameter. One Sentinel-1 image pixel represents 20 m of land area on earth. After extracting the image parameter values, the laboratory results of soil nitrogen nutrient content are entered according to the sample taken.

3.5   Data Preprocessing

The data that has been combined between the soil nutrient sample data with the results of the sentinel-1 extract based on the coordinates are then carried out pre-processing the data. The parameter data that has been extracted from the Sentinel-1 image are then processed using the Spyder editor application using python language as a code language to build a model. The preprocessing was carried out such as eliminating outliers, standardizing data, and randomizing for sharing training data and test data. The selection process through data that is over or too small with the 5th and 95th percentile is discarded. The amount of data used after the selection was 306 data. The data is then standardized based on standard deviation. All data were randomly selected and separated with a ratio of 90% for training data and 10% for test data.

4   Experimental Results

4.1   Modeling Using Random Forest Regressor

The RFR model adjusted using transformation data, feature importance, and hyperparameter tuning. The transformation data used is transforming the data obtained from the satellite and then selecting which data transformation results have the most influence on the model. The data transformation method used is the brute force method, which is looking for all possible data transformations, then selecting which ones have an effect on the model and which are not [36]. The data transformations used in this study are tan, sin, cos, square, root, rounding, cube root, log, and tanh. Initially, there were 10 variables changed to 100 variables which included pre-transformation data.

The transformed data then features importance. The features importance method uses Gini impurity provided by the Random Forest library. All transformed variables were then standardized and divided into training data and test data with a ratio of 90% and 10%, respectively. After the data is shared, the data is trained to create an RFR model with default settings. The impurity obtained is then sorted and selected with a lower limit of 0.05. The independent variable which initially had 100 selected variables became 22 variables because limit of 0.005 of parameter importance.

The feature variables of importance are standardized and then used to build the RFR model. The next step is hyperparameter tuning. Hyperparameter tuning is the process of selecting the optimal machine learning model parameters through trial and error. The RFR model has its parameters that can be optimized for the RFR, Table 2 shows the summary of hyperparameter tuning.

Table 2. Summary of hyperparameter tuning

Parameter name	Parameter variation	Chosen parameter
n_estimators	10, 50, 100, 150, 200, 250, 300, 350, 400	10
max_features	'auto', 'sqrt', 'log2'	Log2
max_depth	2, 4, 8, 16, 32, 64, 128, 256, 512, None	4
min_samples_leaf	1, 2, 4	1
min_samples_split	2, 5, 10	5

The selected hyperparameter parameters are then remodeled so that if the model is reused, it does not need to go through the hyperparameter tuning process. The model that has been transformed into data has important features and hyperparameter tuning. The transformation data is then examined for the quality of the model. Table 3 shows the quality of the optimized model.

Table 3. RFR model performance evaluation

	MAPE (%)	Correctness (%)
	19.85	80.15
	20.76	79.24
	19.27	80.73
	19.47	80.53
	18.32	81.68
Average	19.54	80.46

4.2 Modeling Using Multi Linear Regression

The second model that is processed is multi linear regression (MLR). Before the data is separated between the training data and the test data, an assumption test is carried out.

The first assumption tested is linearity and the first test assumption has been fulfilled. The second assumption tested is the multicollinearity assumption. In the first case, it can be seen that there are several variables are not linear so that data transformation is needed. The data transformation used is the brute force method as is done in the RFR. The transformed variable is the same as the RFR which produces 90 new variables and is added with the non-transformed variable and produces 100 variables. The first assumption tested is the multicollinearity test. Variance Inflation Factor is used to determine whether the dependent variable used has multicollinearity. A dependent variable has multicollinearity if it has a VIF > 10 [37]. After the selected variable is chosen, After the second assumption has been fulfilled, a model is created based on the variables that have been selected. Data adjusted for the variables used were divided into test data and training data. The data that has been selected is standardized and modeling is carried out.

The third assumption test is the normal distribution assumption. The normal distribution is tested on this model using a normality curve or Q-Q-Plot, which is by comparing the residual quantiles of actual data (theoretical quantiles) and the residuals of predictive data quantiles (sample quantiles). Figure 2 shows the normality curve of the MLR model. The more the residual approaches the line, it can be concluded that the model is normally distributed.

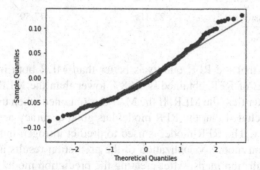

Fig. 2. Normality curve of the MLR model

The fourth assumption is homoscedasticity and is tested using the Breusch-Pagan test [28]. The Breusch-Pagan test results have a null hypothesis, namely, there is homoscedasticity and the alternative hypothesis is heteroscedasticity. If the p-value of the test is below the significant value in this case α of 0.05 then the null hypothesis is rejected and it is concluded that there is heteroscedasticity. The p-value obtained is the smallest of 0.158 and it is concluded that the null hypothesis assumption is not rejected and homoscedasticity. All assumptions that have been made are continued to the model development stage. The model development was carried out by dividing the data in the first phase into training data and test data with a ratio of 90% for training data and 10% for test data. The second stage of building the MLR model is provided by the scikit-learn library. Then the K-Fold cross-validation process was carried out. The K-Fold division is divided into 5 parts and evaluated using the quality of the prediction model using MAPE. Table 4 shows the quality of the MLR prediction model. Table 5 shows the comparison between the RFR and MLR models.

Table 4. MLR model performance evaluation

	MAPE (%)	Correctness (%)
	22.70	77.30
	25.03	74.97
	20.41	79.59
	20.27	79.73
	23.64	76.36
Average	22.41	77.59

Table 5. Comparison between the RFR and MLR models performance

Model	MAPE (%)	Correctness (%)
Random Forest Regressor	19.53	80.46
Multi Linear Regression	22.41	77.59

Table 5 shows that the RFR quality is better than MLR both in terms of MAPE quality. The MAPE of RFR obtained is 2.88% lower than the MLR, which indicates that the RFR is better than the MLR. If the MAPE is obtained when using interpretation [34], it can be concluded that the RFR model has good accuracy and the MLR model has decent accuracy. The RFR model is used to predict nitrogen nutrient levels. After creating a prediction model, visualization of the prediction results is performed using a distribution of nutrition maps. After creating the prediction model, the results of the predictions were visualized using the distribution of nutrition maps using the QGIS application. The map is made with grid specifications - the map grid is made in the form of a hexagon or a hexagon which is likened to the oil palm planting pattern which has a distance between the center points of 9 m so it is assumed that one grid is made to represent one oil palm tree. The nutrient class used to represent the distribution of nutrients uses 5 nutrient classes which are evenly divided and can be seen in the legend of the nutrient distribution map. Figure 3 shows a nitrogen nutrient map using the RFR model.

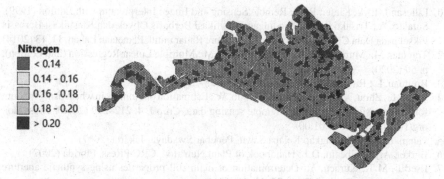

Nitrogen
- ■ < 0.14
- □ 0.14 - 0.16
- □ 0.16 - 0.18
- □ 0.18 - 0.20
- ■ > 0.20

Fig. 3. Nitrogen content distribution map in Jonggol plantation using the RFR

5 Conclusion

The prediction model for soil nitrogen levels was built using the Random Forest Regressor (RFR) and Multi Linear Regression (MLR) algorithm models. The dependent variable data uses Sentinel-1 imagery. The data is trained and a model is built using RFR and MLR. Determination of the best model using the lowest MAPE of the two models. The RFR model gets a MAPE of 19.53% and the MLR model gets a MAPE of 22.41%. Based on interpretation, the RFR Model has good accuracy for determining the nutrient content of soil nitrogen better than MLR model.

References

1. Badan Pusat Statistik: Statistik Kelapa Sawit Indonesia 2018 (2019)
2. Goh, K.J., Teo, C.B., Chew, P.S., Chiu, S.B.: Fertiliser Management in Oil Palm - Agronomic Principles and Field Practices (1998)
3. Safuan, L.O., Rembon, F.S., Syaf, H.: Evaluasi Status Hara Tanah dan Jaringan Sebagai Dasar Rekomendasi Pemupukan N,P, dan K pada Tanaman Kelapa Sawit. Agriplus. **23**, 154–162 (2013)
4. Fageria, V.D.: Nutrient interactions in crop plants. J. Plant Nutr. **24**, 1269–1290 (2001). https://doi.org/10.1081/PLN-100106981
5. Ge, Y., Thomasson, J.A., Sui, R.: Remote sensing of soil properties in precision agriculture: a review. Front. Earth Sci. (2011). https://doi.org/10.1007/s11707-011-0175-0
6. Muñoz-Huerta, R., Guevara-Gonzalez, R., Contreras-Medina, L., Torres-Pacheco, I., Prado-Olivarez, J., Ocampo-Velazquez, R.: A review of methods for sensing the nitrogen status in plants: advantages. Disadv. Recent Adv. Sens. **13**, 10823–10843 (2013). https://doi.org/10.3390/s130810823
7. Shafri, H.Z.M., Hamdan, N., Izzuddin Anuar, M.: Detection of stressed oil palms from an airborne sensor using optimized spectral indices. Int. J. Remote Sens. **33**, 4293–4311 (2012). https://doi.org/10.1080/01431161.2011.619208
8. Ahamed, T., Tian, L., Zhang, Y., Ting, K.C.: A review of remote sensing methods for biomass feedstock production. Biomass Bioenerg **35**, 2455–2469 (2011). https://doi.org/10.1016/j.biombioe.2011.02.028
9. Lu, D.: The potential and challenge of remote sensing-based biomass estimation. Int. J. Remote Sens. **27**, 1297–1328 (2006). https://doi.org/10.1080/01431160500486732

10. Lillesand, T.M., Kiefer, R.W.: Remote Sensing and Image Interpretation 4th Edition (1999)
11. Sutanto, A., Trisakti, B.: Perbandingan Klasifikasi Berbasis Obyek dan Klasifikasi Berbasis Piksel pada Data Citra Satelit Synthetic Aperture Radar untuk Pemetaan Lahan. **11**, 13 (2014)
12. Tranmer, M., Murphy, J., Elliot, M., Pampaka, M.: Multiple Linear Regression (2nd Edition), p. 59 (2020)
13. Breiman, L.: Random forest. Mach. Learn. **45**, 5–32 (2001)
14. Wang, L., Zhou, X., Zhu, X., Dong, Z., Guo, W.: Estimation of biomass in wheat using random forest regression algorithm and remote sensing data. Crop J. **4**, 212–219 (2016). https://doi.org/10.1016/j.cj.2016.01.008
15. Pahan, I.: Paduan Lengkap Kelapa Sawit. Penebar Swadaya, Jakarta (2007)
16. Barker, A.V., Pilbeam, D.J.: Handbook of Plant Nutrition. CRC PRess, Florida (2007)
17. Esetlili, M.T., Kurucu, Y.: Determination of main soil properties using synthetic aperture radar. Fresenius Environ. Bull. **25**, 23–36 (2016)
18. Ulaby, F.T., Bush, T.F., Batlivala, P.P.: Radar response to vegetation II: 8-18 GHZ Band. IEEEE Trans. Ãntennas Propag. **23**, 608–614 (1975)
19. Vincent, P., Bourbigot, M., Johnsen, H., Piantanida, R.: Sentinel-1 Product Specification (2020)
20. Sivasankar, T., Kumar, D., Srivastava, H.S., Patel, P.: Advances in radar remote sensing of agricultural crops: a review. Int. J. Adv. Sci. Eng. Inf. Technol. **8**, 1126 (2018). https://doi.org/10.18517/ijaseit.8.4.5797
21. Lazecky, M., Lhota, S., Penaz, T., Klushina, D.: Application of Sentinel-1 satellite to identify oil palm plantations in Balikpapan Bay. IOP Conf. Ser. Earth Environ. Sci. **169**, 012064 (2018). https://doi.org/10.1088/1755-1315/169/1/012064
22. Dalal, R.C., Henry, R.J.: Simultaneous determination of moisture, organic carbon, and total nitrogen by near infrared reflectance spectrophotometry. Soil Sci. Soc. Am. J. **50**, 120–123 (1986). https://doi.org/10.2136/sssaj1986.03615995005000010023x
23. Morra, M.J., Hall, M.H., Freeborn, L.L.: Carbon and nitrogen analysis of soil fractions using near-infrared reflectance spectroscopy. Soil Sci. Soc. Am. J. **55**, 288–291 (1991). https://doi.org/10.2136/sssaj1991.03615995005500010051x
24. Ehsani, M.R., Upadhyaya, S.K., Slaughter, D., Shafii, S., Pelletier, M.: A NIR technique for rapid determination of soil mineral nitrogen. Precis Agric. **1**, 18 (1999)
25. Harfenmeister, K., Spengler, D., Weltzien, C.: Analyzing temporal and spatial characteristics of crop parameters using Sentinel-1 backscatter data. Remote Sens. **11**, 1569 (2019). https://doi.org/10.3390/rs11131569
26. Kaliana, I.: Development of a decision support system for oil palm fertilizer requirement based on precision agriculture (2018)
27. Matloff, N.: Statistical Regression and Classification From Linear Models to Machine Learning. CRC Press, Davis(US) (2017)
28. Breusch, T.S., Pagan, A.R.: A simple test for heteroscedasticity and random coefficient variation. Econometrica **47**, 1287 (1979). https://doi.org/10.2307/1911963
29. Dietterich, T.G., Arbib, M.A.: The Handbook of Brain Theory and Neural Network, 2nd edn. MIT Press, Cambridge (2002)
30. Liaw, A., Wiener, M.: Classification and Regression by random Forest, vol. 2, p. 6 (2002)
31. Montaño Moreno, J.J., Palmer Pol, A., Sesé Abad, A.: Using the R-MAPE index as a resistant measure of forecast accuracy. Psicothema 500–506 (2013). https://doi.org/10.7334/psicothema2013.23
32. Lewis, C.D.: Industrial and Business Forecasting Methods: A Practical Guide to Exponential Smoothing and Curve Fitting. Butterworth Scientific (1982)
33. Alpaydin, E.: Introduction to Machine Learning. MIT Press, Massachusetts (US) (2010)
34. Filipponi, F.: Sentinel-1 GRD preprocessing workflow. In: Proceedings, vol. 18, p. 11 (2019).https://doi.org/10.3390/ECRS-3-06201

35. Serikat Petani Kelapa Sawit: Dokumen SOP Agronomi Ini Untuk Petani Kalapa Sawit (2016)
36. Nargesian, F., Samulowitz, H., Khurana, U., Khalil, E.B., Turaga, D.: Learning Feature Engineering for Classification. In: Proceedings of the Twenty-Sixth International Joint Conference on Artificial Intelligence, pp. 2529–2535. International Joint Conferences on Artificial Intelligence Organization, Melbourne, Australia (2017). https://doi.org/10.24963/ijcai.2017/352
37. Hair, J.F., Black, W.C., Babin, B.J., Anderson, R.E.: Multivariate Data Analysis. Pearson Education Limited, London (2013)

New Monitoring Framework Intelligent Irrigation System

Mahamed Abdelelmadjid Allali[1,2]([✉]), Kawther Nassima Addala[2],
Nassima Ali Berroudja[2], Mounir Tahar Abbes[2], Zoulikha Mekkakia Maaza[1],
Walid Kadri[2,3], and Abdelhak Benhamada[2]

[1] FSEI, SIMPA, USTO, Mohamed BOUDIAFE University, Oran, Algeria
{m.allali,z.mekkakia}@univ-usto.dz
[2] FSEI, LME, Hassiba Ben Bouali University, Chlef, Algeria
{m.allali,k.addala,n.aliberoudja,m.taharabbes,m.kadri,
a.benhamada}@univ-chlef.dz
[3] LIO Laboratory, FSMA, University Oran 1, Oran, Algeria

Abstract. The Internet has known since its significant appearance growth and touched virtually every area of our everyday life: political, economic, sociocultural, etc. In the last years, it has become the primary source of information. The intelligent irrigation system remains a significant development of the Internet of Things due to the exponential need to make available the right quantity of food at lower agricultural and industrial costs. This work involves studying, designing, and implementing a web application for remote automation of green spaces, "Smart Green," based on a mathematical model. This application aims to control the automatic watering process using an embedded system to optimize water consumption and prevent overwatering. This project consists of three parts: The first part consists of designing an embedded system based on the ESP8266 microcontroller. It allows the automatic control of climate, soil, and plant parameters and sends them over the Internet. The second part is dedicated to building a graphical user interface (GUI) that helps us visualise climatic parameters in real-time (Temperature, Humidity, Soil Moisture) internet connection and save them in a database. Finally, we made a prototype that allowed us to test the performance and the good functioning of our system.

Keywords: Internet of thing · Web application · PID control · Temperature · Humidity · Soil moisture

1 Introduction

The Internet of Things (IoT) is one of the most important existing and potential advances in the information and communications technology sectors. Interoperability among different IoT deployment industries will occur in multiple fields, including healthcare, transportation, smart cities, infrastructure, environment, security, irrigation, and numerous other sectors.

Today, enterprise and industry are focused on Network architecture-based software and the interoperability of Web services. Although the IoT has other particular focuses, the IoT model is an essential field of analysis referred to as the Web of Things (WoT).

© Springer Nature Switzerland AG 2021
S. Boumerdassi et al. (Eds.): SSA 2021, CCIS 1470, pp. 166–185, 2021.
https://doi.org/10.1007/978-3-030-88259-4_12

The WoT aim is to maximise the IoT's interoperability and user-friendliness. Many partners have been working collaboratively for many years to find building blocks that deal with these problems.

This paper addresses different primary IoT technologies that concentrate on algorithms, process algebra, the network's architecture, energy harvesting, wireless communications, and network security. It introduces the strategies of IoT system architecture and recent study findings applicable to the IoT system's evolution and offers current and evolving strategies to develop and design IoT platforms for multi-sector agricultural industries [2].

Irrigation plays a vital role in green spaces and plants that require enough water to live and thrive. So, it should not be overlooked. Among the fundamental problems faced by farmers and landowners are:

- Lack of hydraulic resources and high costs to guarantee irrigation water, especially with the regression in the world's groundwater level, especially in the desert, arid and semi-arid zones.
- Manual irrigation (traditional), which requires excellent daily efforts and time.
- Over-watering, unorganised and inadequate watering causes the water reserves to depreciate in an accelerated manner and results in the deterioration of the plantation and soil quality.

This paper proposes a standard PID and mathematical model, an intelligent irrigation system using Raspberry, with an irrigation technique appropriate for plants grown in a climate-type soil type. Following this section, the remainder of this article is structured in the following manner. In Sect. 2, the relevant works are presented. Section 3 address the solution being proposed. Section 3.3 describes the implementation of software and hardware. Section 4 analyses the observations gathered and explains them. Lastly, the article concludes with Sect. 5.

2 Related Work

A selection of several existing research on cloud-based irrigation technologies illustrates the current state of the art. Next, we will demonstrate some past projects that have a crucial emphasis on smart strawberry irrigation. Moreover, we bring this section closer with a few IoT devices and systems targeted at smart-agriculture, in particular, the cloud-based strategy. A modern irrigation scheduling system created by researchers at Colorado State University (CSU) is known as Water Irrigation Scheduling for Efficient application (WISE). It allows the use of soil water balance (SWB) and weather station data queries from the Colorado Agricultural Meteorology Network (CoAg-Met) and the Northern Colorado Water Conservation District (NCWCD) to make automated decisions about when to apply water.

A mobile application has been developed to assist in activating and mobilising required user interest in the software framework. It is designed to provide users with the opportunity to see and track their soil moisture deficiency, as well as other weather and irrigation details, all shown on a single screen for comparison [3]. In [4], the authors have suggested a cloud-based Wireless Sensor Network (WSN) contact framework for actual implementation and test it. A collection of sensors and actuators is monitored and controlled via this method to gather information on plant water needs. To optimise the device with weather information, a remote web service is deployed.

In [5], Gambi et al. focused on the home automation framework's architectural model utilising LoRa and Message Queuing Telemetry Transport (MQTT). The researchers evaluated how lower power and expense, but also long-range communication systems, affect IoT-based solutions. They developed their system utilising spread spectrum radio communication, such as LoRa. The authors have carried out two experiments: the evolution of the radio coverage region and efficiency assessment. They have focused on the improvement of wireless home control and smart security systems. The entire framework is part of IoT technology. In light of their proposal, many devices were used to implement their suggested approach, such as a Gas sensor, Light Dependent Resistor (LDR), DHT, and Node MCU as a micro-controller. They also used MQTT as a procedure which greatly integrated the suggested system into the IoT process.

In [6] In this research paper, an encyclopaedic coverage is done comprising various compilers, simulator and programmers of various embedded system technologies like 8051, PIC, ARM, AVR and Arduino. In addition, each tool is thoroughly covered with regard to features and availability, providing a full platform for many researchers and hobbyists cum basic users to select the best compiler, simulator and programmer among the available options. And In [7] this research paper, an encyclopaedic coverage is done comprising various compilers, simulator and programmers of various embedded system technologies like 8051, PIC, ARM, AVR and Arduino. In addition, each tool is thoroughly covered with regard to features and availability, providing a full platform for many researchers and hobbyists cum basic users to select the best compiler, simulator and programmer among the available options.

In [8] Najam Ul Hassan and al have developped a Decision Support Benchmark for Forecasting the Consumption of Agriculture Stocks. The proposed methodology uses eighteen socio-economic and environmental factors to forecast next year's upshot with least chance of error. Multiple learning models are constructed using the two methods considered in this research work: Linear Regression parallel with Recurrent Neural Networks. Comparisons show that Linear Regression model by means of most influential factors (economic factors) offers the most effectual forecast values among all the models in terms of the RMSE for all the crops.

An adaptive [9] wheat seed classification technique has been proposed using a digital image processing system (DIPS) and fuzzy clustered random forest (FCRF) techniques. DIP is used to extract the features of the seeds. Further, FCRF is the combination of fuzzy and supervised learning applied in the classification process. This autonomic technique is intended to help the farming industry overcome the issues of manual seed classification. The experiment results show the accuracy of the proposed classification technique with an average performance gain up to 97.7%.

The research paper In [10], a Smart Farming Enabled: IoT Based Agriculture Stick for Live Monitoring of Temperature and Soil Moisture has been proposed using Arduino, Cloud Computing and Solar Technology. The stick fetch the live data of temperature and soil moisture with over 99% accuracy in order to assist farmers in increasing the agriculture yield and efficiently managing food production. This paper in [11] is the first of its kind to present a complete overview of IoT sensor data processing, fusion and analysis techniques. Further addresses how to process IoT sensor data, fusion with other data sources, and analyses to produce knowledge able in sighting to hidden data patterns for rapid decision-making.

The research work by [12] is paper addresses to the proposed system obtained an original APK file together with potential candidate cloned APKs via the cloud network. For each subject software, the system uses an APK Extractor tool to retrieve Java source files through Dalvik Executable files. Finally, the deep learning model is configured to detect cloned apps. In [13] New technologies bring revolution and innovation in every aspect of human life, But they are accompanied by lots of limitations in terms of energy wastage, environmental hazards like carbon or other chemical emissions, extreme consumption of natural or renewable sources and greenhouse effects.

In order to minimize the negative impact of these technologies on the environment, it is utmost important to move towards green technology.is envisioned via the fusion of diverse technologies like sensor communications, cloud computing, internet of things, AI, machine and deep learning. That is the reason researchers are working hard and moving towards green computing, ICT, and IoT, making significant progress towards improvising the quality of life and sustainable environment.

This is why today, farmers need to adopt and use new technologies and exploit what science has achieved in this area. Our project attempts to address these anomalies by developing an intelligent and automatic irrigation system for different agricultural areas by implementing a web application of WoT to manage water use by controlling irrigation by a PID regulator in response to soil moisture changes that meet crop water requirements.

In industrial settings, proportional–integral–derivative (PID) controllers are more commonly used owing to their advantageous cost/benefit ratio. Known for their long history and the expertise acquired over the years, modern microprocessors and software resources, as well as rising demand for better product efficiency while holding costs down, have driven researchers to investigate innovative approaches that will optimise their output and make them simpler to use.

Practical PID Control addresses fundamental problems that can occur when a PID controller is deployed in real-world scenarios. The architecture's primary aim is to concentrate on those functions that can significantly improve performance when combined with a well-tuned parameter setup. Anti-windup techniques, feedforward behaviour, and controller designs both discuss the option of filter to be used. Besides, the PID identification algorithm and model reduction technique selection is an examination occurring in the sense of model-based PID control. The extensive adoption of PID-based control architectures and their related ratios and cascades are also addressed. Recent contributions to these issues are identified and contrasted to other well-established methods. Many simulation and experimental findings explain the multiple methodologies in detail and give a clearer understanding of their strengths and limitations. Practical PID Control is a valuable and insightful resource for researchers, students, and professionals in process control.

3 Smart Green: Overview and Functionalities

Our "Smart Green" project is part of the IoT systems. It is particularly interested in the field of intelligent and automatic irrigation systems. We deem the values that different irrigation devices located in the target environment convey (soil humidity sensor, air humidity sensor, temperature sensor, rain sensor), which will be received by the ESP8266 Node MCU V3 module connected by Wi-Fi. After the values will be sent to the Mosquito server (Broker) via the MQTT protocol, intelligently process this data to make the appropriate decision, which will influence the steering of it and prevent over-watering optimise the amount of water. The proposed solution is based on the paradigm of IoT and WoT systems. The watering theme adopted is based on two types of watering: manual watering and automatic watering. The transition from one to the other is ensured by the platform that we used, Node-Red. This application is intended as a client/server application. For example, since nobody can water your plants when you are away, so the goal of our project is to overcome this problem by offering the "Smart Green" service by Drip irrigation system with which measures the humidity of the ground if it is lower than the setpoint it sends a message, which we transform into MQTT. The ESP8266 picks up the message and starts the water pump. We take the opportunity to save the set point state values in Influx DB to make beautiful graphics on Grafana.

The user can remotely control the electrical equipment in their home via a simple web page using their smartphone or PC by exploiting the Arduino and ESP8266 Node MCU V3 open-hardware technologies, which are undoubtedly the lowest-priced means available on the market. This system will be accessible and controllable in real-time via the Internet "webserver" and extendable by actuators and sensors that the administrator can add and configure following his needs. The user is notified by a message in the E-Mail box when the amount of water is insufficient for irrigation. The user can check and consult the data previously recorded.

Our project's objectives are: Use the various components, namely the sensors, relays, motors, Configure and program the Arduino board to connect the multiple sensors, recover and transmit the data using the MQTT protocol.

Configure and program the Node MCU V3 card in order to:

- Receive data from the Arduino Uno board via serial communication.
- Create a web interface for the digital display of quantities (temperature, humidity, history.) Besides, the control of actuators.
- Communicate by Wi-Fi with the Node-Red server

Configure the router to allow a Wi-Fi device such as a computer or a Smartphone to connect to this router, which will then enable access to the control page hosted on the Node MCU V3 card and thus management activation of the water pump using the PID control algorithm based on soil moisture.

These are the requirements related to the functioning of the system to be developed. The automatic and intelligent sprinkler system should be able to establish the following functionalities:

- Acquire measurements of physical quantities from the sensors used. Allow consultation of data.
- Remotely control automatic watering intelligently (water as much as necessary and as little as possible).
- Local storage of relevant data.
- Review of the acquired data and visualising the statistics on this data over a temporary range Ergonomics of the graphical interfaces.
- Compatibility with any operating system, which is a strong point of WoT systems.

The primary point and soil moisture, the question is: Why monitor soil moisture. Measuring soil moisture is an essential agronomic component for monitoring crop growth and helps improve irrigation decisions, and it is a significant parameter for evapotranspiration [14].

Evapotranspiration (ET): A flow of water continually crosses the plant from the ground to the atmosphere, so there is a continuous exchange of water molecules between the plant and the atmosphere. This process is called perspiration. However, the soil releases significant amounts of water by evaporation. Combining these two terms gives evapotranspiration; it is evaluated by mm/d and determined by the FAO Penman-Monteith method. This method allowed the estimation of evapotranspiration based on climatic variables (temperature, humidity, wind speed, sunshine duration) recorded at the meteorological station, and this natural formula is as [15].

3.1 Presentation of the Study Area

The state of Chlef is located in the north of Algeria is an area with a Mediterranean climate, relatively cold weather in winter, and hot in summer. The rainy period generally extends from October to the end of April and a dry period for the rest of the year. Our region receives only a small amount of precipitation with an annual module of around 334 mm on average. The prevailing winds are west winds during the summer periods. The region receives dry and hot south winds. The sirocco accelerates evapotranspiration, a very sunny region insolation that reaches its maximum in the summer period [16].

The table above represents a summary of the cultures currently practiced in our project (Table 1).

Our irrigation system has two operating modes, automatic mode, and manual mode. The first mode checks the humidity of the soil. If it is not sufficient, the system will activate the water pump; if it is sufficient, the system will deactivate the water pump according to the PID control command. The second mode controls the pump manually by pressing the on and of keys available on our interface.

Table 1. Technical sheets for vegetable crops

	Tomato	*Pepper/chilli pepper*	*Cucumber*
Production area	Annaba, Taref, Skikda, Jijel,GuelmaBlida, Ain-defla, mostaganem, Boumerdes, Tipaza…etc.	All regions of Algeria: coastline, sublittoral, interior plains, and South	Very widespread in the littoral and sub-littoral and Saharan regions
Soils	Clay-siliceous, silty	clay silica	clay silica
Soil moisture	75% to 80%	80% to 85%	70% to 80%
Optimal temperature (days, Night)	(25 °C, 15 to 16 °C)	(20 to 30 °C, 15 to 20 °C)	(22 to 25 °C, 18 to 20 °C)
PH	5,6 to 6,8	6,5 to 7	5,5 to 6,8
Salinity (compared to salt)	Fairly tolerant	Moderately tolerant	Moderately tolerant
Planting date	Early March	April May	March, Half April
Last generally			60–70 days

We designed our prototype's structure (Fig. 1) represents our green space, divided into two parts: one part for electronics (25 × 25 × 10) and the other part for growing plants: width: 50 cm, length 70 cm, and height 20 cm.

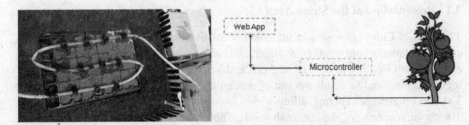

Fig. 1. The structure of the prototype

The wilaya of Chlef is located in the north of Algeria is an area with a Mediterranean climate, relatively cold climate in winter, and hot in summer. The rainy period generally extends from October to the end of April and a dry period for the rest of the year. Our region receives only a small amount of precipitation with an annual module of around 334 mm on average. The prevailing winds are west winds during the summer periods; the region receives warm, dry south winds, it is the sirocco that accelerates evapotranspiration, is a very sunny region insolation reaches its maximum in the summer period [17].

3.2 Design and Regulation

We started developing, dealing with the complexity of computer systems, new methods, languages, and tools to better understand the customer's needs and requirements to achieve a system that meets his needs; among these methods is object-oriented programming (OOP), which includes the UML modelling language. Imperatively, the realisation of an intelligent irrigation system in the IoT domain must be preceded by a methodology of analysis and design aiming to enable the preliminary development stages to render this technology more faithful to the customer's needs [18]. The regulation was defined in the remainder of this section with its methods of adjustment.

The use case diagram is illustrated in Fig. 2. This diagram gives a global vision of a system to formalise the needs in a simple, understandable graphical representation. Therefore, it makes it possible to identify the main functionalities of a system. A use case diagram consists mainly of [19]:

- A use case: portrays itself as an ellipse and describes a unit of outwardly apparent application. The actor who initiates executes an end-to-end service, with a trigger, an unfolding, and an end. Therefore, the use case models a function provided by the unit.
- Actor: is the external representation of a role, a mechanism, or a thing that communicates with a method. The little man below illustrates it.

Regulation in industrial processes relates to applying all the theoretical, material, and technical means to maintain each essential physical quantity equal to the desired value, called a set point, through action on a regulating quantity, despite the influence of disturbing amounts of the system [20].

Those three keywords can summarise it: measure, compare, correct. Each process, therefore, has its requirements. Each device has its terms of use. Thus, the regulation must be designed to meet specific safety, production requirements, and materials-related needs. Regulation is the operation of changing a quantity automatically, such that it continually maintains its value or stays similar to the target value, whatever the disruptions can occur [21]. There are loop-types. We are interested in two forms of loops in this paper: (closed-loop and open-loop).

In our project, we will apply the closed-loop PID command, which monitors humidity at all times from the ground and compare it with the set point. Depending on the difference between our green space's moisture and the set point (the desired soil humidity), we will generate an output signal, which will be proportional. The regulator P cannot eliminate steady-state errors, so we integrate the integral controller to reduce the error that P has introduced. Then, you run the risk of going too far when you approach the set point. Therefore, we are monitoring evolution by imagining the future (derivation) [22].

The advantage of a PID regulator is its dynamic performance, precision of adjustment, and stability. The elements of this regulator referring to the three terms P (Proportional), I (Integral), and D (Derivative), operating on the error signal to produce a control signal.

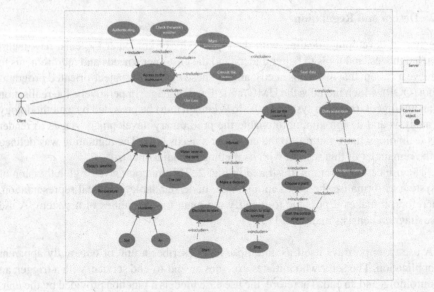

Fig. 2. Use case of Smart Green

If $u(t)$ is the signal control sent to the system, $y(t)$ is the measured output and $r(t)$ is the desired output, and tracking error $e(t) = r(t) - y(t)$, the general form of a PID controller is [23]:

$$U(t) = Kp\,e(t) + K_i e(t) + K_d d/dt\,e(t) \tag{1}$$

Where P, I, and D are [20]: (i) Proportional action (P) it reduces the static error (improve accuracy): The larger the action (K large), the more the static error is reduced, the higher the action, the greater the oscillations during the regime transient, an excess of action (very high k) leads to instability of the system. (ii) Necessary action (I): it eliminates the static error: the smaller the constant, the stronger the integral action. Extreme action (too small or too large) leads to system instability (due to the increase in phase shift). (iii) Derived action (D): the larger the K_d, the stronger the derivative action and reduces the overshoot or the oscillations obtained in proportional action alone, accelerates the measured response, and improves system stability (provision of an advance phase). The derived action is limited by an excess of action, which can lead to the system's instability.

The actuator controls the "Water pump": We used in our project the experimental approach Ziegler and Nichols. The main objective of the irrigation pump regulation is to adapt the soil humidity to the crops. I.e., automatic watering will be carried out when the measures required for watering fall below a predefined threshold, respecting the weather around the system and prevent the soil moisture from exceeding the allowable value. How soil moisture control operation is:

- Y: The sensor's digital value, the instructions are retrieved from the database and compared to this Y value.

- C: This is the target or target value that the measurement must reach. When changing the setpoint, the control loop operates in "servo" mode. When the control loop eliminates the effects of disturbances, it operates in "regulation" mode.
- If Y < C2: Y is lower than the setpoint, then there is a watering pump's triggering.
- If Y > C2: Y is greater than the setpoint, adequate feedback is triggered and introduced a correction.
- If Y = C: Y is within the set range, there is no feedback.
- If Y C: Y is within the set range, there is no feedback.

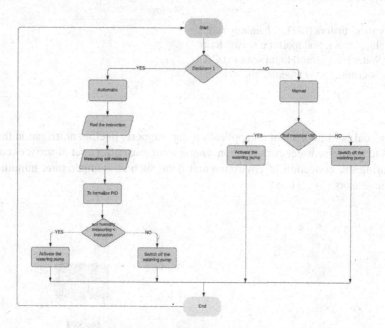

Fig. 3. Organisable Watering system

3.3 Implementation and Realisation

This section presents the implementation and realisation application, "Smart Green." Our goal is to implement an application that supports smart irrigation using sensors to minimise water consumption. Our system must offer a set of services capable of ensuring environmental data collection, such as (temperature, humidity) from the sensors [24].

Environment (material and logical) explains the materials utilised in material sensors and other logical use in the dashboard.

First is dedicated to representing the list of materials necessary to realise our WoT "Smart Green" system. Second, to make our web application and operate the connected object, we used several languages programming, mark-up language, scripting language, etc., so we used the development tools adequate with these languages. Java. The first is for the resolution of the water model (Table 2).

Table 2. Material and logical

Material	Logical
Arduino UNO REV3 card	Programming languages (Arduino, HTML, CSS, JavaScript, Python, NoSQL, SQL, MySQL
module ESP8266-12E (NodeMCU V3)	Development platform and software tools (IDE Arduino, and Node-Red)
Raspberry PI 3 modèle B+	Data Management (FluxDB, Grafana, PHP Mydmin)
Sensors and actuators (DHT22 humidity and temperature sensor, Soil moisture sensor, Rain sensor, Water level sensor, Light sensor (LDR Shield), 4-channel relay module, The watering pump	

Our goal is to implement an application that supports intelligent irrigation through sensors to minimise water consumption. Our system must offer a set of services capable of ensuring the collection of environmental data, such as (temperature, humidity,…) from the sensors (Fig. 4).

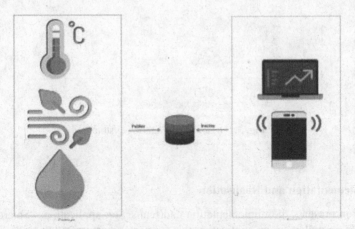

Fig. 4. Hardware and software platform

The Smart Irrigation Device is built into the smartphone application system, enabling the farm field's irrigation to be tracked and managed efficiently. A new function of the mobile application framework is to access the data gathered directly from the sensors and processed in Firebase's cloud storage through a Firebase link, which is the cloud that links various kinds of hardware and the cloud database. The mobile application's main GUI is the system's home screen menu. It is intended to ensure each user has a secure password and to protect the privacy of another client's information. If the user has successfully authenticated the program, another menu emerges that helps the user customise the irrigation device. To use the method, the consumer must choose any of the choices. If the consumer chooses the control choice, they are faced with controlling the water pump either to force "ON" or "OFF" or to place it in the AUTO mode so that the pump's control is dependent on the sensor's setting in the device. The control system then guides the consumer to join ThingSpeak.com. This procedure shows different sensors to indicate the entire farm field's soil condition. Figures 1 and 3 show the flow embedded into the mobile application framework from the Smart Irrigation System (Fig. 5).

Three sensors interesting are: (i) Humidity and temperature sensor DHT22, (ii) Soil moisture sensor and (iii) Water level sensor, we describe detail script essential are two sensors soil moisture sensor and water level sensor:

Soil moisture sensor	Water level sensor

`int sensorPin = A0;`
`int Val;`
`void setup () {`
`Serial . begin (115200);}`
`void loop () {`
`Val = analogRead ( sensorPin`
`);`
`int output_value = map(`
`sensorValue ,840 ,530 ,0`
`,100); /* de trop sec vers`
`trop humide */`
`Serial . print (" Valeur`
`analogique : ");`
`Serial. print (Val );`
`Serial . print (" Pourcentage`
`: ");`
`Serial . println (`
`output_value );`
`delay (1000); }`
	`int sensor_pin = 8;`
	`void setup ()`
	`{ pinMode ( sensor_pin , INPUT`
	`);`
	`Serial . begin (115200);}`
	`void loop (){`
	`int value = digitalRead (`
	`sensor_pin );`
	`if( value == HIGH ){`
	`Serial . print ("Le niveau`
	`d'eau dans le reservoir`
	`est suffisant ");}`
	`if( value == LOW ){`
	`Serial . print ("Le niveau`
	`d'eau est trop bas "); }}`
	`75`

3.4 Web Application "Smart Green"

A web application (also called Web App, from English) is an application that can be manipulated using a web browser. In the same way as websites, a web application is generally placed on a server. It is handled by activating widgets (a component of the graphical interface) using a browser, web, via a computer network (Internet, local network, etc.) [25].

The advantage of the web application to WoT is:

There is no longer a need to install software on each workstation, which vastly reduces maintenance costs and eliminates certain incompatibilities.

A well-designed application can be used by different terminals (computers, laptops, tablets, and smartphones).

There is no longer any geographic constraint, and we can envisage access for nomadic users in complete security thanks to the encryption of data through the Internet.

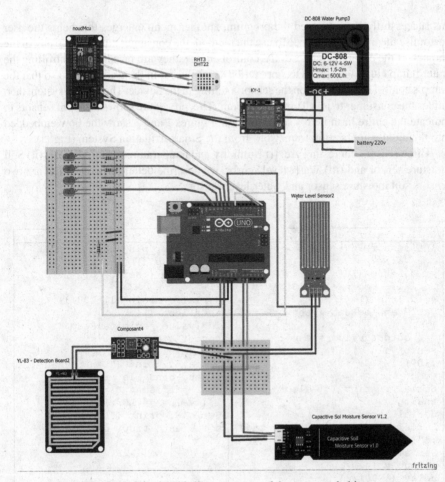

Fig. 5. Connection of all components of the connected object

These applications can manage multimedia data (texts, photos, videos), and users are comfortable because they are used to using a browser in a private setting.

To update the application, modify the application on the server and all workstations instantly access the new version Node-RED Application:

Node-RED is an application representing the logical layer of our system. It is an efficient software to design IoT applications focusing on simplifying programming since blocks of predefined code called "nodes" execute the tasks. It uses a visual programming method that encourages the connecting of code blocks. Connected together, form a flow [16].

3.5 Server-Side Application

We have developed a Human-Machine interface in a web application (Fig. 6) to control our plants remotely. This type of interface is widely used these days because it offers the

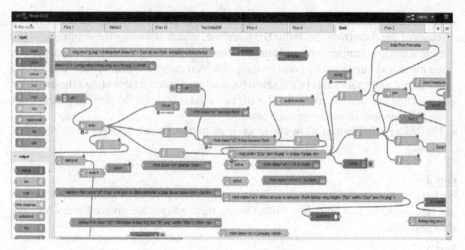

Fig. 6. The work plan from Node-Red

possibility of controlling a system from any computer connected to the Internet without installing additional software or drivers. To access this application, just open the web browser and enter the address of the application. In our case, it will be the IP address of the server follow the port number "127.0.0.1: 1880" because the application is hosted locally. Next will display the dashboard, which contains six parts:

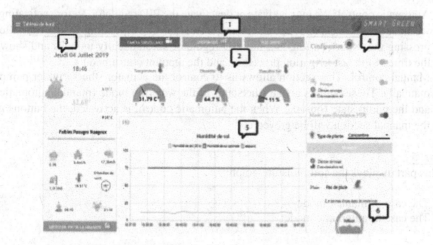

Fig. 7. The dashboard of the Smart Green application

Part 1

This part concerns navigation to other pages:

- The "surveillance camera" button allows us to navigate to a page where we can see our green space in real-time.

- The "History" button will enable us to navigate to the history page so that Grafana retrieves the data from the InfluxDB database, which shows us the evolution of the measurements (temperature, soil humidity, ambient humidity) on a time range, bypassing the mouse cursor over a point on the graph. A rectangle appears with the recording date, time, and exact value of the saved parameters. Hence, a table shows the irrigation period and the amount consumed for the two modes in detail. Moreover, panels show the total amount of water for each plant.
- The "More info" button allows us to navigate to a technical sheet for more details on crops.

Part 2
We have three coloured gauges, which give us the current value of each climatic parameter (air humidity, soil humidity, temperature); these gauges are updated every 30 s and change colour.

Part 3
This section displays the weather, CHLEF weather evolution, minimum and maximum temperature, wind, amount of rain and atmospheric pressure… etc. and a weather trend for the next few days (Fig. 6).

Part 4
This part concerns the configuration necessary for irrigation. It allows us to choose between automatic mode by regulation or manual control. It is separated into two sections.

- Automatic control: We may activate or deactivate the PID regulator. Before activating, we have to choose the form of culture to see the corresponding instruction after pressing the "start" button, and the PID regulator automatically unlocks and shows the time of the last irrigation procedure and the amount consumed.
- Manual control: This section allows us to control the actuator (the sprinkler pump) manually. These buttons give us the status of the watering mode (manual/automatic) and the pump state (on/off). When the automatic control is activated, the buttons in the manual section will be greyed out.

Part 5
This part displays the soil moisture graph:

- The case of manual mode:
- The case of automatic mode:

Part 6
This part concerns the notification by e-mail; the system alerts the user if the quantity of water in the tank is insufficient.

4 Validation and Results

To analyse the amount of water used according to the crop need, we will treat three types of crops with different life cycles and different soil moisture guidelines to draw attention to the water requirements that change depending on the plant type. Then we will validate the choice values of the PID coefficients (K_p, K_i, and K_d) that we have chosen by showing the robustness of our system and its capacity to adapt to changes in plants and thus soil moisture requirements by the result of an experiment whose set point is suddenly changed.

- Case 01: We will choose the plant = Industrial tomato, 'planted in the soil = 'sandy clay,' with optimal soil humidity (setpoint) = '77.5%'. The result of the experiment is illustrated in the figure (Fig. 7).
- Case 02: We will choose the plant = 'cucumber,' planted in the soil = 'clayey,' with optimal soil moisture (set point) = '75%'(Fig. 7).
- Case 03: We will choose the plant = 'pepper' planted in the soil = 'clayey', with optimal soil humidity (set point) = '82 .5%'. The result of the experiment is illustrated in Fig. 7).
- Case 04: We suddenly changed the setpoint from 75% to 82.5% (Figs. 8, 9, 10 and 11).

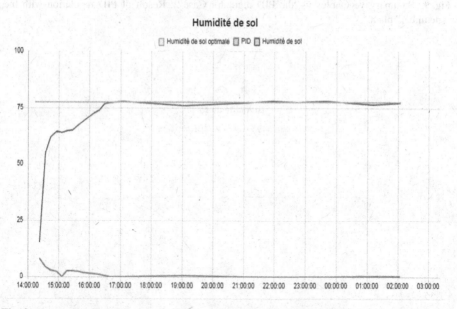

Fig. 8. Summary vegetables vs. the PID regulator Case 1: Result of PID regulation with the "industrial tomato" plant

From the two different cases, we can say that we were able to achieve our goals:

- During the crop's life cycle, we have given the necessary quantity of water for the plant with moist soil, and water stress was avoided.

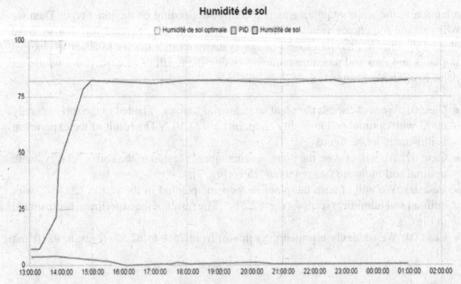

Fig. 9. Summary vegetables vs. the PID regulator Case 2: Result of PID regulation with the "cucumber" plant

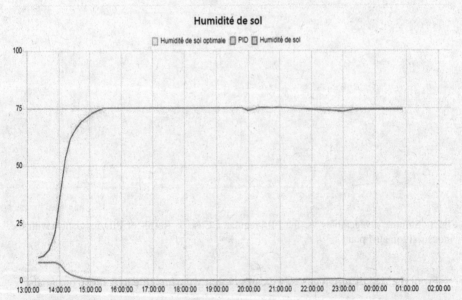

Fig. 10. Summary vegetables vs. the PID regulator Case 3: Result of PID regulation with the "pepper" plant

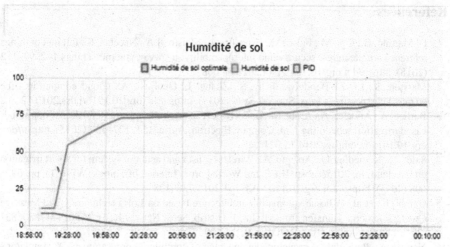

Fig. 11. Summary vegetables vs. the PID regulator Case 4: Result of PID control in the event of a setpoint change

- The control oscillations have been reduced as much as possible to avoid damage to the actuator.
- We have reduced the energy consumed and wasted water.

5 Conclusion

In this paper, we have proposed a system Automatic sprinkler system. Besides, implementing a WoT system for saving water used in green water spaces has allowed us to learn and use several development platforms, tools, and languages, including Node platforms. -RED, Arduino IDE, and InfluxDB.

This project's particularity is the physical realisation of a "Smart Green" irrigation system based on WoT technology, representing the first experience for us. Several concepts are acquired concerning the software part and the hardware part, of which we created a WoT system to automatically manage watering green spaces using PID control. The difficulty lies in optimally adjusting the parameters Kp, Ki, Kd. We used the Ziegler Nichols (ZN) approach to determine the parameters of the PID.

Our system has four parts: hardware, software, communication protocols, data storage. First, the material part: we created a connected object placed in the target environment for watering, and the software part: we have created a web application with the Node-Red platform, which plays the role intermediary between the connected object and the server. It receives the data transmitted from the connected object via the Wi-Fi protocol. It sends them after that to the server via MQTT protocol.

Acknowledgments. This work is part of the PERFU project; the title is "Optimisation of resource management in IoT networks," and Code C00L07UN020120180001 is supported by the Algerian Ministry of Higher Education Scientific Research.

References

1. Di Martino, B., Rak, M., Ficco, M., Esposito, A., Maisto, S.A., Nacchia, S.: Internet of things reference architectures, security and interoperability: a survey. Internet Things **1–2**, 99–112 (2018). https://doi.org/10.1016/j.iot.2018.08.008
2. Marston, S., Li, Z., Bandyopadhyay, S., Zhang, J., Ghalsasi, A.: Cloud computing - the business perspective. Decis. Support Syst. (2019). https://doi.org/10.1016/j.dss.2010.12
3. Bartlett, A., Andales, A., Arabi, M., Bauder, T.: A smartphone app to extend the use of a cloud-based irrigation scheduling tool. Comput. Electron. Agric. **111**, 127–130 (2015). https://doi.org/10.1016/j.compag.2014.12.021
4. Sales, N., Remedios, O., Arsenio, A.: Wireless sensor and actuator system for smart irrigation on the cloud. In: 2015 IEEE 2nd World Forum Internet of Things (WF-IoT), pp. 693–698 (2015). https://doi.org/10.1109/WF-IoT.2015.7389138
5. Gambi, E., et al.: A home automation architecture based on LoRa technology and Message Queue Telemetry Transfer protocol. Int. J. Distrib. Sens. Netw. **14**(10), 1550147718806837 (2018). https://doi.org/10.1016/j.dss.2010.12.006
6. Nayyar, A., Puri, V.: An encyclopedia coverage of compiler's, programmer's & simulator's for 8051, PIC, AVR, ARM, Arduino embedded technologies. Int. J. Reconfigurable Embed. Syst. (IJRES) **5**(1), 18–42 (2016). ISSN 2089-4864
7. Nayyar, A.: A review of arduino Board's, Lilypad's & Arduino shield. In: 2016 3rd International Conference on Computing for Sustainable Global Development (INDIACom). INSPEC Accession Number: 16426549 (2016)
8. Ul Hassan, N., Khan, F.Z., Bibi, H., Khan, N.T., Nayyar, A., Bilal, M.: A decision support benchmark for forecasting the consumption of agriculture stocks. IEEE Consum. Electron. Mag. https://doi.org/10.1109/MCE.2021.3063547
9. Singh, P., Nayyar, A., Singh, S., Kaur, A.: Classification of wheat seeds using image processing and fuzzy clustered random forest. Int. J. Agric. Resour. Gov. Ecol. **16**(2) (2020). https://doi.org/10.1109/ACCESS.2021.3050391
10. Nayyar, A., Vikram Puri, Er.: Smart farming: IoT based smart sensors agriculture stick for live temperature and moisture monitoring using Arduino, cloud computing & solar technology. Int. J. Sci. Technol. Res. **9**(2) (2020). https://doi.org/10.1201/9781315364094-121
11. Krishnamurthi, R., Kumar, A., Gopinathan, D., Nayyar, A., Qureshi, B.: An overview of IoT sensor data processing, fusion, and analysis techniques. Sensors **20**, 6076 (2020). https://doi.org/10.3390/s20216076, www.mdpi.com/journal/sensors
12. Ullah, F., Al-Turjman, F., Nayyar, A.: IoT-based green city architecture using secured and sustainable android services. Environ. Technol. Innov. **20**, 101091 (2020). https://doi.org/10.1016/j.eti.2020.101091
13. Solanki, A., Nayyar, A.: Green Internet of Things (G-IoT): ICT Technologies, Principles, Applications, Projects, and Challenges. https://doi.org/10.4018/978-1-5225-7432-3.ch021
14. Chen, F., Qin, L., Li, X., Wu, G., Shi, C.: Design and implementation of ZigBee wireless sensor and control network system in greenhouse. In: 2017 36th Chinese Control Conference (CCC), pp. 8982–8986. IEEE (2017). https://doi.org/10.23919/ChiCC.2017.8028786
15. Majhi, B., Naidu, D.: Differential evolution based radial basis function neural network model for reference evapotranspiration estimation. SN Appl. Sci. **3**(1), 1–19 (2021). https://doi.org/10.1007/s42452-020-04069-z
16. Bouras, E., et al.: Assessing the impact of global climate changes on irrigated wheat yields and water requirements in a semi-arid environment of Morocco **9**, 19142 (2019). https://doi.org/10.1038/s41598-019-55251-2
17. Bersini, H.: La programmation orientée objet. 2017 Manuel (broché)

18. Agnihotri, N.: Top 15 des plates-formes IoT Les plus populaires. https://iotfunda.com/about/. [published le 14/12/2018, consult le O1/30/2021]
19. Toumi, D., Mihoub, Y., Moreau, S., Hassaine, S.: Real-time implementation of adaptive discrete fuzzy-RST speed control and nonlinear backstepping currents control techniques for PMSM drive. In: Hatti, M. (ed.) Artificial Intelligence and Renewables Towards an Energy Transition. Lecture Notes in Networks and Systems, vol. 174, pp. 361–373. Springer, Cham (2021). https://doi.org/10.1007/978-3-030-63846-7_35
20. Bajer, L., Krejcar, O.: Design and realisation of low-cost control for greenhouse environment with remote control **48**(4), 368–373 (2015).https://doi.org/10.1016/j.ifacol.2015.07.062
21. Schiavoa, M., Padula, F., et al.: Performance evaluation of an optimised PID controller for propofol and remifentanil coadministration in general anaesthesia. IFAC J. Syst. Control **15**, 100121 (2021). https://doi.org/10.1016/j.ifacsc.2020.100121
22. Karunanithy, K., Velusamy, B.: Energy-efficient cluster and travelling salesman problem-based data collection using WSNs for Intelligent water irrigation and fertigation. J. Meas. **161**, 107835 (2020). https://doi.org/10.1016/j.measurement.2020.107835
23. Balaji, R., et al.: Advanced implementation patterns of Internet of things with MQTT providers in the cutting edge communications. J. Mater. Today Proc. https://doi.org/10.1016/j.matpr.2020.11.090
24. Silanus, M.: node-red. http://silanus.fr/sin/?p=984. [published 18/02/2018, consulted 02/07/2021]
25. Sciullo, L., Aguzzi, C., Di Felice, M., Cinotti, T.S.: WoT store: enabling things and applications discovery for the W3C web of things. In: 2019 16th IEEE Annual Consumer Communications & Networking Conference (CCNC). https://doi.org/10.1109/CCNC.2019.8651786

Author Index

Printed in the United States
by Baker & Taylor Publisher Services

Printed in the United States
by Baker & Taylor Publisher Services